In the Theatre
of Dionysos

In the Theatre of Dionysos

Democracy and Tragedy in Ancient Athens

RICHARD SEWELL

McFarland & Company, Inc., Publishers
Jefferson, North Carolina, and London

LIBRARY OF CONGRESS CATALOGUING-IN-PUBLICATION DATA

Sewell, Richard C., 1934–
    In the theatre of Dionysos : democracy and tragedy in ancient Athens / Richard C. Sewell.
        p.   cm.
    Includes bibliographical references and index.

    ISBN-13: 978-0-7864-2993-6
    softcover : 50# alkaline paper ∞

    1. Theater — Greece.   2. Greek drama — History and criticism.   3. Democracy and the arts — Greece.   4. Athens (Greece) — History.   I. Title.
PA3203.S49 2007
792.09495 — dc22
                                                  2007020125

British Library cataloguing data are available

©2007 Richard Sewell. All rights reserved

No part of this book may be reproduced or transmitted in any form or by any means, electronic or mechanical, including photocopying or recording, or by any information storage and retrieval system, without permission in writing from the publisher.

Cover image ©2007 Clipart.com

Manufactured in the United States of America

McFarland & Company, Inc., Publishers
  Box 611, Jefferson, North Carolina 28640
    www.mcfarlandpub.com

To the actors, technicians and students
in whose work, joy and excitement I've luckily shared,
including my dear Kim, Gavin and Bryn

Table of Contents

Introduction: An Amateur Time-Travel Memoir   1

I. In the Theater of Dionysos

An Actor at Play with the Past — Athens, 2005 5
A first view of the Theater of Dionysos at Athens, where theater began in the West.

Three or More Greeces 11
A sketch-map of Greek history; where the century of the playwrights fits in.

A Braid of Three Strands 14
Religion, poetry and game competition — three elements crucial to Greek theater.

Arion 17
The poet who shaped the poetic form from which theater evolved.

A Thespian's Dionysia 21
The predemocratic turmoil in Athens. Thespis, an actor-inventor brought to Athens by the dictator Pisistratus; the founding of the festival that came to include dramatic contests.

II. Aeschylus and War News

Arms and the Man and the News 31
First surviving playwright, from Athens' religious suburb, Eleusis. Athenian democracy. The Persian attack. Aeschylus' participation in Marathon.

... and the New 37
  A second wave of Persian attack, and the emerging theater of that time. Salamis.

How This Theater Worked — the Early Years 44
  The running of the dramatic contest and the early plays.

III. First Plays and Other Newness

Philosopher as Playwright 60
  The fifth-century synthesis in the world at large, a nameless revolution as seen behind The Suppliants.

Suppliants, Persians *and* Seven 68
  Social and political implication of the plots of Aeschylus' first three plays.

IV. Prometheus, Then Orestes

Forethought 82
  Challenges in Prometheus Bound, *both religious and in practicalities of staging.*

The Cry on the House of Atreus 93
  The Agamemnon on stage. A close look at the first production of the Oresteia *cycle: the mechanics and overall idea of tragedy. The first use of a solid* skene.

A Son Comes Home 101
  The Libation Bearers, a variation on a murderous theme.

The Gods Come to Athens 106
  The Eumenides and the play's salute to the Areopagus.

Afterthoughts 115
  How did its audience react to The Oresteia— *how do we? Aeschylus as philosophic tragedian.*

V. Sophocles and Euripides — Worse War News

An Unpleasant Few Minutes 121
  Distrusts and furies in ancient and modern Athens.

Theater Life after Aeschylus 124
  Sophocles, a man of his world, and Euripides, a man outside his world, explore what Aeschylus initiated. Athens evolves toward an empire.

Of Ajax and of Heracles' Wife 128
  Sophocles' first two plays.

A One against a Many 134
  Political and social resonance in the first performance of Sophocles'
  Antigone.

Problematics 141
  Some conventions of tragedy we find least appealing: messengers,
  stichomythia (stylized dialogue), choruses tangential to action ...
  and so forth.

Two Electras, Sophocles' and Euripides' 146
  Two playwrights contrasted via their plays on a theme from
  Aeschylus. Sophocles as tragedian of psychology. Euripides as
  tragedian of the bizarre. Writers in a city at war.

VI. Then and Now

A Twinge 171
  Parallels between Athens and current U.S./British foreign policy.
  The disaster of the Peloponnesian Wars reflected in Sophocles and,
  more uniquely, in Euripides.

Hubris in a Theater of War 175
  The phenomenon of dramatic tragedy in a context of war.
  The defeat of Athens and the atrophy of the art of tragedy.

The Art of Old Age 180
  The unique last plays of Sophocles and Euripides.

Charon's Steps 183
  The withering of an art.

Then Afterthought Said... 188
  A summing up — the creative value of digression, irrelevance and
  history.

Bibliography   195
Index   199

Introduction

AN AMATEUR TIME-TRAVEL MEMOIR

Each of us lodges, lifelong, in a one-windowed cell. Lifelong is not long; we're confined to a short span. Love and the spectrum of feeling let us sense the cells in our vicinity; the daily news hints of others at greater distance. We communicate mostly by taps through the walls. But by way of the arts we can look out through other windows for hints of the great lay of the land outside. One sign that those other views give is that this hive of cells of ours is four dimensional. Besides those of us interned here at the moment, there are yet huger past and future populations, real as ourselves but looking from windows on some other story of years. Without art, those other stories may seem very dead; with it we grasp that they too hold life. Mozart, architect of palaces of magical noise; Li Bo, young forever in Imperial China; Ibsen, born old in asphyxiating Norway; Emily Dickinson and Miss Murasaki, biting back such similar tears so many centuries and thousands of miles apart — their work lets us join them a bit. Their arts convincingly transcend our confines.

Suppose the arts actually do function as hormones and pheromones that pass signals through the cells of the organism of humanity in time and space. If so, then they are even more significant to the future than to their own day. They share in keeping our organism human across millennia.

This notion is too big to lay sure claim to. Our culture is devoted to the present. "State of the art," "breaking news," "planned obsolescence," "instant messaging," "fifteen-minute fame," "with it"—our catchphrases and mind-set carry an overwhelming sense of *now*, of the headlong thrust democracy is geared to be and that an innovation economy demands. Our lifestyle rushes counter to attending to the past or giving much credence to a future. To argue that the arts relate to all times is to swim upstream against a Niagara Falls of opinion, yet this book emerges out of that belief.

Transcending time may not be the only, or the most vital, thing arts do. We embroider and elaborate for many reasons, and applied arts—medicine, for example, or farming—serve life in worthy ways different from the arts smugly called "fine." The fine arts do not bother to prove anything. In a Yeats play an anonymous man whose rights are challenged says a great line, that he will give only the proof of himself that a hawk gives that it is not a sparrow. The fine arts offer only that hawk's proof of worth. They are what they are, now and in the Athens I write of.

As credential for this book I can offer only the proof a sparrow gives that it is not a hawk. I am neither Greek scholar nor historian. I am a lifelong lover of theater who has acted, directed, been playwright, built masks, cut costumes, taught theater history, written program copy, made props. I shared in founding a classical repertory troupe; Dekker, Shakespeare, Johnson, Goldoni, Molière, Corneille, Sheridan, Goldsmith, Ibsen, Rostand, Chekhov, Wilde, Shaw, Synge, O'Casey, Gregory, Giraudoux, Molnár, Anderson, Gibson and Pinter were playwrights who underwent the fortunes of war at our hands. The list seems less to the point when I add that we never did a single Greek play. I have worked on some of those in schools and colleges.

Whatever I may have to offer has seemed at its best in working on plays of the past. I am drawn to how they show what in us is a transitory trick of the light and what, if anything, is semipermanent.

Theater is often the least fine, most untidy of arts. Its practicalities are cluttered with the physics of light and sound, the chemistry of paints and glues, the gimmicks of magic shows. Its skills encompass music, physiotherapy, private and public aspects of psychology, carpentry, tailoring, linguistics and make-do scavenging. The dimmest understanding of a play grills us about sociology, about history, about what "doodle" meant in the London street slang of 1751. Theater is forever slapping my ignorance in the face and demanding, "Educate yourself!" No one person could ever be adequate to it. All this claim for theater would be extravagant without the recognition that other disciplines may speak just as pressingly to their own aficionados. Still, theater has been unique for me, and I shape this book to show, a little, why.

The book was, and was not, written at the foot of the Acropolis. In the spring of 2005 my wife, Kim, and I kept a long-made appointment with Greece, and one morning we came to the ruins of the Theater of Dionysos. I suddenly found myself pulling together (or being pulled toward) a piece of writing unplanned till that moment. Near this book's end, when context has accumulated, I will describe that experience. An illusion of completeness seized me as I scribbled notes and paragraphs; I have gone on writing as though I had settled onto a stone seat right there till I had finished. This book has happened with that one old site sharply and stereoscopically before my eyes.

What is here I owe to scholars; the ways I know and judge what's here, aptly or fantastically, I owe to the practice of theater in times intense and dark. The theme is the evolution of one art in one century in one city. Greek tragedy is Athenian tragedy. Every surviving piece (*The Bacchai* perhaps excepted) premiered in the Theater of Dionysos. Athenian citizens wrote all of it. It emerged, defined itself and atrophied with the rise, thriving and first collapse of Athenian democracy. I won't define tragedy, but only watch it grow, bloom and go to seed in an angrily political and darkening world. Tragedy did not ignore that world; it partook of it in ways too seldom noted, and was shaped and scarred by Athens' policies and war abroad. As freedom now bows more and more to the expedients of security and militarism, that ancient war becomes more and more a mirror.

The fine scholarly books on this subject are fine in the scholar's way; they are at pains to be objective. This book, I confess and warn, is subjective; it is about someone looking at theater's past from inside theater—and from inside war. I hope it does not violate the known past, but it extrapolates from it. No doubt I miss great tracts of forest for the trees; I have seen some trees vividly, moss and all.

Here are facts, rumor, gossip, speculation and fragments of faulty collective memory (including my own). They trace how a special way of telling stories unfolded along with a special way of conducting communal life. I'll pause to play along the trail. I will tell with a straight face unlikely things that others told long ago. When I make my own guesses, I will try to be clear that I am doing that. I had not known my life had collected such a scrap-bag of snippets, but here I piece them together, a crazy quilt of whys and hows. Why should there be a chorus? Why divide up plays into two arbitrary halves, tragedy and comedy, when life makes no such division? Why are the Greek plots so bizarre when their intent is so serious? How did poetry become a basic language of drama? Why would performers prefer masks to their own faces? How did preoccupied, commerce-driven and war-torn cities come to expend such energy on their theaters? How were some problematic scenes staged? A few of the questions may seem bafflingly trivial, but when you squint to see the world in a grain of sand (or get that grain out of your eye), trivial and crucial blur together. Archaeologists tell us there is no more illuminating part of a city to excavate than its trash heap.

Note: Most events in this book take place in a century conventionally dated in hundreds of years "before Christ" (B.C.). It seemed to me that forcing the reader to stumble over "B.C." after so many dates would not only weary that reader but would distance him from happenings that were intense and immediate to those who lived them. For this reason, the identifier "B.C." is not used, but should be inferred, for dates between 500 and 400.

Insofar as those years had numbers at all for the people within them, the numbering was often according to Olympiads, counting from the first pan-Greek games at Olympia. Each city also had its own date reckoning, usually by the name of some presiding official.

I

In the Theater of Dionysos

AN ACTOR AT PLAY WITH THE PAST—ATHENS, 2005

It is April. Blood-red Greek poppies already bloom among the broken marble detritus and a scattering of still recognizable seats. Tiny, daisy-faced chamomiles and whiskered grasses nod to the breezy hillside where I sit. Sparrows speak their patois; a few tourists twitter down below in a similar vein. I'm surprised how off-the-crowded-paths this site is today.

The fortified masonry and ledges of the Acropolis tower behind. Up where slope turns into cliffface, some pipe spindles of staging show archaeology at work. They rise in front of a wide gape of shadow, and I wonder, is it the cave of Pan? Myrrhine in *Lysistrata* tells her horny husband that Pan's cave would be a good place for lovemaking. If the hole there was the sacred grotto, she'd have gestured straight over the heads of her audience to point it out. But my notion is wrong. Pan's cave was on the north side of the Acropolis; my shadow behind me at noon shows I'm southeast of it.

Far off before me and to my left hangs a vaster protective wall than the Acropolis cliffs: Mt. Hymettus, famed for honeybees. Its upward curve has turned back the tide of land-hungry city construction. It is mottled hazily with woods and rock, not so much a mountain as a very long ridge of mountains fading into violet.

Here I look down to battered paving in the shape of a *D*. Its bulge is toward me; its straight line is a crumbling waist-high wall where carved, yard-tall warriors stand and stride — and one giant (Atlas maybe?) crouches. On the far side of the wall an open jumble of marble hints unhelpfully at toppled structures. Did plunderer or preservationist range those blocks and drums in that semblance of order? Among them rise a few dark steeples of spongelike cypress and lighter puffs of pine. Through an iron fence between those trees and a street of town houses, black-and-white uniformed magpies patrol back and forth. To them and the sparrows, modern and ancient are all one. Keeping the Parthenon up behind me from looking too big, a milky sky opens its eternal hugeness. "Man is the measure of all things," says the Greek. "Maybe," says the sky. And Hymettus hums to itself.

So this is it. The half bowl of seats and gaps for seats scoops up to me and on up beyond. Fractured marble flags down there abut a now-vanished platform and fallen facade. These are the Theater of Dionysos. They are where it first happened — *it* being my life, among other trivia. This place I have never visited has been a center to a compass arc for fifty-six of the years the Fates have so far given me. Any who do my kind of work and play might say, "Here is the pivot, the hub of my wheel." Right here, almost exactly twenty-five hundred years ago, on a spring day (for Dionysos' great festival was a spring one), it's believed that Aeschylus, son of Euphorion, a veteran of Marathon and later to fight at Salamis, changed choral chant and response into what we call drama. That change came when his production included not just a soloist and chorus singing to each other but a second soloist, an antagonist countering the protagonist with friction and interplay. Aeschylus didn't win a prize that year. Perhaps the mutation felt too odd to the judges. Still, his originating idea would not go away.

Well, yes and no. It's a flawed truth that Aeschylus began drama. We might grope back for the moment when first some African monkey imitated another monkey just for the rarified satisfaction of imitation. Evolutions have no beginnings — except the Big Bang, if that. All unfolds from what went before; to speak of Aeschylus is to start (like a good play) just before the high point of the story. So. No cave of Pan, no primal Aeschylus. I sit and try again to take in this place.

For a while I stare down on the *orchestra* ("dancing place"), ruins of stage front and sparse fragments of *skene* ("tent," and only eventually "scene.") I try, in vain but with pleasure, mentally to peel away layers between now and the grand then.

I. In the Theatre of Dionysos

Back past Byron, past the exploding Parthenon, the Crusades, back to the convert emperor, Constantine (about 300 A.D.), this site has been in the hands of Christians or of Muslim Turks. For devout monotheism, Muslim or Greek Orthodox, this spot was tainted by heathen rites better forgotten, incomprehensible nakedness, demonic excesses. Monotheists cannot afford tragedy; tragedy looks at divine injustice as well as justice. They can't afford real comedies either. The next world shakes its head at comic revelry in this one.

The most recent seventeen centuries of this theater then, seen like video run backward, show a vision of *lapidation*: a gradual, haphazard restoration of lost blocks of marble. Various churches and fortifications are unbuilt and the looted stones hauled here again by monks, slaves, workmen and their straining oxen — all trudging backward in the mind's eye as I slip down through those hundreds of years. Occasionally an earthquake contributes its mite to the process: earth shudders a column back into vertical or pulls into plumb a twisted wall. Rain restores in minute increments the contours of carvings on the low face of the old stage. Trees shrink to seed, grasses are a flickering spume of green like the diaphane of fire on brandy.

Did poor people build and raise families here under Turkish rule and in the Middle Ages? I imagine they were mostly house builders and minor masons who stole away, slab by slab, the ascending semicircles of seating. My mind's eye makes them return their loot, rung by rung, up and up past any trace of where seats are now discernable, to the threshold of that cave up in the cliff.

When that recession seems done, I am under Roman rule, looking at a typical, smallish classical theater. We have all seen the pictures. The front row is not open seating but an arc of high-backed marble chairs, smug and privileged thrones. One surprise: between those front seats and the orchestra floor rises a fence wall of marble slabs, awkwardly high. Those who sit in the thrones cannot see feet or even knees of the chorus when it dances close. A New Englander is reminded of the barrier that rims an ice hockey arena. My idea of free-flowing emotional current between audience and performers is chafed. Perhaps the barrier keeps in the magic of the performance space; more likely it keeps out the impertinence of the crowd.

A wooden stage floor stretches out atop its waist-high front wall enriched with frieze. That frieze is painted, like much of the decor. Garish? Yes, but live where all daily objects are the brown of wood, the red brown of clay and rust or gray browns of dust and lead — where only sky and sea are pure blue, only trees and grass briefly true green and only blood and poppies commonly bright red. Without plastic, color printing, aniline dyes, with eyes no longer jaded, we'd savor painted sculpture. Any mountainside in the circuit of our life could offer us the mellow pallors of natural marble.

The stage is narrow, reached from the orchestra by a central flight of five steps. Actors up there are oddly remote from the chorus on the dancing floor. Upstage of them rises the *skene* facade: central doorway, symmetrical side doorways, standardized and colorful niches, two, maybe three stories, a display case for statuary and Doric, Ionic and Corinthian pillars in relief or full round.

In 200 A.D. (I round the number again) the Romans had been making a pet of Athens. Vile Commodus had just died; a next vile emperor ruled. Despite obese success and downright Texan self-congratulation, some Romans prized every Greek thing that could be bought, stored away in scrolls or set up monumentally. Had they had elevators, Greek poetry would have been sung softly in them. To ornament Athens, Roman magnates were proud to build stoas (malls, more or less) shrines, temples, parks and porticos for the schools to which they shipped off sons to be polished. "Polished" meant rubbed smooth by this *polis*, this unique city. Romans underwrote plays and concerts. A five-minute stroll from here along the base of the Acropolis, they had built a rival theater concert hall, the New Odeion, move solid than this Theater of Dionysos, better preserved and still used.

Now comes an oddity. While I push back another five centuries, from 200 A.D. to 300 B.C., the Theater of Dionysos hardly changes. It jiggles a bit; perhaps a story is added to the facade, here or there a broken statue is replaced, the diaper pattern in the flagging of the orchestra may get redesigned. But the overall effect is static, generation after generation, across a wider gulf than the one that separates us from Shakespeare's grandparents. Here is a culture in stasis, posing for its portrait.

The Romans aren't here yet. The thirty-eight-year-olds of 300 B.C. had been born when Lycurgos (not the Spartan lawgiver but a local finance minister responsible to Alexander the Great) was arranging a round of restoration at the Theater of Dionysos. Twenty-three-year-olds had been born when Alexander's surviving generals were each seizing his corner of a world they'd conquered. Those generals' heirs now fight one another savagely off and on, mostly on. Times look bad. When these young people will be in their forties and fifties, Gauls from the forested north will invade a debilitated Greece. Those marauders will eventually wander off to what is now Turkey, where their Gallic descendants (tamed more by Asia than by passage through Greece) will be "Galatians" and receive epistles.

Arnold Toynbee, a historian now himself historical, points out that counter to our impression, war is not the statistical norm. Most folk most of the time have lived in peace, troubled more by drought, plague, childbirth, old age, toothache and slavery than by mad Ares. In this 300 B.C. Athens, peaceful for the moment, Epicurus is teaching philosophy, proposing people might as well try for happiness. He suggests its pursuit is not helped by religion. He's a genial, sensible man, though his name will be a byword for one who burdens himself with a trained palate he must pay to satisfy. The new Sicilian poems of Theocritos are being passed around; they evoke country ways so charmingly that back-to-the-land thinking, the pastoral style, is born, a frail undertow beneath the human flooding from countryside into cities. Plays are performed this year here as in Greek towns all over the Mediterranean's East End, wherever war is not staging one of its hideous revivals.

A horse nearing home jostles its excitement into the rider. I feel the tug of a home barn now. The progression of images of this theater that I'm conjuring for myself draws close to the hundred years between 400 and 500 B.C. That's where the familiar names lodge: Aeschylus, Sophocles, Euripides, Aristophanes, pug-nosed Socrates, Herodotus the traveler... That is the time of the planning, carving and laborious up-winching of the Parthenon, the grope in the minds of arrogant Democritus and suaver Anaxagoras toward the idea of an atom, the grand-terrible, squabbling experiment of democracy. That is the dazzling century.

An odd thing happens to the Theater of Dionysos as one passes from its 338 B.C. Lycurgan reconstruction back through 400 to 500. After its long Greco-Roman stillness, it fidgets under scrutiny. Just when one would most like to see it clearly, it changes and keeps changing. The raised stage blurs into uncertainties. The hockey barrier drops away. The high, elaborate back *skene* shrinks and not only grows simpler, humbler and more susceptible to varied décor but also becomes impermanent, literally a booth or tent. With a jolt, the orchestra floor enlarges; it moves some yards back and slightly to one side. The hillside slope itself grows less steep, not yet dug into a conic section. Abruptly, instead of any scenic backing at all, there is a drop off at the far edge of the orchestra circle. One sees what the stagehouse blocked from view for so long: the roof of a little temple of Dionysos. That, in 500 B.C., does not hide backstage; it is part of the scene beyond the scene. The whole view, however, is hazy with uncertainties. At about 540 B.C. it vanishes down one of time's trapdoors.

Wise, murky Heraclitos of Ephisos (who lived into that dazzling century and, as refugee understood instability) said, "You cannot step in the same river twice." I cannot step into that Theater of Dionysos I was seeking. For a depressive moment I feel the weight of an odd Greek term, *epigones*, coined for the orphans of the seven warrior nobles fallen attacking Thebes in support of one of Oedipus' sons. Roughly it means, "those born after it's over." Here we are epigones — might as well live with it! As I'll admit later, I'm here partly as a refugee from myself and I feel like getting up, strolling off into the modern city and finding a taverna for lunch.

Still, we do ponder unknowable happenings of our vanished childhood. It is addictive to rummage here among the spindrift for what it was that tossed the sea-change event of theater up into the world. All who come to Greece are in quest of their own past, self-consciously or not. This part of Greece is Attica and — by truth of a pun — it is in fact an attic of one of our old family homes. The pun is not even absurd: in Greek Revival architecture of the 1800s the fashionable broad, sloped roofs produced an upper half-story, which for its Greekness was called an attic.

We compose images of the past from a limited number of pixels, and some of those are surely out of place. Most honest scholars and record keepers admit their assemblages are phantasmagoric. Archaeologists, boot deep in clay, measure with precision; they analyze pebbles spectrographically, they label shards with the patience of Solomon's djinns numbering the sea sands — yet finally even archaeologists have to guess. An immutable mutability of statistics assures us some guesses will be wrong. Here in Athens I'd like to touch something I can be sure of. I can't.

I *can* set the pixels into some order, step back and see if a picture coheres. I fill blanks with scraps of old gossip that careful skeptics reject. Fashions in debunking and re-debunking history come and go.

What our forebears believed of their forebears was part of their consciousness, their present. Their conscious present is the past we seek.

Three or More Greeces

Which Ancient Greece am I looking for? History means what was written; the first Greece is prehistory. Any writing it has is checkmarks of inventory or glyphs of ownership. Greek speakers migrated into the area by 2000 B.C., give or take vague centuries. They took to sea, depopulated and repopulated the islands. The mythic wonder tales filter down from this dreamtime Greece, and the great playwrights portrayed it, overlaying their own ideas and lifestyles onto a deep past.

The wise, terrible judge-kings of Crete, called or not called Minos, did or didn't build unfortified, multi-gabled Knossos. There Theseus, an Athenian princeling (if such a place had princes then), did or did not overcome the Bull of Minos, the Minotaur. The Knossan royal insignia was a *labrys* axe; "labyrinth" the elaborate palace was called by mainlanders like young Theseus. They thought it a maze built to bewilder. For a guess at what that world might have been like, try Mary Renault's *The King Must Die*.

Next to the excavated palace at Knossos, from two sides of a paved rectangle, broad steps shelve up where some two hundred could stand, each rank viewing over the shoulders of the next. It is in some sense a theater; a "seeing place" that word meant. It is too small for the bull-leaping sport Cretans painted; watchers would have gotten gored. *The Iliad* says that the craftsman Daedalus designed "a dancing place" for Minos' lovely daughter, Ariadne. This may be it.

That theater was built between 1700 and 1400 B.C., when Egyptians, whom Cretans traded with, were imperial. Egyptian liturgies from those times suggest pageant scenarios. Did the priests perform dramas in the vast, columnar temple privacy for an audience of painted stone, or out in the sand glare, awing and entertaining court and populace? Egyptian temples offer nothing like a seeing place. Tantalizing! In Egypt we find scripts but no theater space; on Crete we find theater space but no scripts.

I am imagining a Greek itinerant actor for whom this Theater of Dionysos here was modern. On tour he visits the ruins of Knossos and thinks, "Here it began…"

On the prehistoric mainland, Argos, Sparta and Athens had no theaters. Theseus may have ruled from this Acropolis, which was craggier then, its top not yet leveled to build temples on nor its steep sides vertical with hewn stone. Around the Aegean gold burial masks, "cyclopean" masonry, Cretan murals, puzzlingly tiny carvings and puzzlingly huge urns testify to the give of trade and the take of war. A bit before 900 B.C. Kings Agamemnon and Menelaus did or didn't sack Troy. Earthquakes, volcanic tsunamis and incursion of the wilder upon their more sophisticated kin finally reduced that old way of life to anarchic poverty, a "Dark Age."

A reemergence from dark to a dazzling second Greece eventually brought this Theater of Dionysos to Theseus' city — along with so much else. To the littered dates of that process use a mental sketch-map of four numbers: 900, 776 (easy for an American), 490 and 333.

900 B.C. approximates a border between mythic and literal. Around this time Greek-speaking northern Dorians invaded, iron swords against bronze, then settled. In landlocked Laconia they seized scattered towns, which they called, in their blunt way, "The Scattered" (*Sparte*). There a grim Spartan discipline evolved from Dorian ferocity; laconic Laconians became the only Greeks not fond of talking. A bit later Homer sang his *Iliad* about getting even and his *Odyssey* about getting home. Even Laconians valued poets.

776 B.C.— the first Olympic Games — Greek speakers only! A pride one must call national is coalescing among divided, city-loyal peoples. The Olympic Games have a unique Greekness. Kings and dictators don't risk competition; they can never afford to lose. Gamesomeness is one seed of democracy. No other cultures rewarded athletes so wholeheartedly, nor went naked so casually, nor assumed (among kindred) an equality in contest. Greek cities grew well off enough to sprout colonies in Sicily, Italy and on the Black Sea, but even far-flung colonists sent sons home to Olympia to compete.

Time was reckoned by Olympiads, so 776 is a first fixed date. Romans reckoned from their city's fratricidal founding a mere twenty-three years later. Romans seem younger arrivals because Rome didn't show much grandeur till Greece had about run out of glory. Greeks tally history from a game, Romans from a brother-murder.

490 B.C.— Marathon. The Athenians (aided by one small neighbor town) make a Persian invading force recoil. The Great Kings in

Persepolis will nurse vengeful plans for ten years and try again, vastly. In the Gulf of Salamis Athenians will smash that fleet and feel a surge of civic confidence and prestige. From this date Athenian drama launches into fame. Aeschylus fights at Marathon; Sophocles as a boy dances to celebrate Salamis; Euripides is born, some say, during the battle. All three owe their careers to their city's brilliant century.

If you remember numbers easily, throw in **399 B.C.**, a sundown to that brilliance when the recently defeated city executes old Socrates. After that, Athens' political influence dwindles—not because of that judicial murder but of linked causes. The last surviving Greek tragedy has now been written.

333 B.C.—Alexander the Great's wonder year, when he cuts the Gordian knot, one peak of his crazy success. A single Greek-speaking man is taking charge of the entire eastern Mediterranean and Asia Minor. He will go on as far as the Indus River. Ten years later he will be dead and the Greek heartland exhausted. Greek lifestyle, however, defines civilization in the Western World and Near East for centuries to come.

Rome became political and economic master, and Roman skill did things Greeks had been superb at imagining. After six hundred years, a third, unsmiling Greece followed. In Byzantium, Greek in name and language, haggard, ascetic monks redefined the heart of the cosmos as the haggard, ascetic Christ-face looming in dim gold mosaic. In the court of the emperors, regulated almost to autism, an unwieldy bureaucracy's byways of backroom diplomacy and literal backstabbing gave Byzantine its present meaning. Theater was out of the question. Greek excellence had come out of the lovely Cretan labyrinth of Minos and now disappeared again, after two millennia, into a darker labyrinth of Byzantine theology and imperial rigidity.

An actor grasps a role by finding *beats*, scene segments when a single "I-want" drives the character. Meaningful dates mark beats when a new impulse changed the way some scene of a society was played. Larger than the beats, actors may talk of the "spine" of a role or of a whole play. (Hairs get split about these terms, so I won't define *beat* or *spine* more closely.) Something organic produced Greek theater. *Spine* is a good metaphor for it. *Twine* might be better, several strands intertwisted. Religion, competitive games and a tradition of poetry braid in my mind just now as major strands.

A Braid of Three Strands

Down beyond the fence to these ruins school kids trounce a soccer ball up and down the street with hue and cry. The magpies are used to the rumpus. We understand competitions in sports. We share the vicarious thrills of wins and pay for them with irrational pseudo-despairs over losing. That the world was not always crazy about athletics seems to us more odd than that the Greeks were. But competitions as religious fervor and poetic exultation are things to ponder.

In Greece, holy festivals usually *were* contests: "Who can do a thing most excellently to honor excellent gods?" In light of that, a foot race, a discus throw, even a brutish and degrading boxing match was a kind of prayer. Praise-songs to athletes were part of their victory mead and praise-songs to local heroes and spirits were entries like athletic feats. At the Pythian Games near Delphi the poetry competitions had come first. Competitiveness and spirituality teamed together, and bards, migrant in quest of patronage, sang or trained choruses of local chanter-dancers to compete.

In what way did Greeks believe in gods? Not as a tidy twelve from Olympos. By the time belief was that well organized, it was no longer belief, it was story. Merchant voyagers met gods under shifting names and natures. Artemis (Diana) at Ephesos was so fecund she had thousands of breasts; Artemis at Delos was so chaste and warlike that folk said her Amazons cut one breast off so they could draw the bowstring better. On dark nights Artemis was hellish Hecate; bending to ease childbirth, she was the midwife, Eilithyia.

Where hair rose on your neck, where you shivered at a cold splash of the otherworldly, there the gods were. Priests were not rich nor overfeared. Much religious feeling was grounded in places holy for being beautiful. Delphi, holiest of all, is stunning for its sheer vertical cliff slopes, eerie for its fuming earth crack* and sweet for icy mountain

---

About that crack. Delphi was the world navel, the oracle where even Persia and Rome sent gift-bearing delegates to learn from Apollo. Apollo was not sole deity there. He had seized the shrine, they said, from an old earth goddess and her serpent, Pytho. "Pythia" as each generation of Delphic priestess was called, seated herself over a vent in the rock, gasses rose and she, drugged into touch with the All-Knowing, muttered dark responses to inquiries.

Till recently we were taught that there was no such vent—excavation had found none in the ruined temple of Pythian Apollo; however, in 1995 archaeologist John Hale and geologist Jelle de Boer collaborated, and geology revealed what archaeology had missed. A deep fault does run directly under the temple at Delphi. Its limestone shows traces of naturally

springs. There was a dancing delight in nature to which Christians, Jews and Muslims can seem blind. If Greek visual art has little landscape, that must be because the Greeks felt their skill was not up to it. They loved their steeps and coasts almost to rapture. Theirs could also be a thinker's religion. Herakleitos said, "The mind that steers all things through all things is willing and unwilling to be called Zeus." He did not speak for all Greeks, but he was not blaspheming. In plays, characters may talk of "God" in the singular, making us ask if the translator imposed modern beliefs. By a linguistic oddity, the name Zeus, (when not the subject of the sentence) seems to be a form of the adjective *godly*. Talk of Zeus rings polytheistic in some ears, almost monotheistic in others. Zeus could also simply be the sky. Folk said "Zeus rains" as commonly as "It is raining."

Religion everywhere has angry gods from which one seeks salvation. Greeks had those, but out of the nightsoil of Hades they grew their best hopes. Young Persephone, queen of both death and springtime, figured with her mother, Demeter ("Grain-mother" or "Godmother"?), in a mystery cult at Eleusis within a long walk of Athens. That holy place kept its secrets; we know only that it offered hope beyond the grave to the initiated soul. Bacchos Dionysos, the vine god, a cult deity newer to Greece, naturalized himself especially among the socially repressed, the women and the poor. There was vivid folk memory of the spread of his worship and of resistance to it. Ecstasy, mania, orgy the cult was called, but, like Demeter, Dionysos promises life more abundant; his myths fused with hers. Like the vine, he was resurrected each spring; like wine, he opened minds to things joyously or terribly beyond reason. Such gods say to their devotees, "I cannot tell you why you suffer, but I suffer with you." A god's sorrows comfort the sorrowful.

How Dionysos became patron of theater can be traced through two early poets, Arion and Thespis. Why Dionysos became that patron is subtler. Ecstasy means literally "standing outside," or "being beside yourself." Did Bacchic ecstasy lend itself to acting? Certainly being drunk on stage does not. Still, though all performers strive for self-control one way or another, there is free-wheeling loss of self in role-playing. Most of us prefer not to accentuate that. Thinking about it

formed ethylene, a sweet-smelling gas that produces euphoria and seizures. So much for debunking. Wesleyan University's spring 2004 publication details the discovery.

too much feels either like self-delusion or psychological hypochondria. It is a paradox — as are the most profoundest things about theater and about religion.

One of the Greek religion's paradoxes was that it had no holy book, no fixed credo. It was as open-ended as life. Every good word about pagan Greek religion is refutable. To seek theater in Greece is to find Greek life with its self-contradictions, religious and otherwise. In ancient Greece you came across sanctified cruelty, stupor and pig-headedness, even human sacrifice under extreme stress or in the outback of Arcadia. But when you compare other religions' worst behaviors, praise feels valid. Of separation and non-separation of religion and state in the great days of Athens, there are tales to tell eventually.

Poets were felt to talk of gods as meaningfully as priests. A priest repeated old rites, but poets when enthused ("in-god-ed") could rhapsodize new news of the gods. Greek bards never wholly lost their folkrole as shamans. They often sang of daily life in the street and lively nights in the bed, but if they could "articulate sweet sounds together" (Yeats' phrase for poemmaking), they were in touch with the divine.

Greek poetry *was* sweet sounds, sung, often to a lyre. A fair parallel to a Greek poet is our folk singer with guitar. ("Guitar" is, via Spanish via Arabic, *kithara*, a lyre with a louder sound box — an amped lyre, you might say.) Poetry not only had pitch, it was also and primarily rhythmic, though in a way we would be hard put to hear. For us, speech rhythm is patterned by how we stress or do not stress syllables, loud or soft. Greek drew vowels out long or clipped them off, and the Greek ear heard pattern in long and short. To try to reproduce those rhythms in English is to make apple pie with crackers; the basic ingredient is hopelessly wrong.

Theirs was a smaller, known world of landscapes and inscapes. Friendly neighbors whisper to impatient Electra in Sophocles,

> One who lives by Krissa's cattle-grazing shore will not forget.

All hearers knew that Electra's longed-for brother had been raised near Krissa, and many had eaten raisins in those pastures under Delphi's looming mountain, watching chariots race at the Pythian Games. Later in that play, a recounted chariot crash feels to us like digression; for its audience it had context.

Greek word endings let poets say, "Xerxes built swift ships," "Ships swift built Xerxes," or "Swift built Xerxes ships." A line that fizzes with scrambled words may go flat in translation even apart from lost melody and rhythm. Also, contemporary speech was just one available building material for poems. A current poet would cringe to write anything as old-fangled as "Xerxes wrought fleet barks," but Greeks freely mixed dated words with the up-to-date. Aeschylus, an extreme poet, was a bolder coiner of idioms than Shakespeare and played with ancient prayer formulas, poetic dictions of other cities, folk-spell and phrases from *The Iliad* and *The Odyssey*. Speaking a timeless chant of awe and magic, the plays and poems are at once rite and entertainment. They still touch us if we lean a bit toward them.

ARION

The works of Homer, "Father of Poetry," almost defined a Greek to the Greeks. What linked together their city enclaves was the tongue they spoke. If a nationality is a kind of intangible organism, this organism's circulatory system was its journeying bards, keeping language and traditions mutually intelligible from city to city and generation to generation.

Credit for a role in theater's evolution is seldom given the poet Arion — yes, the Arion with the dolphin. His mythlike story points up things about geography, lifestyle and one of the deep roots of drama. Arion was real, an adult around 620 B.C., born on Lesbos off the coast that was Asia to his people, Turkey to us. " Ionian" and "Aolian" the Greeks there called themselves and their dialects. They were cosmopolitan; their great ports, Mytilene, Ephesus, and Miletos shrewdly sent respects to non-Greek inland kings but conducted their own affairs and felt as sovereign to themselves as cities on the home peninsula. Greece in those days was the whole horseshoe of mountainous shores around three sides of the Aegean, the islands scattered in it, plus colonial Sicily and southern Italy. Think of Greece as much as a body of water as an area of land.

Arion traveled. Festival days when a poet might win fame and reward varied from city to city, so poets were migratory. Arion spent some part of his life in Corinth, whose perch high between two gulfs brought it trade and luxury. Its Acrocorinth, higher than this

Acropolis and with its own fresh springwater, seemed unassailable. At the time Corinth typified an unpleasant stage in political growth. It had expelled its king, the apex of a warrior aristocracy, only to slip into the hands of dictators, supporters of the business class and cynical claimants to the loyalty of the farming poor. Such a dictator was called a "tyrant," perhaps for living in a *tyrsis*, a tower fort — the word came at last to mean about the same as *king*. Sophocles' title *Oidipous Tyrranos*, gets billed as "Oedipus the King." The second-generation tyrant Periander of Corinth, whose forty-year rule spanned both sides of 600 B.C., was a horrible, long-surviving old hyena who could have given lessons to Pinochet or Idi Amin, but he was a generous patron.

Corinthians were as fond of gold as people always are, but Greek life style on the whole had a grace of simplicity. Conspicuous consumption was not a particularly Greek vice. Our alpha dogs display with designer wealth-trash, executive jets, and cosmetics of costly botulism and the scalpel. To show off, rich Greeks typically turned to public works or patronage of schools or of the arts. In return for patronage, a Periander expected praise from poets he hosted. Greeks had a keen appetite for *kudos* — respect, praise, good repute. Periander's ilk were dangerous, yet for them one's honored image in the minds of others satisfied like drink. A craving for kudos sometimes made them use wealth and power better than humans usually do. Still, it is hard to appreciate Greek poets when they are singing paid-for praises — and neither buyers not sellers blush. Arion put at least some of his gift to better use.

Periander financed a western tour for Arion, to Sicily and the instep of Italy's "boot." Colonials were always glad to hear the accents of the home cities. Arion competed and won. Such a man's performance was very much a show; he was, of course, a master of his lyre (hence the word *lyric*), and there was often a striking costume. We know little about what was worn, but it drew the eye.

Arion not only performed solos but also trained local youth, maidens or both to chant and move. He worked up a unique genre of performance for festivals of Dionysos. Sicily's volcanic soil and clement weather are blessed by the Wine God, and dwellers there blessed the Wine God in return. Arion's ecstatic chants used a double chorus of fifty dressed in goatskins like the god's satyr followers. The group tossed its excitement back and forth as it danced. Judges bore a keen eye for the excellence of the choruses as they gyrated and stamped. The base patterns of poetry were called "feet" for reason; feet accentuated rhythm with heel and toe. As the two halves of the chorus countered each other, there were "turns" and "counterturns"—the Greek for those is *strophe* and *antistrophe*. For centuries those terms clung to antiphonal verse patterns echoing one another. Literal-minded latter-day teachers assured their students that choral movement among the Greeks consisted in turning to the left and then to the right! Another quirk of word suggests that the basic move was circular, natural for dancers when their audience stands around them on all sides.

Arion's performances were unique enough to have a special word, *dithyramb*. ("*Di-*" hints at doubleness; what a "*thyramb*" was is argued.) Judging from later dithyrambs, they were not just praise; they were stories. A chorus of fifty was specified and recalled, suggesting that it was an unusually large number. Even if a chorus is divided so that only twenty-five speak at once while the other half moves, that big a group makes clarity devilishly difficult. But the effect, well done, is stunning. In choral work words now take second place to music, but there was equality in those days; the words mattered.

Somehow the tradition of Arion and his choral invention has to square with the ethnologists' vision of theater as emerging from folk festival and primitive magic. Arion brought the sophisticated art form of competitive poetry to the harvest revels where field hands in improvised blood-paint and leaves frightened and delighted their fellow villagers by personifying the roving satyr trains of Dionysos. One pictures something like the Twelfth Night children in Hispanic countries, who sing and beg through the streets in the guise of the Three Kings of the Christian Epiphany. Imagine such a folk band taken in hand by some former-day Carl Orff, who composes for them new, demanding text and music: this was art song, not folk song. It has to have been the role-playing as satyrs that made the dithyrambic chorus different from other groups that professional poets trained.

Arion was a hit in cities like Sybaris, with its sybarite reputation for pleasure seeking. I think of the Greek West as a California. People immigrated there for the soil; they stayed for the lifestyle. Prizes at festivals were proudly simple, a garland, a goat kid or crock of good wine, but the wealthy added their showy generosity. In such places poetry could be as profitable as our rock stardom. Arion was a rich man when he took his prizes and gifts aboard a ship bound back to Corinth. His luggage included gold wreaths, rings and (the kingdom of Lydia's innovation of 680 B.C. having reached west by way of the Greek city of Argos) coins. Of that voyage the extraordinary fable is told.

The crew knew what Arion had with him. Just before their home landfall they conspired and turned on him, ready to kill. He begged them to let him perform a last chant. Even for pirates a poet was very nearly a holy man. They must have watched uneasily as he took his lyre and stood up in the stern to sing. When his song was done, he leaped into the sea.

The treacherous crew continued on to Corinth and reported that Arion had chosen to stay behind with his prize monies. But a dolphin, drawn by the poet's song, had dived under him, buoyed him up and carried him to shore. When Arion arrived to tell Periander what had happened, the crewmen were still in town. Perhaps they were spending ill-gotten loot in the famed brothel temple of Corinthian Aphrodite, nightclub to the world, which made Corinth an ancient Las Vegas.

That Periander punished them can be guessed by a grim story from Herodotus. Periander once walked in a wheat field with an older, neighboring tyrant, a cousin with whom he could be frank. The younger asked how tyrants hold on to power. The elder made no answer, (tyrants are never unaccompanied) but as they strolled, kept striking with his staff to knock off wheat heads that grew taller than average.

Periander understood that wordless advice: Corinthians who stood too tall under his rule did not live long — nor, surely, did sailors who tried to kill his favorites. But either Periander felt no threat from poets or devoutly feared the Muse as a goddess; he did well by Arion. In later times people pointed out a bronze statue of a dolphin with a rider, set up on the cliff at Taenaron that beetles over where Arion had been borne ashore. It was an offering statue, they said, commissioned and set up by Arion as a thanks to the sea-god. Herodotus, in the first book of his travels, writes of seeing it.

Take the stories for their worth. What matters is that the dithyramb, an intense narrative by a double chorus, fifty chanting dancers, became a tradition at Dionysian festivals. What had been a local style became known throughout Greece with Arion's name attached. Celebrations of the god of the regrown vine had their dithyramb as our Christmas has its Handel's *Messiah* or our Passover its *Haggadah*.

Corinth in the 600s B.C. seemed destined to greatness. The Isthmus made it a crossroad: Sparta to the south was already rigidified in political paranoia, rejecting all innovation. Athens to the northeast was smaller and faction-torn. Thebes to the north had a rich plain and a lake but no harbor to keep it in touch with the world. Why did Athens come to take the lead and Corinth to play a secondary role? My comparison to Las Vegas is not a flippant dumbing-down. However you define *goods* or *The Good*, Corinth was more a sieve that goods poured through than a basket that held them.

In Athens, a generation after Arion, a performer poet named Thespis took the next step toward drama. To imagine him, one needs a sense of the Athens that welcomed him.

A Thespian's Dionysia

When Thespis came there, Athens was at that phase of political metamorphosis that Corinth had been in Arion's time. Like the Corinthians, Athenians had driven out their king, though by a subtler revolution. A King Codros (date unsure) died without issue; consensus found no one worthy to succeed him. Kingship was divided among a priest king, a war king, a king-to-date-years-from, and so forth. I'm simplifying. Clans and economic classes jostled fiercely together, and *king* (for which there are several words) came to mean those to whom powers were parceled out. Over time kingships that had been for life were term-limited and elected, first from the old aristocracy, then from a wider community. But a prosperous peace is not secured by multiplying officials.

Twice, as the city verged on anarchy, respected individuals were asked to bring an acceptable order into public life. In effect they were to be constitution framers, though the concept of a constitution did not yet exist. The first of those men, named Draco — I'm not making that up! — imposed strictures so severe that his name still clings to draconian legislation. He did get the city's laws written. (For example, Draco decreed that homicides be tried openly in the Areopagus, replacing blood vendetta with jury verdict. That becomes a great play's theme some hundred and seventy years later.) But Draco's support of conservative status quo in a non-static city could last only as long his intimidating personal magnetism. Once he died, aristocrats, merchant seamen and up-land farmers were again at three-way odds. Other cities' bloody revolts and counter-revolutionary tyrants like Periander made vivid a dire need for compromises no one really wanted.

Athens some thirty years later put itself in the hands of one Solon, about a decade before Periander of Corinth died. Solon was trusted for sense and sensibility (he was a poet among other things) and for un-Dracolike geniality. His reforms shaped much that was workable in Athens as long as self-rule lasted there. The assembly he created or strengthened seems to have functioned under the archons (multiple "kings") roughly as a parliament functioned under the monarchy of the Renaissance in Britain. To himself he must have seemed a failure. At sixty-seven, still vigorous, he had called his work as lawgiver done and traveled for many years, seeing the world. He chose to wait for the recipe he had given his home city to cook.

He returned to find his oven smoking. A young cousin, Pisistratus, was worming toward tyranny. Too old to mount a political campaign, Solon took to poetry.

> Sure as thunder after lightning, sure
> as clouds will drop their snow and hail—
> raise a despot and you lay a city low!
> There's a truth it's time you all should know.

Solon's polemics don't tempt great translators. At last he hung up his shield outside his door, a statement that he was done with public life.

Pisistratus had a flair for political theatrics. Staging an attack on himself, he asked the assembly for a guard of fifty. Once he had his private army, his fellow officials were easy to intimidate. Demagogues always have a call for security ready in their carpetbag of tricks. To Pisistratus' credit, his ruthlessness had limits. Avoiding a typical tyrant's bloodbaths, he usually maneuvered to have opponents exiled. Twice during his long career he too was temporarily exiled. He made his second return by his most shameless ruse. He marched home to the Acropolis with a strikingly tall young woman in helmet and armor leading his followers. They spread the rumor that Athena herself had brought him home to bless her city! We smile, but worse men have gotten themselves high office by claiming divine moral mandate.

Pisistratus did the arts much service, good or ill. Some poets had begun writing their chanted verses, and Pisistratus called to Athens a commission of *rhapsodes*, or reciters, to collate and write out *The Iliad* and *The Odyssey*. For Homer and his "sons" (traveling rhapsodes), the Muses had been not nine but one, and one of her names was Mnemosyne, Memory. Poetry had been a musical thing of mind and tongue, phrased for indelibility in the ear or else soon lost. Rhapsodes did the prodigious, memorizing whole epics, but any poet had his own works ready on his lips, along with pieces by others that might be called for over the wine. Now the nature of poetry was shifting. Crucially, writing hastened a separation of poetry from music. An alphabet could preserve speech, but a notation to freeze-dry music in a similar way was lacking until long, long later. Transmitted by ink, a poem was tuneless, a frozen bird, plumage but no song. Melody (and memorization), however, remained vital to performance: when a specific muse later became linked with tragedy she was Melpomene, She-Who-Sings-Sweet.

It was Pisistratus who, as patron to Thespis, ensured him a place in Athens. Thespis, native to Icarion, a nearby town tucked into the hills above Marathon, worked like Arion with local choral backups he trained. Rather than sing varied genres of verse, as most poets did, he seems to have turned all his skill to dithyramb. The cult of Dionysos had deep roots in Icarion. One could not live by one springtime god alone; traveling like other poets from festival to festival, Thespis must have made his name saluting varied gods and heroes. When the celebration was not Dionysian, the chorus was no longer necessarily of satyrs, but the form Thespis used was dithyrambic. We're told he traveled with a cart, carrying properties or costumes with him, and made his own masks. His shows were not only words and music; the eye was invited to feast along with the ear.

Thespis' crucial innovation was that in performance he stepped forward, telling, boasting and grieving *as* the mythic being he celebrated. To uncritical onlookers he may have seemed a "channeler." Dionysos was a divinity of ecstasy out of another world. An individual, suddenly standing out among dancers, speaking as magically as a spirit might, was in some sense that spirit.

Characters in epics often speak for themselves. The winged words of Odysseus, Achilles and others fly back and forth in first person throughout Homer, and rhapsodes spoke those lines with personalized passion. But in the leap of full embodiment a performer suspends emotional distance, surrenders self to other and *enters* a role. It can seem to the outsider suspiciously like demonic possession or identity theft. To many people, for good or ill, acting is uncanny. Reservation about actors (and attraction to them) has been endured or capitalized on through the centuries. Famous performers, more than other artists, draw adulation out of all proportion to their worth — and I think trigger some covert fear. We, as naïve as Greeks, sometimes elect our actors to high office on the strength of personae they have played. Greeks and Romans too used actors as persuasive ambassadors. Thespis took on the charged role of role-player. Before him that had been the province of shamans and prophets. Now it was to belong to people who consciously thought of themselves as artists.

There's a good story that just may have happened if Solon lived to be very old and rather a curmudgeon. Solon, whose motto is "learn something new every day," comes to see Thespis' work. After the show he goes up to the young man. Bystanders hush: what praise will old, famed wisdom speak to young, flushed success? Solon asks, "Aren't you ashamed to tell such lies in front of so many people?" Well, few old men (Chomsky and Studs Terkel excepted) are at their best when confronted with the new. Thespis must have known he was going to be able to dine out on that anecdote for the rest of his life.

Thespis performed masked. Poet-performers want the world to know who they are. Arion and other Greek bards dressed strikingly, but they would no more have disguised themselves as someone else than Joan Baez would. A poem is at once a general truth and an intensely personal statement, so poets are quintessentially themselves; personal soul is their stock in trade. Thespis, however, like thespians after him, chose that the world should know the character he played — although to see that character intensely and convincingly was to lose sight of the performer. Right there was a fork in the road: what had been one art became two different ones.

Why do theater practitioners and sensitive audience members even now feel uneasy with a theater space in which spectators must cross the set to take their places? The master convention of theater is this: figures who walk in the defined space are any persons from time or imagination *except the persons they actually are.* It follows that the theater space can be any place in this or another world *except this actual theater space.* We exclude nothing but actuality. When this convention is novel to spectators, a mask is a key; it smoothly opens their mental door to that perception.

A mask's limitations are clear. Our prime organ of communication is the face, not the tongue, miracle though language is. A mask's advantages are subtler. It throws focus onto the words. It ensures an otherness a barefaced player must work for. It liberates the shy, heightens a player's strangeness and covers up the near blasphemy of pretending to be a demigod or a hero. It is also selfless; it tests an actor's generosity. When you are in a mask, the play is hardly about *you* at all.

What kind of mask did Thespis wear? Masks had figured in ritual before his time. Bacchic roisterers painted their faces with ocher or blood and leaves. Bloated Gorgon faces grimaced with protruding tongue on shields and roof peaks to ward off evil. Athena herself wore Medusa's snaky head on her breastplate. Ethnologists coined the term, *apotropic,* for devices that keep demons at bay. At some rites in rural Greece priests wore apotropic masks. But the roles Thespis created needed the sort of faces sculptors were just then carving for gods and heroes. In the next generation masks covered the whole head, helmetlike; the old ritual masks may or may not have.

The oldest pictured Attic theatrical mask is on a vase fragment from Thespis' time or a bit later. It is a very basic face, handsome in a folk art way, a bit neutral like all but the best of the era's statuary. It is shown frontally, so that there is no telling whether it covered the head. It troubles us because it seems almost a meter tall, to judge by the young man who carries it. A dancer with a head half as big as his body strikes us as cartoonish.

A mask that huge would have loomed over chorus and onlookers. In a festival the crowd might have been uncritical. Thespis wearing such a thing would have been a bearer of a god head — those of us who've seen the Bread and Puppet Theatre will know such a mask has eerie authority. However, there is no knowing what event that mask was intended for, comic or serious. Also, at the period of this vase, children were drawn as diminutive adults. Probably the mask carrier here is a little boy. A foot of someone walking beside him at the edge of the fragment is almost of a scale to wear the mask without oddity.

My guess is that Thespis' masks were of near normal size. Those of the next generation were. Were they molded leather like the masks of commedia dell' arte or of linen rigidified with glue? Given the stench of hide glue, which elderly theater practitioners still recall, leather seems preferable. Either way, they would have been shaped on molds of sculpted clay or wood. Thespis lived to see exquisite, idealized near realism being done in sculpture. Surely his masks were craftsmanly and subtle once he enjoyed patronage.

Patronage came. Pisistratus must have first seen Thespis at work in the agora at one of the year's four Dionysian festivals, and the ruler's eye did not miss the way the young man's work swayed a crowd. Pisistratus incorporated Thespis' dithyramb into an aggrandized version of the Dionysian celebration at Athens, the "City Dionysia." A countryside Dionysia already existed — a rural god was being lured into urbanity. A historian, reluctantly praising Pisistratus, tells more clearly than I would how art and politics fused. (I abridge but use his words.) Pisistratus

> forced the rich and Well-fathered of Athens to keep the oath that Solon had exacted of all citizens before he deliberately went on his travels.... [Pisistratus] guarded the interests of the peasants, redistributed the lands of exiled nobles, built an aqueduct and undertook other public works that employed the poor.
>
> Not content with making more impressive the Great Panathenaic festivals in which athletes from all over Greece competed, rhapsodes recited Homer and musicians sang, Pisistratus founded the Great Dionysiac festival to appeal to the people — for Dionysos was a favorite god of Dustyfoot" [peasant farmer].... A central feature was ... a dialogue between god and man. Pisistratus and his two sons ... favored the gods and heroes the populace most loved. In favoring Dionysos the god of ... the union of man with god, of death and resurrection, [he] was drawing on the deepest beliefs of the poor, on ancient religious hopes and fears that the nobles, with their Olympic deities in general did not share. The mysteries ... promised eternal life to all, even slaves" [Stringfellow Barr, *The Will of Zeus*].

There is a lot to chew in that. It recognizes that Pisistratus was no run-of-the-mill dictator tyrant. Either profoundly or cynically or confusedly, he must have believed in government as a service to the governed, the principle that his cousin Solon's laws had sought for. His two exiles without major bloodshed bear witness.

I like Barr's calling Thespian dithyrambs "dialogue between god and man," assuming "man" as humankind. The Greek chorus embodies the collective human community as well as some specific group caught up in a specific event. Thespis, in the role of Dionysos or another demigod, speaks directly to them and is spoken to. Mystics describe intimate *meeting* between human and cosmos; here, in nascent theater, it happens in the open air among a throng.

Barr points to Dionysos as a partisan god in the poor's struggle to share in power. Moses versus Pharaoh and the Egyptian nobility, Jesus versus Romans and upper class Jerusalemites, Mohammed versus Medina's rich merchants — religions, like most people, are radical when young, conservative near death. (Is that why young conservatives seem abnormal and old radicals faintly comic?) We hardly think of Bacchus Dionysos versus the Greek aristocracy, but the conflict left traces, Euripides' play *The Bacchae,* for one.

Economics hint at why Pisistratus welcomed and supported Thespis. Could Thespis have known he was being used to exalt a political agenda? If he knew, did he agree and more importantly could he afford to care? Theater is so labor intensive that it has almost always required patronage. Before it was fully born, theater's potential as a social tool was recognized. Theater professionals can have other impassioned aims but should not forget the power in what they do. Power brokers censor it or utilize it. Pisistratus hired Thespis and, by spiritual subcontract, hired Dionysos as well. Dionysos, like the tyrant's impoverished supporters, understood suffering; a performance piece about suffering spoke to the god and to the people. Tragedy is an aspect of social politics from its start.

At last, under the regime of Pisistratus, I dimly glimpse something here at this specific site. Not on the Acropolis, but down here at town level there had been a fane (holy ground) to Dionysos ever since his worship had arrived in Attica, and there was a small temple. Pisistratus had construction undertaken here; the great circle of the dance floor, the *orchestra* was laid out. Some trace the circularity of orchestras to threshing floors where tethered oxen tread round the pivot of their stake to trample grain from chaff. Once the threshing is done, a dance to the vegetation god takes place in that round. Isn't it simpler to picture that wherever dance happens in plaza or marketplace, the crowd drifts in from all sides, naturally forming a circle?

To flatten ground on the slope for the first Great Dionysia's dance space, a retaining wall higher than a man had to be raised on the side away from the hill and toward the temple. From the temple steps the dancers would have been above eye level, but from up toward the Acropolis many could watch. This playing space was less for the God in his house and more for the people who gathered in open air.

Actors will see how that arrangement surrendered the communal interaction of playing in the round. The gain was a rudimentary upstage and downstage never to be had in a plaza or threshing floor. Upstage and down let players put their audience at a distance, approach it more intimately or even turn backs on it. Perhaps only performers sense how much artistic leverage this adds.

Entry from down behind that retaining wall was possible. Performers learn instinctively the curious advantage of arrival and vanishing, a "clean" entrance or exit. To come up from out of sight would have had a visual effect like rising up out of the earth or out of thin air. Surely Thespis, bearing a novel, masked identity, must have taken advantage of that. "Lo!" "Behold!" "Presto!" are primal cries of theater because "Surprise me!" is always the unspoken request of the audience.

The three- or four-day City Dionysia was inaugurated in the spring of 534 B.C.. It was to grow to five days a generation later, when comedies were added. Solemn and erotic mingled in ways weird to us. Dionysos' statue, having been conveyed by night outside the West gate on the Sacred Way toward Eleusis, was marched in prancing triumph home through the city to his temple and the new playing space. As at other festivals, tall phallus poles were paraded through the streets. Some popular rites of India where religion and rumpus converge help us imagine how a crowd that exuberant could be brought to focus attention on intricate verse.

Rules of contest are known but not the order in which rules evolved, nor how they changed nor how firmly they were enforced. Dithyrambic choruses in the old vein had pride of place: on the first day choruses of men and of boys competed. Later there were to be ten of those, one from the ten tribes of Athens, but the ten tribes were part of a democratic city restructuring that came after Pisistratus' sons were driven out. At first the number of entries will have been open ended.

Other composer/arrangers of dithyramb soon seized on Thespis' innovation of individual encountering chorus, evolving the new form, distinct enough to need its own contest. Ritual presumes repetition, competing demands the opposite, variation. Inevitably, in quest of variety, the subject matter expanded from Dionysos into the whole realm of folk heroes.

The rules get spoken of as if unchanging: an entry of three serious pieces and one "satyr play" by a given presenter in a day, three days of entries. Were there, from the first, two other proto-playwrights (as opposed to dithyramb composers) to compete with Thespis? Did they, from the first, each stage four proto-plays? Later, all pieces exhibited were premières. Were the required four pieces a hurdle set up at first so that those with a developed repertoire — and therefore some claim to quality — would enter? I pose the questions only as reminder that the event was evolving, not fixed. Sensing that what they watched was different from dithyramb or anything else, the audience called the event "doings," which in Greek is *drama*.

Did a satyr play differ much from the comedic street improvisations of the time? Probably mostly in linking the contest ceremony firmly to Dionysos through his rout of satyr followers and in sharing the dithyrambic pattern of chorus and lead singer. The satyr play's separation from more solemn dramas must have evolved over forty or fifty years: a merrier and always Dionysian story following the more serious ones till tradition and taste made two species, as different in temperament (though as like in general shape) as wolf and fox.

Among the earliest professional (that is, full-time) comedic performers in Attica was Susarion, who in Thespis' boyhood, supposedly, brought that kind of fun from elsewhere to Icarion, Thespis's hometown. Would an itinerant entertainer bring his skills specifically to so tiny a hill town on the north flanks of a marble quarry mountain? Surely Susarion visited many Attic villages — but he was remembered especially for his visit to Icarion because there Thespis watched him and imagination was kindled. If one could talk hilarious nonsense from inside an assumed role, Thespis must have thought, why not talk earnest poetry? Susarion's followers, in Aeschylus' time were still plying their mockery in the marketplaces. Comedies were not competitions at this point; any number could play. That may have been what nudged Aeschylus toward his innovation in tragedy. So, comedy was one of tragedy's forebears. Comedy was to grow so popular as to be awarded its own day of contests, but before comedies had that formal role, the word *tragedy* was being used in Athens not as an opposite but as a thing of its own.

In Thespis' Icarion the prize at a choral contest had been a goat, and the word *tragoidia* ("goat-song") dates at least from him. Explanations of the word over the centuries have been ingenious. A monkish medieval scholar proposed that the term applied to a play that "began prosperously like a goat's beard, and ended miserably like a goat's tail!" Goat-songs dealt with struggle and suffering but might reach a solemn, worked-for resolution that could be called happy. *Tragedy* was not yet a synonym for *horrible calamity*. Aristotle says the language of the theater before Aeschylus was "laughable"; he probably means he thought it absurd, but it could be that it had a deliberately comic side. Between Thespis' day and Aeschylus,' as the subjects of tragedies became darker, the obligatory satyr play defined itself in deference to a lingering taste for the whimsical. No doubt a ritual recollection of satyrs in the first dithyrambs helped keep satyr plays both distinct from other comedies and also organic to performance of tragedies.

At those early City Dionysias deep basics of Athenian tragedy were in place: the festival, the uphill-slope viewpoint for watching performance, the several troupes vying, the primacy of a double chorus's responsive chant and dance, the masks, the assumption that even urgent talk would be in well-wrought verse, the focus on suffering and strife. Most importantly here was the present tense, the essential it-is-happening-now-and-you-and-I-are-here of theater, along with its contradictory here-is-elsewhere-and-these-people-are-other. As a festival it had permanence; as a competition it had to keep growing; as poetry it was memorable. There was more to come.

II

Aeschylus and War News

ARMS AND THE MAN AND THE NEWS

Last night Kim and I saw the Greek National Theater's Young Company in an inventive, bizarre production of Aeschylus' *Oresteia*. They paraded their audience, with clowning down the street around a corner, to an unfinished parking garage and unfolded a free-wheeling, viscerally impassioned version of the trilogy, herding us from dim floor down to dimmer floor till the final confrontation with the Furies and the trial of Orestes was in the minelike dank and rubble of an unfinished cellar. Past and present embraced like angry lovers where this city will eventually park cars.

The Oresteia is about the gods bequeathing responsibility for justice to humans, a deed they accomplish in establishing trial by jury. Aeschylus believed that bequest had been made to his fellow Athenians, and his long life was over before they had completely bungled the administration of it. That the Gods, remote themselves from justice, expect humans to be just is a huge, unwieldy thought. The twentieth century tried to pick it up again under the intimidating name of existentialism. *The Oresteia* is very much *our* play. A great piece carves out a place for itself in remote generations.

I try to let awakened notions about Aeschylus (other people's notions — all I know is hearsay) take over the parking space that this old, once holy Theater of Dionysos site is making in my head. What vehicles were here? However, between shadowy Thespis and solid Aeschylus and his peers who make this Theater of Dionysos matter, Persians and their wars get in the way. Those wars need accounting for.

Pisistratus' heirs were two sons, less scrupulous than their father. Most second-generation dictators are either hyenas or toy poodles. The Pisistratidae were a bit of both. They had seen their father go in and out of exile and had no intention of imitating that. They charmed friends, assassinated opponents, threw great parties — and were overthrown. One, trying to use his privilege to horn in on a love affair between two young men, was stabbed. The other Pisistratid son, Hippias, took his brutal revenge (the faithful mistress of one of the assassins was among those tortured), but the fire was in the hay. Athens hailed the stabbers as liberators and revived its traditions of popular rule. Hippias and an entourage of his clansfolk fled east. They left behind in Athens a custom of Dionysian drama already too deeply grown into the city's life to be rejected.

East of the Aegean, the Ionians, long so free and intellectually so alive, had now been absorbed into the Persian Empire, a stern landlord. Many Ionian émigrés to Athens, bringing a mental wealth of poems, books and skills, had also brought uneasy reports of Persian might. Hippias went to the Persians. If Darius the Great King would reinstate him in Athens, he would be the Great King's vassal. Darius, indifferent, asked, "Who might these Athenians be?"

Hippias cooled his heels for six years in the Great King's court; however, Ionia rebelled (piecemeal, wrangling city with city), and in 497 B.C. some Ionians burned their nearest Persian provincial capital. The huge Persian Empire retaliated. Within four years Ionian Miletos, home of poets, artists, philosophers, doctors and shrewd merchants, more culturally rich than the Athens of the time, went up in smoke; its captured men were slaughtered, their families marched off into slavery. When Darius learned the Athenians had sent ships to aid Miletos, he summoned Datis, his most skilled sea-general. He also called Hippias.

Those happenings backgrounded the boyhood of Aeschylus, son of Euphorion. If he was born in 525 B.C., he was ten or eleven, the age when one grows aware of the world beyond the end of the street, in the triumphant days when Hippias was driven from Athens. Or, if the translator Richmond Lattimore guesses right, he was in the womb at that happy time and about fifteen when the big news was the fall of

Miletos. A shadow as of drifting smoke over Aeschylus' work tempts me (irrationally) to the road less traveled by. For our purposes, assume with Lattimore that Aeschylus was born in 512 B.C. or thereabouts. Oppressive threat from Persia hung toxic in all Greek air through the years of his adolescence.

Aeschylus' family belonged to the small-town nobility of Eleusis. The mystery rites of Demeter and her daughter were the principal business and preoccupation of that little holy city, and various priestly roles passed down among the old clans. To them still came men seeking ritual purification from blood guilt and other transgressions.

> His birth under the shadow of the famous sanctuary of purer religious aspiration ensured to his youth ... the subtler influence of the holy Mysteries of the Mother and the Maid, [helping prepare him] not as a mystagogue but as ... the teacher of his people through the medium of dramatic art.

I'm condensing H. W. Smyth, who Englished Aeschylus for the Loeb Classical Library edition. Mr. Smyth wrote in the 1920s, when essayists still could effuse, but he is right that no one grew up in Eleusis unaffected by the age-old eeriness of the place. Strange. Greeks talked about everything, but they did not talk about what was said and taught at Eleusis. They acknowledged that being in this world involves not saying too much about the next one. If only more of our own religious men and women had that humility!

Whereas Sparta created serfs of those it co-opted into itself, Athens had been growing at this time by wisely sharing citizenship with neighboring populations. It was the policy Rome was to follow. If Athens had stuck to that generosity, instead of fearing aliens, it might have lasted as a power as long as Rome did. Eleusis had been a part of Greater Athens for over a century now; any resentment at its absorption into the larger polity had passed, and Eleusians were staunch Athenians; but the place still kept a unique, proud piety. Even if Aeschylus was not an initiate (and lips were sealed on that subject), he knew at least what we know, that the story of the Maid's decent into Hell and yearly resurrection was in some way *played*, acted out, at the mysteries. Eleusis and Aeschylus are appropriate to each other.

Seductive bits of gossip flirt with our desire to know the unknowable; a true scholar resists them like the hermit Saint Anthony repulsing the succubae. I yield. One such story from Aeschylus' boyhood teases to be believed. It tells of his being sent out to scare birds from a vineyard when grapes were ripening. In the heat and the quiet he fell asleep. The god Dionysos walked up though the vines not to scold but to tell him, "Make tragedies for me." He woke and found he could. Some poets discover their own imaginations in ways that vivid. Dionysos himself often figured in the kind of dramas to which Aeschylus would have been taken; having seen the god would be very helpful. The few things we can be fairly sure of show Aeschylus to us as a soldier in an outward world. It is good to have one hint of an inner world that was to sprout such tendrils of the cosmos.

Young men of Aeschylus' class were groomed for their city's military and its public life; they would have gymnastic training, would own a shield, spear and sword and serve their two years in the border guard. A difference between their freedom and ours: there was little room in their freedom to be apolitical. A nonparticipant in public life was called an *idiotes*. That meant a private person, but the connotations were negative. Enfranchised citizens of Athens belonged to a minority among a majority of foreign nationals and slaves; a birthright Athenian was by definition a public official or on call to be one by lottery. Aeschylus had to feel himself a part of his city's politics; training one's speaking skills was becoming almost a duty for his generation; it became a paid profession for sophists and rhetoricians for the generation that followed. In his world a flare for poetry was not inconsistent with soldiering and office holding.

Exiled aristocratic families — "oligarchs" we call them — had played an off-stage role in driving out Hippias, but it was the democratic impulse that prospered when freedom came home. One of the returning aristocrats, Cleisthenes, surprised and outraged his fellows, furthering populist causes by fair means (and foul now and then). His proposals widened the confines of citizenship and broke up old clan voting blocs, substituting *demes*, which voted by location. He formalized exile into ostracism by popular vote. Cleisthenean ostracism could be exercised against any one figure in a given year who was perceived as a danger to the city. It was exile that involved no loss of property, nor disgrace — in fact it might swell one's prestige — but one had to stay away from Athens for ten years (later five). Although Athenian democracy actually dates from Cleisthenes, he and his immediate political followers are scantly recorded. It is as though a view of American democracy looked from William Penn and Peter Stuyvesant to Wilson and FDR with only a glance at Jefferson, Jackson, and Lincoln. Sometimes the Athens of the whole dazzling century gets called "Periclean," ignoring that Pericles, impressive though he was, was to step late into a story others had initiated. He would dominate only the next to last scenes of a great era and the onset of a ruin. In Aeschylus' days Pericles was a lad with an unknown future.

In the 490s the Persian threat drew two Athenians into enough prominence to be virtual heads of parties. Aristides was justly called "the Just," and Themistocles should have been called "the Sea Fox." Themistocles foresaw that power for Athens (and for himself) meant sea power. A year after Miletos fell, Themistocles, though still young, engineered votes for an improved harbor at Pireus. The world's commercial fleets are distant heirs of his efforts. Themistocles was selfish, pragmatic, brilliant and shameless; born poor, he became rich. Aristides was cautious, generous and scrupulously honest; maybe born rich, he died poor except in kudos.

Aeschylus, with his stubborn sense that in spite of appearances the cosmos is on the side of justice, should have been of Aristides' party; however there are some hints in his plays that he favored Themistocles. Everyone in Athens had to be on one side or the other; the two leaders were that distinct. In their teens they'd even both wanted to marry the same beautiful girl from Ceos Island. She died, but their rivalry lived. Through the long storm that came, they acted as sail and ballast to their city.

That storm broke at Marathon. A first Persian attack fleet had gotten smashed against the cliffs of Mount Athos; two years later, in 490, a second crossed the Aegean, taking time to destroy island after island as it came and letting escapees bring the mainland the news. Commander Datis knew terror was a stronger weapon than surprise.

Aeschylus had a sister and two brothers, if not three, one called Cyneigiros. That odd name means Dog-Rouser or Hunter — a playful nickname? Among family-proud people it is surely the name of a younger son. The Persians reached Attica's north shore at Marathon. The brothers, as part of a full contingent of able-bodied Athenians, marched out and camped in a spot sacred to Heracles among the scrub pine hills south and above where the Persians had beached, on the north shore of the plain. Ikarion, once home village to Thespis, was close enough for its women to bring them bivouac bread — it's a small world. There came a weeklong wait. Who knew what the Persians were waiting for? The Athenians, with a band of allies from little Plataea, waited for Spartan reinforcements from the south. That those would not come till the moon was propitious was the news the great runner, Pheidippides, finally brought. As he had loped the heights on the borders of Arcadia through buzzing heat and the thudding of his own feet and heart, Pheidippides had heard the god Pan ask why the Athenians ignored him. The Spartans would not send help; Pan, in return for worship, had vowed that he would. But a smudge of smoke above Euboea Island over across the water confirmed grim rumors of what the Persians had done to the small city of Eretria. No god had helped there.

Campfire talk said Hippias, now old, was down in Datis' tent — was *he* thinking of his brother, twenty-four years dead? Or of how in boyhood he with his father, Pisistratus, had passed over this plain on return from an exile?

The Persians did not charge up hill into the wooded camp; their proud cavalry could not maneuver to advantage there. They must have decided the little Greek force was afraid; they began to reload to sail round Attica and strike Athens directly. They swam the horses out to the ships first. At that the Greeks charged, taking the last mile at a run to get in under the Persian arrows. Aristides was one of the generals who large-mindedly yielded command to an abler soldier, Miltiades. The Miltiadean strategy of thin center and reinforced left and right has served often since. The bonded Greeks closed pincers around a chaotic melee of Persians.

Athenians fought by clan groups. Aeschylus will have been beside his brother when, in the surf, that young man seized the gunnels of a boat some Persians were escaping in. An axe blow severed hand from arm. A youngster so wounded stands a moment not believing fate. A brother runs to his brother. When the heart pumps wildly, arteries are quick to empty. A first-time soldier, however canny, can be amazed that, when a thing that wrong has happened, the battle does not suddenly stop. Cyneigiros died.

A time for tears was not yet; Datis' fleet could round Cape Sounion and descend on unguarded Athens. The victors quick-marched home the twenty-four miles. Aeschylus, who was one of the wounded, jolted along with his gashes raw in their bandaging. When the Persians tried to land, they saw on the shore the battle standards they had fled from the day before. They turned back toward Asia for reinforcements.

Aristides had been trusted to guard the gold in the Persian camp at Marathon. As bleak comfort to mourners like Aeschylus, Aristides reported 6,400 Persian corpses and only 192 Athenians and Plateans. Call the number 193; the splendid Pheidippides, who had run the 150 miles to Sparta for help, run back to Athens with news that no help was to come, run to Marathon and fought there and then run back to Athens with the warning that the Persian fleet might come at any hour, died of exhaustion in the agora. The cave of Pan in the Acropolis faces north toward the Marathon road; it was dedicated to fulfill the promise sunstruck Pheidippides made to Him Who Cast Panic upon the Persians.

Aeschylus was drawn young to the anti-worlds of drama and of war's dreadfully real doing and undoing. If he seems grandiose to our taste, he had a right to grandeur. I don't know a single moment in his plays when he glorifies warfare.

...AND THE NEW

The Persian Wars have been retold often and well. I won't recap the scope of them nor belittle inspired deeds truly equivalent to D-Day.

The Persians were no barbaric axis of evil. Their worldly aristocrats ran an empire that was vaster than China was at the time. Their scribes wrote three languages and had superimposed what Egypt and Babylon could teach of math, business, and architecture upon what their nomad grandfathers knew of the conduct of good life. Their enemies saluted their unpredictable moments of human decency. Their tolerant state religion, Zoroastrianism, saw life as a primal struggle between good and evil, a view that was profoundly to affect how Judaic, Christian and Islamic morality would evolve. Darius must have been pulling Hippias' leg when he said, "Who are the Athenians?" The Great King had had dealing with the oracle at Delphi (if not devoutly, then shrewdly; Delphi's wide influence seemed susceptible to gold). He and his wife, Atossa, came to rely on a Greek doctor who had practiced in Athens. Would it have mattered deeply then if Darius had won and the Greeks had lost?

Most of us won't matter to the world in a hundred years. The Persians resembled us in that. Their government and business were like others; their contributions to humanity were much the same ones other governments and businesses make. But now and then an individual or culture synthesizes, out of experience and out of the thoughts of prior millions, some newness. All who come after are different from what they would have been without such a person or culture.

In those 400s B.C., Greece was not merely making news, it was generating the new. Had Marathon gone the other way, had the usual flooded out the unique, we might still be snugly a thousand years of technology behind our two great threats, the atom bomb and the chemistry of petroleum. We'd be equally far from any attempt to reject slavery, to equalize the sexes, to control toothache or population or to imagine a poor man winning a lawsuit. Whether we'd live better or worse in that not-parallel universe, we'd be unrecognizable.

Athens' ten years between 490 and 480 are hard to imagine. When the Persian fleet pulled away, a quick return blow seemed certain. A lion had been kicked in the face. Would Datis turn his ships around? Would Darius have him strike elsewhere? Eventually word came that the fleet had dispersed back to its many home ports.

The temporary victors did not all behave well. Within the year Miltiades disgraced himself, using unchecked command to extort money from the island of Paros under threat of wholesale slaughter. He was tried and imprisoned, and he died of gangrene or of suicidal chagrin.

Each spring the City Dionysia was held, as were all festivals. One of the babies born in 490 or thereabouts was Pericles. The births, the buyings and sellings, the politickings, marrying and burying went bravely on. One always lives on the incline of one volcano or another. Athenian theater shared in the making of that newness I spoke of, or at least in reflecting it. Either before Marathon or (following Lattimore's logic) after it, Aeschylus submitted his first entry in the Great Dionysia. Out of the whorl of huger events, no notice has come down to us of what his entries were. Was it at that debut or later that he veered from precedent, bringing on stage a second actor? He could hardly have done it if competition rules had been already firm. We can't know the moment that seems, to any actor, so pivotal. That second player was a transformation that made drama unique and new.

At simplest, two characters display conflict rather than recount it; show matches tell. But the innovation goes deeper. Aeschylus might not have claimed he'd made performance into an image for his city's way of trying to govern itself, but he had. It is no accident that this theater and this democracy were born — and were to grow senile — together. Drama "makes moment of the individual" (Walt Whitman's phrase), bringing us to see an issue from both sides as viewpoints exchange, person to person. That kind of exchange becomes crucial when one's personal choices are made among the thronging personal choices of others in a relatively free society. Thespis had put a collective human chorus, in conversation with a divine or semi-divine *protagonist* (a word that grew to mean the character the audience sides with, as well as the main contestant for a prize). Now in Aeschylus' time an *antagonist,* a "counter-struggler," embodied a play's conflict, the other voice. Two distinct characters bounce the energy of their wills back and forth. Nothing in theater matters more than that tennis of persons.

Today, mounting a play in our major cities grows so costly that monodrama is reemerging as a performer's necessity — and the mother of a fashion. Still, when I go see a friend in a one-actor show, I miss the electric crackle of player versus player; an evolutionary step in theater is missing. Aeschylus is at least owed some joking apology in the program.

News of Marathon spread in the Persian Empire, as in Greece. Individuals went from land to land with an unpassported freedom we have lost to our fanatic nationalist dread of the illegal alien. A sacredness clung to travelers. They risked robbery on the roads, but the homogeneous towns welcomed them for relieving monotony and bringing news. Egypt (which had franchised a resident-alien city of Greeks in the delta) was as chafed by Persia's yoke as Ionia had been. It heard of Marathon and rebelled. Aging Darius became absorbed in that and in family feuds; four years after Marathon he died. The new Great King, Xerxes, reconquered Egypt, then turned to assembling the vastest, most varied army the world had yet seen — all to avenge Marathon. Why did Xerxes think so huge a force was needed, or Greece worth it? Darius had grown a bit daft about Greece. After Athens helped the Milesian revolt, he had assigned a table servant to whisper in his ear at every supper, "Sire, remember the Athenians." He'd planted his obsession in Xerxes. Does a leader of a vast nation actually go to war just because his father had gone to war? One has seen it happen.

The oracle at Delphi, levered by Persian gold or logic of numbers, veered from its usual ambiguity. Its clear prophecies of Greek defeat seemed self-fulfilling: Greek community after Greek community sanely yielded to Persia until Xerxes' war looked won before he reached Europe. In Athens, Aristides was ostracized not out of distrust but to clear the way for Themistocles' policy of fleet building (though one voter said he was just "tired of hearing that man called "The Just"). Knowing they were specifically aimed at, the Athenians could not surrender and the Spartans would not because they defined themselves as never-surrendering soldiers. Athens and Sparta knew their backs were to a wall. What kind of wall became an issue.

An Athenian commission to Apollo at Delphi inquired about defense. Apollo's mouthpieces told them, "Wretches, leave my altars!" Disobeying, they vowed to starve there till granted better word. Moral blackmail wrung from the oracle a vague comfort to carry home: that wooden walls might save Athens. Since the way up to the Acropolis had once been barred with timber and thorn-brush, some elders proposed enduring a siege on the height behind such walls. Themistocles seized on the phrase " wooden walls" to mean ships. He urged evacuating the city to Salamis Island off Pireus harbor and attacking the Persian fleet to cut off its army's supplies. Spartans might think themselves better soldiers than Xerxes' hundreds of thousands of conscripts, but Athenians knew from seagoing experience that they were better sailors than Xerxes' men — excepting only his small minority of Phoenicians.

The strategies by which Themistocles got his motions carried were typically devious. A poet named Phrynichus, older than Aeschylus, presented a tragedy, *The Fall of Miletos*. It is thought that Themistocles arranged to have it staged to help rouse the city to defend itself. The play indeed roused the city; the entire audience was in tears remembering the fate of a sister city — many viewers knew refugees from that calamity or had lost kindred in it. The city assembly fined Phrynichus and banned the play, but Themistocles had made his point — and openly political theater had entered the stage of history.

The Fates gave Athens an extraordinary gift that same year. New silver mines were discovered at Laurion out toward the Attic point, opening what Aeschylus was to call "a fountain running silver." The city had at hand wealth to pour into harbors and triremes and to make skilled oarsmanship a well-paying trade. It is crucial that the Greek war galleys were rowed not by slaves but by salaried free men.

At the climax of the invasion Themistocles tricked both his own people and the Persians into an engagement each would have otherwise postponed. The recurved shore of Salamis that faces the mainland forms the bay of Eleusis; access to the bay is through two narrows, east and west. Themistocles gathered his fleet in the bay; the Persians were approaching from eastward, and to encounter them in the shifting currents of the narrows made sense. When some allies talked of flight, Themistocles took an appalling gamble. He actually sent Xerxes word of their vacillation. The Persian fleet divided, sending a contingent around Salamis by night, closing off the far inlet. Had Athens lost, Themistocles would be remembered as an outrageous traitor.

Aeschylus was again among the defending warriors, this time on shipboard. All his wounds except the deepest, Cyneigiros, had healed. Moods were ferocious; at the last city assembly on the mainland a mob had killed a man for counseling surrender and even stoned his wife and children in a frenzy of patriotism. The dawn of that battle was horrendous for Athenians crowded onto the island shore. Smoke from the city they had abandoned was visible where a red glow had stained the night. The Persian horde was leaving them nothing to come home to. Stubborn grandfathers who had chosen the Acropolis must have been dying up there as Athena's temple and the fortress burned.

Military discipline was strict, but civil law dissolved among the displaced crowds. Embers of long-extinguished superstition flared. A fanatic hereditary priest sacrificed some captured women and children from a Persian baggage train. Mei Lais happen and are forgotten. The frantic ape gibbers in us all when threatened. Aeschylus' tripartite *Oresteia* was to deal with curses traceable to the gods' revulsion at human sacrifice.

No aid would come from the south to the evacuees. Everyone knew that the Spartans and Corinthians, hoping to defend their Peloponnese at the Isthmus, were raising a wall there. Wiser heads could take only grim comfort in the futility. A glimpse of the huge Persian vessels revealed what numbers the Persians could land on the far side of any such wall, outflanking the Spartans as Persian troops had outflanked the courageous Spartan holders of Thermopylae a few weeks earlier.

By tidy irony it was Aristides, returning under a general amnesty to fight with his fellow citizens, who brought Themistocles and the ship captains word (no surprise to Themistocles) that there were Persian galleys at the west mouth of the bay as well as the east. No Greeks could sail away — it was now fight or die.

> The fox knows many tricks, the hedgehog knows
> One good one.

The line was from old Archilochus, one of the first and bitterest warrior poets. His iambic rhythm was especially speakable. Aeschylus came to use it for dramatic dialogue. (Much later Marlowe and Shakespeare used English iambics for the same reason.) Were verses in Aeschylus' head on Salamis beach? Why not? A poet is still a poet when weighted with weapons he waits in line to go aboard a warship. In the mind of an Aeschylus, Archilochus could express the contrast of Sparta's one thorny strategy to the many ruses of the Athenian leader, or maybe the contrast of Themistocles to Aristides. Themistocles had his Athenians in a two-mouthed bottle; they had to attack willy-nilly. However, the Athenians knew these winds and currents, and their smaller ships could maneuver where bigger Persian vessels, mustered from captive Egypt, Tyre, Sidon, and Ionia, wallowed and cracked together for want of sea room. Warships of the time were seagoing battering rams that smashed enemy vessels at waterline with jutting timbered prows. It helped to be small and quick to turn, to thrust in and quickly back oars clear of the carnage. Why listen to me? Let Aeschylus tell it; he was there. He puts the story in the mouth of a war-shocked Persian.

> First the floods of Persians held the line,
> But when the narrows choked them and, rescue helpless,
> Smitten by prows, their bronze jaws gaping,
> Shattered entire was our fleet of oars!
> The Grecian warships, calculating, dashed
> Round and encircled us; ships showed their belly:
> No longer could we see the water, charged
> With ships' wrecks and men's blood.
> [*The Persians*, Lattimore translation, Univ. of Chicago, 1956]

The translator lets Aeschylus' tangled grammar come through, words jamming together chaotically like the ships. Themistocles' gamble, justifiable because there was no other option, paid off. Again as at Marathon the Athenians lost few and the enemy perished in huge numbers, at least by Greek tally. There has to be some truth in their figures, since Xerxes, who had come not only in person but had brought women and children of his family along, hurried back to Persepolis, taking two-thirds of his army with him to protect his person! One vast third remained in Greece without supply lines.

The startlingly handsome youngster chosen to lead the dance song and play the cithara at the celebration on Salamis was one many had noticed. He had already won a double prize for wrestling and music. His name was Sophocles. In the crowd was a tavern owner (his tavern now burnt across the bay) whose wife had borne a son in their tent among the citizen refugees. She had had a lucky dream that the boy would win crowns, so the parents planned to raise him as an athlete. They named him Euripides. It was a name that could have been passed down in a family from Attica's north coast where the Euripus flows between the mainland and Euboea, but it can mean "son of the good tidal rip"—appropriate to a child of Salamis!

A dazed, triumphant population returned to blackened rooms and courtyards, to olives hacked down to fuel the destroying fires, to pavings dug up in quest of hidden goods. What bodies could be found of the elders up in the Acropolis were buried with honors, as were the hacked and blackened statues of the gods, with their still-smiling faces. The toppled gravestones were set up again. Too many cities have reperformed that slow, grievous ritual. It was late September; roofs were needed before the winter's rain and frost. It helped their morale that Greek lifestyle was simple; houses and furnishings were mourned for but could be remade. Gold and silver coinage they had carried with them, also the wealth of scrolls, *The Iliad, The Odyssey* and other epics that had been copied out when the dead elders in the looted acropolis had been boys.

News came that, on the day of Salamis, Carthaginians had invaded Greek Sicily. Carthage, North African by locale, was Near Eastern by origin. It had been colonized from the port of Tyre, now a Persian subject city. Xerxes' councilors must have coordinated that attack so the Greek west would not sail to aid its mother cities as Athens fourteen years back had tried to aid Miletos. The Carthaginians were routed by the army of a tyrant of Syracuse whose heir was to patronize Aeschylus. In the struggle Athens and Syracuse were both victors. Athens' story would have Herodotus as well as Aeschylus to tell it, and Herodotus was one of the all-time great tellers. Syracuse was served by lesser word-shapers; its heroisms glow less.

The next year Sparta at last showed what it could do in offensive battle. Combined Greek forces commanded by a Spartan king crushed the vast, dispirited army Xerxes had left. They fought within sight of little Plataea, whose boys had stood with the Athenians at Marathon.

Aeschylus fought there too, a man of thirty-three perhaps, with his first victory at the City Dionysia some years behind him.

How This Theater Worked—The Early Years

The Theater of Dionysos had new seats. The front row of judges' chairs were perhaps of stone.* They weren't the line of thrones whose remnants are down there today—those came when the tragedies had become showcases for Athenian power; ambassadors and guests of the city filled many of them, along with generals and archons. The Dionysian priest's central one still shows the god's name carved in it. Back before 500 B.C. several rows of wooden benches had been ranged on the hillside. At a Dionysia when Aeschylus competed, those benches collapsed, in a landslide of yelling spectators and an uprooted tree. Before next spring some new and less improvised seating was in place, though the slope was not yet shaped into the fanning geometric cone it would one day be. The foresighted brought cushions, and much of the hill was steep enough so that you could wear a sun hat without irritating those behind you. Along with solemnities aimed at the great gods, performers made whimsical vows to Krotos ("Clatter"), the little god of applause, as the predawn crowd assembled. These were people of the sun, up at first gray glimmer and, except at full moons, usually asleep when the stars shone again.

Watchers at a good play become citizenry of an imaginary country; book readers or video viewers at home lack that crucial communion. Like a pigeon flock or a run of herring, an audience has what in guidance systems is called cybernetic intercommunication; it mutually self-adjusts. People laugh where alone they would merely smile; they pass through the emotional currents of the story exchanging signals that touch them en mass. From on stage one vividly feels their unanimity—or a disconcerting lack of it. Most good playwrights

---

For a very current insight into an accoustical advantage achieved as stone seats began to replace benches, see the brief article on page 89 of The Economist, *March 31, 2007. Drs. Nico Declerq and Cindy Dekeyser of the Georgia Institute of Technology have analyzed how the seat backs were crucial in bouncing and amplifying the spoken voice while minimizing wind rustle and crowd murmur. Without that fortuitous effect, perhaps the audience would never have grown as it did and included every stratum of society. Declerq and Dekeyser worked at Epidauros, on a late example of the peak of the evolution of true Greek theaters, but the effect they note must to some extent apply to the earlier, smaller theaters.*

have been actors: for playwrights the audience is their school in two senses.

There is a canard that women were not allowed in the Theater of Dionysos, but they were; they contributed their presence. Women sat apart from men, as in many of our synagogues, where the separation is read less as a slight than as a signal of respect. Whimsical witness to women in Aeschylus' audience can be inferred from the tale that the Furies in his *Oresteia* were so hideous that pregnant women miscarried at the sight. That anecdote would not have worked even as a joke if everyone knew women were not admitted to theater.

Inaugurating the day's performances, Dionysos' hereditary priest had the first turn either on stage or at the altar of the temple downslope from the orchestra. A goat died for the god's breakfast. The god was generous with the meaty bits; they were lotteried out to onlookers while he savored the smoke of bones and fat. Judges' names were drawn also by lot and at the last moment to foil bribery — some incident of hot dispute must lie forgotten behind that cautious custom. The selected judges moved to their reserved place with the priests in the front row. The judges didn't qualify particularly as critics, but that did not undermine the honor of their praise. Dionysos himself voted too, by way of lottery. Luck of the draw still passes for the judgment of an intervening angel, and our own critics pass no competitive exam. Theatrical success, like all success, goes often to the gifted, but sometimes to the booby.

Second and third prizes were no defeat. The real loss — not being selected to exhibit — had been endured privately months before. Hopeful entrants had submitted their works to a city official, an archon, and three sets of plays had been chosen. That gave former winners an edge and must have often opened the sluices of favoritism. It boggles us that some town father, elected or chosen by lot, read dozens of four-drama entries and made an informed selection. Did every Athenian have genius, taste and patience? More likely each entrant presented himself to recite a segment of his work at a kind of acting audition and editorial submission in one. We assume a divide between popular and rarified arts; *Grease* and *Einstein on the Beach* have different audiences with little overlap. That chasm had not opened as widely among Greeks, and if a given archon had no taste for poetry he surely invited in others to listen with him so as not to disgrace himself with a really bad selection.

Days before the festival a crier in the agora had announced the contestants and had named the plays. Since there were no posters or programs, the audience probably heard that announced again just before the performance. Was this crier's shout the source of our assumption that a single, author-given title is a thing any work always has? In a bookless world where else would the notion have taken root? Rhapsodes had been asked for the song of Achilles' wrath at Ilium before people formally called it *The Iliad*. Many authors feel that summing up their work in a word or two is like attaching a handle to a sculpture. Two of Sophocles' plays were called *Athamas*, two *Phineas* and several by more than one title. Naming was flexible.

As the century wore on, the Dionysia was to become encrusted with more and more of Athens congratulating Athens. There was a saying that the way up to power is hard but the way down is harder. The same is true of celebratory custom; it is easier to add to an event a community takes seriously than to leave out anything once added. That mix of one-upmanship and tradition still drives weddings and parades to extravagant, joy-stifling extremes. Eventually the ten elected Athenian generals jointly poured a libation (the one time a year when they functioned publicly together); the orphan sons of those fallen in battle were paraded in armor; even the city's collective wealth, gold and silver, hauled down, from the treasury in Athena's temple, was shown to the crowd. By the time all those state events were taking place on the first morning of the contest, an unlucky playwright, no matter how patriotic, must have groaned to be assigned the opening day. The pageant made his plays an anticlimax. But this came after Aeschylus' years.

If the three serious dramas of a given entry played at dawn, at pre-siesta midday and toward sundown, was the after-piece, the satyr play, done at night? It is tempting to picture those high jinks by torchlight and full moon. Stylistically it would have bracketed the satyr plays from what they followed and there was certainly a tradition of Bacchic night revels. There are objections. With our streetlights, glowing signs and shop windows, we hardly picture how black the streets in an ancient city were at night. Only the rare house that towered to a third story might have had a window facing a street, and that would be a mere shuttered glimmer in a murk that belonged to different gods than the bright day. Still, there *were* nighttime events, torch races in honor of Pan, for instance. The Dionysia was held during the folkloric full moon of March, when hares run mad. The Leneia, a February festival that eventually also included play competitions, was also held at the full of a moon. In fragments of Aeschylus' *Prometheus Firekindler*, satyrs singe their hairy fingers at the new red dancing toy that spits sparks. Only one satyr play, Euripides' *Cyclops,* survives, and there are parts enough of another, Sophocles' *The Trackers,* to give some sense of the whole. A nighttime performance would heighten the visuals in both. I am convinced some tragedies were performed at sundown and into dusk, but my conviction is no proof.

What went on here in the Theater of Dionysos during Aeschylus' career involves a mare's nest of contradiction. Some say Aeschylus started the use of masks. Then what of Thespis, one asks? Some say it was Phrynichus who added the second character. To take Aristotle's word is to give Aeschylus that credit; Aristotle knew Aeschylus' grandchildren's generation and lived in his city — other "authorities" were further off in time and lived elsewhere. Let me admit again how much I am writing fiction. As I stand here, staring rapt at the Theater of Dionysos, I toy with the colored bits and nuggets. I shied from sharing them when I taught theater history because most of them lack solid proof. About masks, my guess is that Aeschylus (along with fellow poets?) started using masks in the plural, giving his whole chorus a characterizing anonymity that only the protagonist had had in Thespis' day. Wasn't the chorus masked earlier? Certainly dithyrambs were sung without masks. The kudos that repaid a talented, elite youngster for being in a chorus would diminish if no one in the audience could recognize him. The prestige of drama needing some years to rise, by social capillary action, high enough to make masked participation rewarding. That is conjecture. Aeschylus' second actor, like the principal actor, used a mask — more than one, since he and Aeschylus might each play several characters.

For shrewd (maybe discouraging) insight on historical sources, read Edith Hamilton's essay *Fifteen or Fifty?* in her book *The Ever-Present Past.* By way of one query, (how many performers made up a chorus?), she sums up the problem with all such knowledge: that fragments of evidence can be hardly more reliable than the average of human accuracy — which is pretty low. Hamilton is insightful although dated, (words like *grandeur* and *glorious* come easily to her), and she can be joltingly politically incorrect. But ultimately we're all dated, soaked in the fluids of our own times.

Did one chorus cast act in all of a day's three tragedies and in the satyr play? Chance to compete was called "being awarded *a* chorus," which suggests they did. Some guess that during Aeschylus' career a playwright's chorus of fifty was broken up to save expense or length of rehearsal, giving each play twelve or thirteen performers. I doubt that the paring down of choral size happened in that way. Expenses mattered immediately after the Persians sacked the city—but it is then that plays give strongest hint of huge choruses. Athenians were astoundingly willing to lavish money on the arts as long as the lavishers could take public credit.

When Thespis had represented Dionysos himself, it was the chorus, his following flock, who were the "us" that watchers could principally empathize with. It took much of Aeschylus' career to shift his audiences' predisposition from relating most to the chorus to relating to the soloist, whom we call the *central* character and whom we see so clearly as the heart of a play. Masking the chorus might have served to distance the chorus a bit and so push individual characters more to the foreground. Of Aeschylus' seven surviving tragedies, four are named for their choruses, only two of the latest for the protagonist. (*The Seven against Thebes* is named for foemen never seen on stage.)

In Aeschylus' earlier plays chorus and ideas are the core. One starts, in those oldest survivors, with a great poem about the feel of a predicament, spoken by a group who experience it. The poem radiates (good poetry *does* radiate by digression) into reference and comparison of parallel events, and it dives intensely into the emotional foam of that predicament. Individual characters trigger or embody that predicament, but the audience is clearly intended to share most directly in the plight and passions of the chorus. I think this kind of play-as-poem is what Richmond Lattimore means when he writes of "lyric tragedy." By century's end the chorus was to become a decorative fringe, but for now it was the essential fabric.

So, we know Aeschylus from only seven plays: *The Suppliants, The Persians, The Seven against Thebes, Prometheus Bound* and three from one year's trilogy: *The Agamemnon, The Libation Bearers* and *The Furies,* (collectively *The Oresteia).* Those—with fragments and hearsay titles—show Aeschylus' preference for choruses of women (played by males). The tally among complete plays is five female choruses versus two of elderly men. Why so? It is very twenty-first century to assume some sexual motive, but where homosexuality was widely accepted, would the titillations of drag amount to much? It may well have had to do with diction. A typical voice carries further in lower registers but, especially in a mask, enunciation is clearer in tenor range because there is less burr. There's also a matter of emotional intensity. Despite their freedoms, Athenian men, like men in most cultures, were expected to be relatively stiff-upper-lipped; women were allowed wider demonstrations of feeling. Demonstrativeness is what is wanted of a dramatic chorus.

Choruses, male or female, cried out. We have few grief and pain exclamations aside from obscenities — really only "alas," "alack," "woe is me" and "ouch." "Alas," "alack" and "woe" are so extinct now that some actors have a hard time saying them on stage, and "ouch," though grandly descended from the Irish mourning cry "ochone," has grown trivial. (Perhaps the film *E.T.* is the last English-language performance piece in which "ouch" has full force, and it is said by a puppet.) We clench our teeth; our screams are inarticulate. Not so the Greeks. They had a full phalanx of grief cries: "ie!" "nea dua!" "aiai!" "oi moi!" "popopo!" "feu!" and many more. Choruses use such cries over and over. They drive translators to despair and are stumbling blocks for us who are tempted to giggle in reading. Anguished outbursts come in many styles, but very slight cultural behavior differences can clog our capacity for empathy. Shylock's Near Eastern grief looks funny to Venetians, and Greek outcries can ring false in our ears, especially in the choruses. Our poetry no longer includes gasps and groans.

Typically the chorus sings alone four or five times as characters come and go (and soloists change costume backstage). Out of the alternation of choral song and episodes of individuals' action a convention was to emerge among Romans that a play had (as if by some law of nature) five acts. That assumption lingered through the Renaissance all the way down to the early nineteenth century and even gave rise to a good deal of not very helpful theory about inciting action, rising action, climax, descending action and resolution.

Contrast between chorus and individual characters was heightened by the choruses using a special dialect. Maybe that convention emerged from the use of scales and melodies from elsewhere: traveling dithyramb composers from far-off cities brought their homeland music with them. (Major and minor in our music are remnants of the many scales — *modes* — then available, and Aeschylus' elder contemporary Phrynichos was remembered by old men in the comedy *The Wasps* for his "sweet and sexy tunes from Sidon" — a Near Eastern trade port.) But the custom may root in myth. Dionysos is pictured as having invaded from far away with his ecstatic foreign horde; outlanders' speech and song patterns could have been part of the revelers' guise since before Thespis, one more way of being strange. That stylized dialect can be compared to the rural-from-no-real-place speech patterns that Bob Dylan brought so pervasively to our recorded, folksonglike, popular music. Think of it as a strategy for stepping across class and ethnic barriers.

Aeschylus didn't work with his choruses wholly alone; he had a favorite dancer. We'd call that man a choreographer, and in him we glimpse the beginning of that network of collaborative trusts and reliances that now makes theatrical art such a communal life experience for its practitioners when the process goes well — and so difficult when it does not. Companionship in work is one great blessing given actors and musicians, unlike more solitary artists, and as with most blessings, self-control and relaxed generosity are needed if it is not to turn into a curse. Aeschylus feels like the kind to have had the self-control; I wonder about the relaxed generosity. His visions feel too complete to welcome much input from others.

Choric moves and sound patterns have left tantalizing jargon ("*emmeleia*" [intra-song?], "*stasimon*" [standing?] and so on). I've already mentioned *strophe* and *antistrophe*. Calling such terms "jargon" is no slur; *jargon* is linguist's jargon for the special terms any trade or skill evolves. When the trade ceases to be practiced, meanings get lost. Even within a thriving trade, jargon is fluid from generation to generation and means various things to various practitioners. Imagine devoted scholars two thousand years hence trying to define what twenty-first-century performers once meant by "strike," "riff" or "ball and change," or "combination." Most of us after a mere hundred years have already forgotten what nineteenth-century performers meant by "O.P." or "in one." The chorus danced. As to how, the unjustifiable guesses of an eccentric Isadora Duncan or a Rudolph Steiner are as valid as yours or mine.

And they acted. Cleo, Muse of History, teases anyone who tries to trace an evolution of acting. Variations on the phrase *more lifelike now* recur in nearly every favorable comment anyone has left about a difference between the acting of a given present day and the acting of a prior generation. If we believe the world's fans, there have been thousands of years of unbroken progress in technique, always toward the goal of more lifelikeness. The day's actors are startlingly real to their day; yesterday's were stilted and (we *do* have a word for it) hokey. There's an essential present tense in theater. An audience's willing surrender to an actor is as much at work as what an actor in fact does. You can push the philosophy of this deep, if you like: that our reality is what we are willing to perceive or perhaps able to perceive. Labyrinths of esthetic theory open off that mysterious relation of seer to seen. Isms and counter-isms echo as far afield as to the respected physicist Schrödinger assuring us a cat in a box is neither alive nor dead till we observe it as one or the other! Schrödinger talks only of things submicroscopic, but his image reminds us that all edges are fuzzy.

There is some such indeterminacy in the effect of an actor on stage. The acting is as live or dead and the music is as sweet or revolting as we think it. Both performer and audience have a vested interest in believing the opposite, in *knowing* that excellence is an objective, seekable reality exterior to themselves — and therefore, in some way, they make it so! Each time we grope a few blind inches around that vast elephant, our fingers tell us we've now touched the hidden truth. We may have gone round and round the elephant several times already. More likely it is so vast that we have spent all our history feeling a wrinkle in its trunk.

Mockery aside, the acting here was big — it played to a big space, was gestural, was vocal, and used the skills of dance. One aspect if it, strange to us, gets light from a Platonic dialogue. Plato's *Ion* is brief but not very recommendable. (Euripides' *Ion* is about a different person, a human bastard son of Apollo.) In the Platonic dialogue Socrates talks with a self-enamored professional rhapsode, Ion, who claims he knows Homer better than any man alive and seems proud to know nothing else. Socrates, bemused, ties the fellow's ego into baffled knots. If that Ion was a real person, the dialogue is cruel mockery — mercifully it was written after both characters in it were dead. Performance is not the focus in Plato's *Ion*, but in it Socrates takes absolutely seriously the idea of otherworldly inspiration, an enrapturing, divine seizure. The concept humbled deep artists, though it smugified shallow ones like Ion into humbuggery. The tradition of actors meditatively communing with their masks before a play must go all the way back to Thespis. Makeup mirrors still receive that gaze. There was (and some tacitly still believe there is) a serious element of the sacred in acting and in watching acting, because there is a serious reaching outward from the self. The long gowns actors wore were not just showy; they were intentionally priestlike. Even now a diva may go on stage as a peasant heroine, or a film star parade her bosom to an opening, in a dress that would feed a barrio's children for a month. Vestments of orthodox religions and the equally striking costumes of some rock and punk bands are easy to sneer at from the outside, but from within the experience they are suits of light; for believing fans they sparkle with a reflection of sacred fire.

From before Arion's time *choragos* had been one of the words for a composer poet of a chorus, johnny-do-all and principal performer. *Chorus-teacher* was another. *Coryphaeus*, spelled not with a *CH* but with a *C* or a *K*, means simply "crew head" or leader — the term used for the strong-voiced and reliable captain of a chorus. Once the Pisistratids no longer supported the City Dionysia out of their own, that's to say the city's, pockets, a new figure grew into prominence, the *choragos* as producer. (I'll try to be clear by calling the nonperformer who put up the money the "producing *choragos*.") Being producer was seen as an honor and obligation. Whichever wealthy citizen took on the job had real expense and trouble, providing, within limits settled between himself and the poet-composer, whatever the play required. It was great luck for the poet to be assigned a producing *choragos* generously committed to proving his munificence. The producer's recompense was in kudos: to him even more than to the author-director went the prize of a leafy crown and a handsome bronze tripod. Proud victors began setting those atop pedestals in what came to be known as Tripod Street, which curved off into town from below the theater. One such pedestal, a mini-tower thirty-five feet high, still stands. It gets called the Tower of Demosthenes now; that political orator later liked to sit in its shade to work out his speeches. I'm only half tempted to prowl and see it. The tripod itself, being bronze, was long ago conscripted into some war effort.

Despite the city's reaction to *The Fall of Miletos,* censorship was almost unheard of; when it occurred it was symptomatic of cowardice. The comedian Aristophanes was later to be prosecuted for speaking ill of his city. The charge against him was that he had done it not at the Lenaea, a winter festival attended mostly by Athenians, but at the Dionysia "in front of strangers!" It was foreigners' eyes and wartime which made that washing of dirty linen shameful. Aristophanes was acquitted. The Lenaea, by the way, had a traditional playing space somewhere in Athens, no one now knows just where.

The playwright Phrynichus was not deterred by his fine from composing the *Persians*, about the recent war, and two years after the battle of Salamis Themistocles, equally undeterred, was producing *choragos* to his *Phoenecian Women*, which had a chorus of widows of the Phoenecians (second only to Greeks as sailors) who had manned the Persian fleet. Aeschylus chose a parallel theme in his *Persians*, five years after that. His chorus in that play is old men; using women would have been too close to what Phyrnichus had recently done. Because so few of the competition plays have survived, it is easy to forget how often playwrights reused and reworked one another's themes; originality was not in itself a virtue, and a successful new treatment was a demonstration of skill. Some have guessed that for a while after the Persian invasions at least one play about the great wars was presented every year.

Still, an assumption grew that ancient, communal stories served the Dionysia best. Current events are incrusted with detail; a poet can hardly pare away enough to reveal an effective core. Also, demands for obvious relevance often come from narrow minds, as if only what is already in everyone's thoughts were worth thinking.

The performance space Aeschylus worked in first was still that big, open circle Pisistratus had seen laid out. An altar at its center remained throughout tragedy's evolution, a tethering stake that kept drama tied in the field of religion. Like a tethered bull, tragedy grazed hungrily at the edges of religion's circuit.

In those days any structure in the playing area other than that one low altar came and went with each play. *Skene* is a word that suggests the temporary. Only Aeschylus' last play needs a roof and doors. If setting required house or temple, something eye-catching was put up. It had to be gone a few hours later unless an author's three plays used one setting; even then it had to be erected in one night and gone by the next, so it had something of a tent's flimsiness. Re-costuming and masking unseen could happen below the drop off at the back of the orchestra, or out at either side where the two *parodoi* led on stage from up right and up left, or in a tent, whence the word *skene* eventually migrated onto the scene.

Language crams every new thing into its old mouth somehow. *Parodos* meant byway, "*hodos*" being a road. *Parodos* became jargon for the chorus's entry chant. There's a pun — or confusion. *Ωide* with a long O is a song; *parodos* sounds rather like "entry-song," and *exodos* (a chorus' finale), like "exit song." Later translators of the Torah into

Greek were to title the tale of going out of Egypt *The Exodus,* thinking of it either as "Song of Departure" or "Outbound Road." Later still, as the Greek will to define was blending with the Judeo-Christian will to believe, church fathers preempted a theater term to speak of their One God as Himself, His Own Son and also a Spirit in all believers. They spoke of "masks" of God, *personae. Masks* sounds blasphemous, but *Three Persons* is a term from orthodoxy. Groping through human speech for the superhuman, they were more beholden to theater than they'd have cared to be.

Much ingenuity went into striking the eye here. Embroidered tunics and draped cloaks modified priestly and everyday cloths, seeking "a sense of the familiarly unfamiliar." (Leslie du St. Read's phrase neatly pins down a paradox of good stage design: be new and strange yet steal no undue focus.) There are on-stage chariots in Aeschylus' *The Persians* and *The Oresteia,* perhaps in *The Suppliants* or *The Seven against Thebes.* We're reluctant to put animals on stage but horse-loving people noticed droppings underfoot as little as we do the petroleum fart of cars and motorcycles. Some lines in *The Suppliants* hint that each of Danaus' daughters had an attendant maid on stage with her, swelling their numbers almost to a mob — but those lines may have been added in the next centuries when stages were often vast and needed extras for visual filling.

Skeuopoios (technician) is a term used in theaters in the next century, but there were craftsmen before they had any special notice. As late as the nineteenth century scenic artisans were simply "the carpenters." A gulf of snobbery opens along the vague fault line between skill and art. In Aeschylus' career theater *skeuopoioi* must have begun to come into their own.

Supernumeraries and properties were only limited by the generosity of the producing *choragos* and by the space itself. Extras need costume (perhaps not masks) — and (if they were not slaves) compensation for hours in training, though being in the chorus was an honor. The actor as professional evolved after a taste for theater spread out from Athens. It did spread; cities soon began building their own theaters like this one, and plays that had been done in Athens were what people elsewhere wanted to see. Rather like Broadway in the United States between World War I and the '70s, or London's West End, Athens was where a play had to happen if it was to be desirable and where a playwright had to work to win full respect. Each play, mounted raw, stood or fell on one encounter with its audience. Businesslike Broadway and the West End have their out-of-town tryouts; the Dionysia did not. Even to make that comparison over-contemporizes. We hate to admit it, but art and business are opposites. Art is a form of giving, commerce a form of taking. The two may act as systole and diastole in a society; more often they simply have nothing in common. Current hopeful hype to the contrary, business is as clumsy at producing good art as art is at producing good business. Athenians would think preposterous our attempts to run our charities, social services, arts and universities like businesses. Steeped in commerce, we cannot imagine other ways. The Athenians could. Maybe they had more of the vice of pride than we and therefore a bit less of the vice of greed. At their rare best they strove toward excellence for the same reason some climb Everest — because it is there.

It was not until 449, seven years after Aeschylus died, that actors were eligible for individual prizes at the Dionysia, signaling recognition of performer as apart from poet. Eventually there was work for troupes of traveling actors to live on, but not, probably, while Aeschylus lived. Mary Renault's novel *The Mask of Apollo* imaginatively reconstructs the itinerant actors' world that eventually evolved, but Aeschyus as poet-playwright-performer traveled first without a troupe.

Aeschylus at thirty-six (Lattimore's reckoning) was famous beyond Athens. Commissioned by the Syracusian tyrant, he journeyed to Sicily, as Phyrnichus had done before him, to write and stage a play. His play was *The Women of Etna*, for founding ceremonies of a new city, Etna. His play is lost — was it about victims of volcanic Cyclopes or the invading Carthaginians, still sharp in memory? Fragments of *The Women of Etna* flicker a light on the dramatist's craft: its action seems to have had several different locales. This hints at something vaguely like out-of-town-tryout; Aeschylus experimented in distant Sicily with an approach to playwriting not much tried at home.

In constructing the plots of plays, dramatists have a choice of two basic stratagems. They can follow a smoldering fuse cord of incidents, as an epic does, moving our imaginations from spot to spot and through weeks and months or, instead, they can focus on one point in time and space where event-fuse meets explosive. With original plots, playwrights who use that second, focused strategy must convey their backstory through fairly elaborate exposition. But when plots are from generally known tales, backstory is no great problem.

An open air orchestra like the Theater of Dionysos is congenial to focused plotting. Its magic circle seems a solid place; things look as if they were happening here in real as well as imaginary time and place. Instinct assumes that the here of the story is persistent and continuous; characters and key events seem to arrive at one location during a sustained now. Greeks favored this focused dramatizing. However, the fragments of *The Women of Etna* suggest that in it Aeschylus took the less traveled road, moving, epiclike, from incident to incident and locale to locale.

Shakespeare's audiences and audiences in the old capitals of India and China followed stories that leaped over days and years and from spot to spot in the epic way. Were Athenians less willing to lend a play their imaginary forces? Surely they were not less imaginative. An answer lies in Greek taste. Greek aesthetic has to do with simplicity. Their tragedies have few homely details and few idiosyncrasies; such things were relegated to comedy. No one in a Greek tragedy would ever say to a ghost anything as untidily earthy as "...now, old mole, can'st dig in the earth so fast?" nor could a Greek write the line from *Midsummer Night's Dream* that sums up the secret beauty found in imperfection:

> In their freckles are their savors.

Greeks did not savor freckles. Their sensibility went for the clean, flowing line in sculpture and décor. That taste included letting as few external circumstances as possible distract from the stark event, and so they had little patience with setting new scenes over and over. They used the empty space their orchestra gave them and liked its emptiness.

Taste only gradually turned into convention. A generation after the great tragedians, Aristotle, as first analyst-critic, proposed that a well-made play should seem to unfold within one circuit of the sun. From him, later theorists eventually proclaimed unity of time and of place as fixed rules. Molière's tight plays show what pride of skill French writers once took in honoring those "unities." Aristotle was looking back at what had worked (especially what had worked for his own favorite, Sophocles). Aeschylus, Sophocles and Euripides were feeling forward to find what would work. Aeschylus, in that groping, occasionally plotted not just by way of the multiple scenes *The Women of Etna* appears to have had, but with big time jumps as well.

One tosses the words plot, myth, and story about. Everyone knows what they mean — and no one does. One Greek word covers all three, *mythos*. We feel differences of meaning but with no fixed consensus. For us such words point to something like this: by means of speech, pictures or actions we perceive a set of events as a *series*, linked to make for us some kind of sense. Our hunger that the universe, or at least human life, makes sense is very keen.

The most obvious kind of sense is cause and effect: the queen wanted an apple; the king drowned fetching it; the queen died of grief. Cause and effect is a chain. There is also a circularity of linkage — call it poetic justice or poetic injustice. The queen's wish caused her at last to have nothing to wish for. A third way of linking makes not what I'd call story but which might be myth. It is parallelism: the queen died, the fountain dried up, the winter came. At its most primitive that is sympathetic magic; in subtler form it is how, for example, Aeschylus links the one active figure in his *Prometheus Bound* to the rest. The cursed and wandering cow maiden, Io, wanders into that play without cause and out again without cause, but she fits as a parallel to Prometheus. She is a direct parallel, another victim of the callousness of Zeus and more subtly a reverse parallel by being damned to perpetual flight while Prometheus is damned to perpetual stillness. Cause and effect, poetic justice and parallelism seem to be three things that make a story cohere. All three ways plots hang together are in Aeschylus, often at once. He loads his plate.

Along with its will to make sense, a story craves an end. It can't stop in midair; it needs to finish the arc, to hit earth. We may wish a story to reflect reality, but at last it must round off and tidy up in a way that life never really rounds off or tidies up. Reality never comes to a halt (till we do); a story does. Inevitably then, the close of even the most realistic story will be in some way an artifice.

In real life a death is as close to an ending to a story as we can know, and, though the heart rebels, death is one irrefutable way a story can end. That absurdly simple reality contributes to our preconception of a tragedy. And yet only one of Aeschylus' seven surviving plays ends with the death of a central character. If seven is too sparse a sampling out of his seventy-plus plays, one can add that of Sophocles' seven as well; only two end with a main character's death (though there are deaths *within* the plays). One of those two, *The Oedipus at Colonos,* ends with such a blessed release that the chorus simply closes by saying,

> No funeral song. No tears.
> These things were from God's hand.

It is not death per se then that makes a plot tragic. It is life. In building these earnest, terrible plays out of phantasmagoric folktales, the tragedians, I truly believe, bring the audience to acknowledge what we so blunt ourselves to ignore—how weird, implausible, and in some maddening way miraculous, life is.

Also, neither "story" nor "plot" is always a good translation of *mythos*. Myth of folklore is not a matter of mechanics. I just now spoke of cause and effect, event making sense by relating to another event. We are usually taught to think of folkloric myth as explaining something, but I am not sure that is very insightful. Archibald MacLeish's great dictum, "A poem should not mean, but be," applies. A plot must make sense in order to ask us to believe it. A myth is believed by definition, it has nothing to prove in its own culture. It is what it is, as the Jehovah in Exodus says of Himself. When playwrights dealt with myth, what they did in the way of plot as cause and effect was really more a decoration than a core armature. The core, I believe, was magic being, not meaning.

Aeschylus is the Attic tragedian whose language is least spare—and who mixes some spice of humor with his solemnity. Aeschylus, in fact, has less of that esthetic of sparseness I spoke of than do the other playwrights. By our tastes he is stark, but to his own time I imagine he seemed rather baroque, a bit fraught. To the credit of his contemporaries' breadth of mind, they appreciated him nonetheless.

Even the tyrant of Syracuse treated Aeschylus with respect. What Aeschylus thought of the tyrant is another matter, perhaps glimpsed later in *Prometheus Bound*. Eventually he would return to the lush Sicily. For now he came back to the challenge of his fellow playwrights here in Athens, where the hardest-won kudos were to be had. But he did not abandon his experiment in multiple locales.

Considering the talents the work demanded, a surprising number of Athenians made plays. Writing poetry often leads inward, but Greek drama was not for an introvert. Besides being a musician (and playing and singing one's music at least well enough to teach it), you were a choral conductor, diction coach and sometimes choreographer. You did not write your play, you wrought it as a shipwright does a ship. The playwright was often the lead performer. Open-air acting requires big, sustained lung and larynx power, the chest and throat of an athlete or opera singer. Thespis had set a daunting example.

Aeschylus' brooding, earnest focus was on things philosophical — I'm tempted to coin a word, "theo-illogical." Still, he had to deal with the amalgam of practical expedients and passions a director with sparse technical support must pour into a mold. Wouldn't such hot metal crack a cast? Aeschylus was one of those titans of energy that arise rarely out of our gene pool. He wrote between seventy and ninety plays: four plays make a festival entry; entries for twenty of the over twenty-six years he worked comes to eighty plays. If he won first place eighteen times, he lost twice! The numbers are uncertain, but a wonder — and a tribute to Greek competitive spirit — is that so many others kept entering the contest! Between his first victory in 484 and his final one in 458, he must have gotten very accustomed to standing beside his producing *choragos* of the year to have the priest of Dionysos put the wreath on his brows.

In 472, when his three plays included his *Persians,* the producing *choragos* was a scion of a wealthy, returned family Pisistratus had banished. This was Pericles, bringing himself vicariously into notice. Pericles was so young that it's conceivable he was the performing chorus leader as well. He had wealth enough and presence enough to be both if he and his family chose. Aristocratic by background, Pericles was a democrat and, like FDR or Cleisthenes, was viewed as a traitor to his class by many a bitter oligarch. I violate history to blur our party term *Democrat* with the general noun, but democrats in Athens believed good government should counteract the unavoidable drift of society's wealth into the hands of an ever richer and tighter sub-community. Athenian oligarchs, like our own, found that drift in their direction perfectly satisfactory. Their thought was, "It is not *society's* wealth; it is ours."

In the quarter century after Salamis, theatrical customs were working themselves out here in the Theater of Dionysos. Artistides and then an equally honorable Ephialtes had turns as chief executive (*archon*) of Athens. Sculpture was achieving the astonishing anatomic and gestural realism of *The Discos Thrower.* The threat of Persia was drifting off to the horizon like a terrible storm that grumbles at a distance. It grumbled enough to produce among Greek cities a mutual aid compact and council, the League of Delos. This was founded at the instigation of Athens, and its first assessment of contributions was handled by Aristides, whom all could trust. Painting became an official entry category at the Pythian Games, and women poets as well as men competed at the Isthmian Games at Corinth. Comedies eventually joined the City Dionysia. Times must have looked basically good.

III

First Plays and Other Newness

Philosopher as Playwright

There is no sure order of the seven plays of Aeschylus we have, but for years the oldest was assumed to be *The Suppliant Maidens* (or just *The Suppliants*). Why it seems oldest is significant. Why it also seems to have been produced later in Aeschylus' career is something to be looked at.

The Suppliants is the first play of a trilogy that could be called *Daughters of Danaus*. It is built on an unlikely legend of fifty sisters in flight from forced marriage to their fifty cousins, sons of their uncle, Aegyptos. The maidens have voyaged with their father, old Danaus, to Argos, where they beg the Argive king to protect them from their pursuing suitors. The play is (among other things) about refugees, about obligations that press on those from whom the desperate beg help.

The chorus is the central entity. Old Father Danaus seems oddly at his daughters' beck and call, and the Argive king makes no decision on his own till his people ratify his wish to help the women. That community's vote is the great off-stage dramatic choice. The great on-stage dramatic choice lies with the fifty sisters. Rather than yield to men they hate, they vow to die — and they sound ready to do it.

Scripts were without stage directions; a reader must infer locale from dialogue. Though settings are not described, locale is not a vacuum. Anyone who stages in any era seeks set pieces, and props that define the play's where and when and in the same stroke give habitation to its ideas, its concerns and its mood. That principle is at work in what I take for the very first of surviving plays. At minimum *The Suppliants'* set must be a row of sacred pillars, emblems of Zeus, Apollo, Aries, Aphrodite and others. The women's appeals that obligate the King of Argos to receive and protect are made principally to those idol-pillars. They are not small statues but columnar, solid and high, since from them the daughters of Danaus vow to hang themselves. Recall how effective a threat of suicide at a sacred spot had been when made by the Athenian embassy to Delphi before Xerxes' invasion. To pollute a holy place with violent death was to draw down incalculable wrath.

Except for the god-pillars, one senses from the script an open emptiness. We are to picture a spot distant from any settlement, a beach where arrivers are confronted first and crucially with the gods who govern this land. A raised stage and a façade came in the next century to separate principals from chorus, but here the audience will fix its attention on that big, open orchestra with little to obstruct the imagination. It is the "empty space" that the director Peter Brook posits as an ideal.

There is much to be said (some of it pretty scary) for the idea that plays and film and video are to their society as a whole what a dream is to the individual, that a collective unconscious is speaking. A locale in dreams can be vivid, almost another central character, or tenuous, fluid, hardly there. Event then steps toward us out of a fog, unencumbered by surroundings. In Aeschylus' *Suppliants*, written for open air and in the old tradition of chanted dance-narration, place feels especially undefined; any elaboration of literal stage set seems a reduction, an impertinence. That is one of the qualities stamping *The Suppliants* as transitional between dithyramb and later drama. Even more than at most plays we are invited outside space and time; the event is in some eternity.

As principal actor, Aeschylus played Danaus and the pursuing Egyptian Herald, a contrast of helpless low energy and furious high energy interesting for a performer, with a bravura bit near the end when the Egyptian goes out and Danaus enters (from the far side of the stage) with only brief exchange between King and Chorus for cover.

This chorus is feisty and sure of its own collective mind. Modern readers harshly judge Aeschylus' view of women, mostly from an arrogant slur on women's share in parentage that Apollo makes near the end of *The Eumenides (The Furies)*. We should notice what Danaus and the chorus say about love as the prime essence of marriage at the close of *The Suppliants*. A speech at the end of a play has special weight, even though one should be cautious about assuming any playwright's convictions are summed up in the lines of one character.

In this tragedy the goat's tail is not miserable; at play's end the Argives protect the women from the threatening Herald and his thuggish silent henchmen. The myth and a surviving fragment let us know roughly what happens in the whole trilogy. In the second play, the Argive protection is overridden (how is unclear). The women, forced to marry their loathed cousins, take a sacred oath to kill their bridegrooms that night and go off to their weddings with concealed hairpin knives. In the third play it turns out that one of the women loved the man allotted to her and has let him live. She is put on trial for oathbreaking, perhaps by her father, who had opposed the marriages from the first, but, given his weakness and the intransigent will his daughters show, perhaps it is they who press charges against their sister. Aphrodite appears for the defendant, and we have the goddess's praise of marriage because a later writer quoted her:

> ...love takes hold of earth to join in marriage
> And showers, fallen from heaven drawn to her bed,
> Make the earth pregnant; and she in turn gives birth
> To flocks of sheep and the food of Demeter —
> A marriage that drenches the springtime of the woods —
> For all of this I am in part responsible.
>
> [translation my pastiche]

The Roman poet Horace chanted of Hypermnestra (the bride who does not kill) as *splendide mendax*, "shiningly an oathbreaker" or "splendidly false." He was probably echoing in Latin what Aeschylus had said of her.

Any summary of *The Suppliants* will do it injustice. Danaus' daughters (fifty brides for fifty brothers) feel to us like figures from some house-tale the Grimms collected at a peasant hearth. Very likely a production of it wouldn't help us. The Egyptian Herald is a stereotype; he rages with an absurd accent. Surely he got his laughs, and we would cringe. Broad humor changes radically from society to society, and quieter humor is hard to detect across centuries (or across national borders, for that matter). I feel sure there is intended humor in Aeschylus. Was that uniquely Aeschylean, startling to his audience, or did his vanished rivals too have an impish vein? There is nothing like it in Sophocles, almost nothing like it in Euripides, which suggests it was unique. No contemporaries notice it, which suggests it was not. If it *was* unique to Aeschylus, all who commented on him later avoided mention of it as though it were a kind of Bergerac's nose.

Humor aside, Aeschylus is fascinated here and later with turning an ethical problem over and over; he shows obverse and then reverse of the coin or even palms one coin and reveals another. In this trilogy the suppliants are victims. Then they are murderesses. Then one of them is in the wrong because she *isn't* a murderess. Then, by at least one divine code, she is vindicated. That is not a nihilist's shrug at conflicting moralities, but it certainly doesn't settle for easy answers. In a primitive myth it digs uncomfortably deep into human dilemma.

On the verge of apologizing for *The Suppliants*, I find myself struck by it as never before. This is a beginning. Being present at a birth is exalting yet disturbing. Blood and helplessness are things we associate more with death or injury than with life. Old, gory and grotesque myths, standing shadowy at the mouth of a Pan cave of incoherence, are hard to associate with a great mental emergence. I've felt the same about the Oedipus story; some feel it about the plot of *Hamlet*. But I make myself listen to what is being said in *The Suppliants*: that these foreign women's desperate appeal lays Argos under obligation. Aeschylus is not *preaching* that we, the comfortable, have a duty to take up the burden of the world's suffering — he is no preacher. However, that moral duty is exactly what he is bringing us to look at and respect.

One can find oneself looking very hard. I've suggested three major strands in Greek theater: poetry, festival and competition. There's a fourth, philosophy. As it loomed up in the mental life of the Athenian intelligentsia during Aeschylus' lifetime, it of course affected the plays. An *intelligentsia*, a term U.S. Americans recoil from, is made up of all who care for the life of mind and heart; it is not an exclusionary club of high IQs. Raw IQ often wastes itself on career scramblers who don't give a snap for it except as a tool for getting ahead. An intelligentsia respects the tool.

Let's jump back a few years. Among émigrés to Athens during the upheavals of the Persian Wars, a young man named Anaxagoras arrived.

Whether or not he came in time to share in the first, numb rebuilding, he was a sharer in Athens' reinvention of itself; he became one of its citizens at heart though not by birth. He stayed many years, till at last the devout drove him away. He was a citizen of the universe, one of the constellation of pondering minds we now call philosophers. He must have been a genial and fascinating talker, for he soon found influential friends. Anaxagoras was not one of the greatest contributors to philosophy, but he was a vector. Ideas he and other displaced Ionians brought to Athens from the wider Greek world captured many open Athenian minds. I think of the influx of thought and interests Middle European immigrants brought to the United States before and during two World Wars. What sort of new ponderings did Anaxagoras bring from his home city of Clazomenae, Miletos' equally threatened neighbor?

Thales of Miletos, dead some sixty years by the time of Salamis, was the first ponderer of this new kind to leave a record. Miletos, not Athens, would have been remembered as the center of things Greek if it had not been for the expanding Persian Empire. Thales recognized in geometry ("measuring"—there was no better word for it yet) an attainable certainly. It is unshakably true that when a man's flat shadow is as long as his height, the unknown height of a pillar can be found by measuring its flat shadow. We seldom say anything unshakably true; for some a quest for unshakables becomes a thirst. Only geometry and mathematics satisfy that craving in ways all humans can agree on, but to what places the thirst has led us!

It led Thales, they say, into long-range weather prediction. Foreseeing a huge olive harvest, he cornered the market of local oil presses and funded a life of travel and study by way of the world's first outrageous monopoly! Using lunar records from Babylon and Egypt, he predicted the solar eclipse of May 28, 585 B.C. That made him no money (unless he placed bets, as I suppose he might have), but it demonstrated that even Heaven, at least the Heaven a man can see, is subject to the rule of number. Eclipses are not divine whims. That eclipse, by the way, terrifying Persians and Lydians into temporary armistice, arguably delayed the Persian Empire's arrival at the Aegean coast by forty-one years. Luckily for a generation of Milesians, Thales' insight was not yet understood.

Thales sensed that under the world's disarray there should be something all things are made of—though his language had no workable words for *substance, elemental* or *fundamental*. His idea of water as the fundamental substance was flawed, but his inquiry has led by twists and turns to the table of elements, to subatomic particles and to who knows where next? His ideas were a long lever: one small move at Thales' causal end, a huge sweep of effect at our end. Others are credited with developing the scientific method, but weren't they verbalizing what Thales began? This water-dreamer, according to some ironist, fell down a well while looking at the stars. The story tells more about skeptics of philosophy than about Thales.

Heraclitos who survived the burning of Miletos and thought fire the fundamental element, called Zeus "the mind that moves all things through all things." That mind was just then uniquely upon the move. Anaxagoras believed that Mind itself was the fundamental. It was a taste for such thoughts that he brought to Athens. During Aeschylus' and Anaxagoras' lifetimes many were wrestling with questions that Thales, Heraclitos and their ilk had set loose.

Skole is Greek for "leisure." In Athens and also in Greek colonial southern Italy, *skole*, "school," came to mean especially "leisure to wonder at quandaries." Soon it also meant any group that shared some theory, a school of thought. We sometimes think schooling so laborious we have coined the oxymoron *schoolwork*. Yet it began playfully, and many young Athenians took to it with the passion that seventeenth-century Dutchmen would bring to tulips, twentieth-century Russians to chess or Argentines to soccer. One human excellence is our capacity for play, and philosophy was play. It was play that spanned from thinking about what we now call physics to what we call ethics.

The freedom in a daring mind tosses away nothing until it has peered at it closely. Counteractive to rigidity in politics or religion, it is an essence of democracy. The most antidemocratic moments in Greek life or ours come when things are left unthought for fear they might insult the opinions of a majority or oppose the will of some powerful few.

In the *Daughters of Danaus* trilogy, Aphrodite sums up her role in all generative processes. It is a speech the semicomic minx-goddess of love in Homer's *Iliad* could never have come up with. It was written when people with a philosophic turn of mind were suggesting that the Gods were understandable as forces, principles in a principled cosmos, not just mighty and erratic egos. Empedocles, an atomist philosopher and mystic in Greek Sicily, was writing his insights in verse during these same years; Anaxagoras and the playwrights read them in Athens. Fragments survive to tell that, for Empedocles, Aphrodite (Love) is the mothering half of a great dyad with her rival and partner, Strife:

> ...thus then Aphrodite, when she has moistened the earth with water
> breathed air on it and gave it to swift heats
> to be congealed ...
> and thus tall trees bear fruit, firstly olives ...
> ...late-born pomegranates and luxuriant apples ...
> [*Selections from Early Greek Philosophy*,
> M. C. Nahum, ed., F. C. Crofts & Co., 1947]

My attention dilates away from the dance circle where *The Suppliants* sang to their arc of statuary gods, beyond the horizon rim of Hymettos Mountain. During precisely the years when Thales was forging his ideas on the western edge of the stony expanse we now call Turkey, on its eastern edge where the mountains become Iran, Zoroaster was teaching Persians that the Good God has no tangible form, that the Bad God is to be resisted and that these two are the only gods. In 484 B.C., the year of Aeschylus' first win in the City Dionysia, Siddhartha, whom we will know as the Buddha, is finishing his last seasons in this world. In China Master Fu, whom we know as Confucius, is old but vigorously teaching that people should not do what they don't want done to them.

I'm not wildly overestimating Aeschylus or theater when I speak in the same breath of those contemporaneous Everests. I am peering at one of history's profoundest enigmas. There can have been no exchange of ideas between the Huang Ho basin, the Ganges basin and the Aegean Sea. Those populations were unaware of one another and would have shrugged at one another's cultures had they vaguely heard of them. Yet just before and around what I have called Greece's dazzling century, which I sit here trying to conjure, a whole new level of thought was welling up. Simultaneously in many far-flung places human inner life was irrigated more richly than it ever would be again until, perhaps, now—and we're too close to now for objectivity.

Our times have been radical, but we can understand the cross-pollinations that germinated our inventiveness. It is no puzzle (for one small example) that young builders in Russia and the United States got their first flying machines off the ground at virtually the same date. Exchange of ideas in the fermenting intellectual climate was global in 1903; time was ripe. But twenty-five hundred years before our technological revolution there was a revolution, that was... what? Moral or ethical or self-perceptive, call it what one will, there it is. Burgeoning in far-separated places, it was nowhere a work of some one man: Confucius and Siddhartha were not solitary any more than Anaxagoras was. Each within his own culture shared mental life with other theorist-philosophers and religious and mathematical thinkers and artists. The simultaneity among these separated, originating cultures is baffling.

Confucius, with his vision of a solid social order built on a natural one; Buddha, with his shocked awakening out of our dimensions into huger possibility; and the Greek thinkers, wading as individualists into the never-the-same stream of ideas about the One beneath the Many, are each unique. Yet they share a fundamental: they are in a way the chorus talking back to the god. Human thought is *tackling* things, not just humbly accepting them. Humankind is consciously wrestling with the cosmos, seeking to make it other or better, more endurable or sensible. One thinks of the folk hero Jacob in the myth, wrestling with the angel till he gets a hernia and a name. These people were saying to existence what Jacob said, "I will not let thee go, except thou bless me."

And speaking of Jacob. That last quote is of course from the Torah as Englished in the seventeenth century. Devout monotheists may be pleased (or disconcerted) to have their books included in the let's-call-it Ethical Revolution I'm suggesting. At the time of Confucius, Buddha and Aeschylus, the lighter yoke of Persia displaced the heavy Babylonian one on an exiled population of Hebrews who were then allowed to return to Jerusalem. (Esther's King Ahasuerus from the Purim play is Xerxes.) Solomon's ruined temple to Y-W- (He Who Cannot be Named) was being devoutly rebuilt. Also, the scattered holy writs of Israel were being refound, copied out, revised, assembled (and *forged*, at least in the ironsmith's sense of the word) into the Torah, what many English speakers call the Old Testament. Pisistratus had had divine Homer copied out hardly a splash or two upstream in the river of time! It is one more of the coincidences that accumulate into the huge puzzle I clumsily call an Ethical Revolution. Historians have not much dealt with it. Scholarship has a healthy narrow-mindedness; by the terms of its own agenda it must ignore the truly inexplicable.

Staring at the Theater of Dionysos I will not solve such enigmas. I only blink and return my thoughts to Aeschylus immersed in the creative brew of a Greece where Athens was becoming more and more the unacknowledged capital. I will try to leave the history of the world alone except in so far as at the moment it impinges on us in our here and now. There are riddles enough in *The Suppliants* itself to draw one out onto limbs of speculation.

SUPPLIANTS, PERSIANS AND SEVEN

How can I think *The Suppliants** must be the eldest play in style when it is now known to have been produced fairly late, certainly after *The Persians?* A papyrus fragment found in the 1950s all but proves *The Suppliants* and its companions in the trilogy were produced when Aeschylus was near his fifties or, given the traditional date for his birth, over sixty. The papyrus does not absolutely settle production date, but fixes it between 467 and 456.

Did Aeschylus have an early trilogy, one either refused the first time he submitted it or never submitted, one that (slightly rewritten?) he staged in the 460s? The only evidence for that scenario is in the play itself, its archaic bareness and the explicitness of its having a chorus of fifty. But there are political events that would justify staging this play in the 460s even if it was by then out of date in style.

I owe what support my idea has to a book by Anthony Podlecki, *The Political Background of Aeschylean Tragedy*. His theory hinges on things going on in Athens and all Greece in the 470s and 460s. To untangle them without drawing many more names into the telling, I will over-simplify. May Podleki's spirit forgive.

In many Greek cities the old guard, conservative descendants of aristocrats, tended to trust the Spartans. Those who favored democracy did not. Intelligent conservatives could admire (at a distance) the order, the structured society and rigid moral values of Sparta; thicker-headed conservatives noted that Sparta never let its own poor get out of hand. Sparta could be counted on to help put down popular revolts elsewhere, fearing that they might set its own underlings a bad example. So in Athens many aristocrats (people with ancestry) and oligarchs

---

**Two plays have this name. If the titles of the Greek plays that we have are those the authors chose for them, then Euripides showed nerve in calling his woe-racked play about war widows* The Suppliant Women. *The feeling that Euripides admired Aeschylus well on this side of idolatry may be reflected in Aristophanes. His* Frogs *has Euripides and the ghost of Aeschylus vie comically in Hades for the approval of Dionysos.*

(people with enough money to act as if they had ancestry) wanted accommodation with Sparta; Themistocles and the democrats did not.

Tension rose between Athens and Sparta because, following the Persian Wars, they were the two strongest powers. Athens' business was business, which means expansion; Sparta's business was militant status quo, which means resisting expansion. The Spartans had their own iron-bound Peloponnesian League. They did not join the League of Delos, which made the League more a NATO than a United Nations. Its existence fueled Sparta's distrust. For Spartans Themistocles more clearly than anyone else embodied shameless Athenian slipperiness.

I've called the twenty years or so just after the Persian Wars "good times." They were, relatively speaking; however, times never look all that good to those in the midst of them and Athens was as fermenting and divisive as ever. The upshot of many ins and out of office was that in 472 (while *The Persians* played at the City Dionysia), Aristides was commissioned to look into municipal accounts. Themistocles, it turned out, had taken many bribes, promising to engineer the bringing home of exiles. At times he had not even kept those shady promises. It is tempting to see in *The Persians* a reminder to Athens of all they owed Themistocles. It's true that play must have been finished before the account rolls scandal, but anti-Themistoclean sentiment was hot before it boiled over, and in Athens even an absorbed playwright knew what was being growled in the agora or in the great houses.

Rivals seized on Aristides' revelations, and Themistocles was ostracized in 470, a reversal of fortune for a man many idolized. He did not go far at first, only to neighboring Argos, which welcomed him. He still had wide-flung allies and resources and his reputation as the savior of Greece.

On a map the Isthmus of Corinth is the thin join between north and south. South of the Isthmus the Peloponnese is a four-digited right paw print, palm down; a stubby thumb points east, three fingers jut south. Sparta is just below the center of the paw; Argos lies in the crotch between thumb and first finger. No place is more haunted with myths and restless ghosts than Argos. The Greek besiegers of Troy were called Argives because their leader, Agamemnon, hailed from there. Two hundred years before Aeschylus' day Argos had been the first Greek city to take up the Asian fashion of minting coins, and, more significantly, Argives had once actually defeated a Spartan army. The shock of that was a factor in turning Sparta into a permanent armed camp, fanatically committed never to accept defeat again — and scornful of coinage. (Argos also defeated Athens in a skirmish about the same time; Athens got over it and forgot. One learns from history that sometimes it is good not to learn from history.) However Argos had no Pisistratus to push a growth spurt, no excellent clay pits and potters, no new silver mines. In the glorious century Argos had not grown much, though it was one of the few towns in the Peloponnese outside the shell of fearful clients and serfs in which Sparta had cocooned itself. Just before the Persian Wars the Spartans briefly held it again, only to let it go in a shuffle of alliances when the Persians were coming. Argos was eagerly democratic and despised Sparta.

Themistocles understood that his real support lay not in one city or another, but in democratic movements wherever they welled up. From a friendly base in Argos he began furthering the ousting of old oligarchies in the smaller Greek cities. Democratic revolts drove the old guard rulers from some within Sparta's sphere of influence.

The Spartans resorted to Themistocles' enemies in Athens, sending them compromising letters from him to one of their own kings, Pausanias. Pausanias was the hero whose generalship a year after Salamis had given the remaining Persian forces their deathblow at Plataea. He was also a scoundrel. Like General Miltiades of Marathon, he had overweened, fallen into disgrace with his own people and been starved to death. Among his belongings were writings that seemed to show Themistocles plotting with the Persians. Perhaps the letters were forged. On the other hand Themistocles might well have written them; some fox trick of his to put Pausanias in bad light may have turned and bitten Themistocles' own hand. A joint Athenian and Spartan embassage descended in arms on Argos to arrest Themistocles; friends there could no longer shield him as they had, and he was helped to flee.

"It is remarkable that within a very few years of this," Podlecki writes, Argos should be brought "to dramatic attention at Athens for its willingness to give protection to suppliants, even at the risk of war!" (A. J. Podlecki, *The Political Background of Aeschylean Tragedy*, Univ. of Michigan, 1966).

The Suppliants is very much on the side of Argos, on the side of democracy and on the side of sheltering refugees. This play's Argive king does not protect the suppliants by royal fiat, though ancient kings in other plays make their choices with autocratic assurance. Over and over it is emphasized that the Argive people collectively and unani-

III. First Plays and Other Newness

mously approve and confirm the generosity by literal show of hands. "...and the play sweeps on to the Danaids' prayer for their benefactors.... This great choral hymn is the heart of the play, a benediction for the prosperity of the Argives. The people have [Poldecki quotes the play itself] 'cast a favorable vote' and 'may the people's power, which rules the city, preserve its rights in security'" (Podlecki).

Assume that a current event prods Aeschylus to put praise of Argos' generosity to refugees on stage on short notice in 467. A piece of writing from his youth strikes him as aptly adaptable. A playwright's works are not necessarily produced in the order they are written. Mr. Podlecki lets me eat one small cake and have it too: to understand *The Suppliants* as an early play although knowing it was produced fairly late. Briefly retold, all this sounds far-fetched, but *The Political Background of Aeschylean Tragedy* is detailed and convincing. More certainly, the play is clearly pro-democratic. It is puzzling that some have seen Aeschylus as a conservative aristocrat.

The issue of the Danaids' fate is dim, but the issue of refugees, in Darfur and elsewhere now, is still a darkness visible. The heat of its own day adds a vitality to any play; in the cool of later times it must generate its own warmth. If it can do that, we call it timeless; it has radioactive elements in it though its sun has paled. I don't think there is enough heat left in the bare world of *The Suppliants* to support life for us; it orbits out there, a moon of Saturn. Still, such a sphere tempts exploration.

The Seven against Thebes, like *The Suppliants,* suggests for setting a row of statues, shrines to the major gods. This time we are in the agora of Thebes. The gods are very present and active even in a play much concerned with human affairs. For Aeschylus they always were there; something in him was stubbornly old guard in relation to religion, though new, even heretical ideas kept seeping in on him and he was too honest to exclude them. *The Seven* belongs to a trilogy that spanned from the reign of Oedipus' father to the death of Oedipus' sons. A curse upon the family unified the three dramas; it is hard to judge the over-all from this one play. The American poet Anthony Hecht has done a translation that offers it all the service it can receive; it would be one of the hardest of Greek plays to make touch an audience now.

Plot, part one. In Thebes an embattled king must fight his exiled brother — whose ascendancy to the throne six heroes have gathered to assure — and the citizens are in panic. If there's dramatic reversal in this segment of the play, it depends on visuals of staging. A herald tells of each attacker in turn, particularly describing the semimagical device on his shield; the young king selects and sends out, from among his own six champions, one to face each. Last the herald describes the king's brother, and, now that the silent six champions have gone, the one left on stage to oppose him is the king himself. The frightened chorus knows, and so does the king, that he and his brother are cursed to destroy each other. Nonetheless, he does go out to the doomed combat.

I'm unprovably convinced that much of the meaning and effect of this scene was lodged in the symbols painted on the shields of King Eteocles and his six mute warriors. Those would be images counteractive to the power signs carried by their opponents. A poetry of sight can be as vivid as poetry of word. The chorus is still the heart of this drama. Its women represent the whole noncombatant citizenry, witnesses and victims of a war as unsparing and terrifying as flood or volcano.

Plot, part two. Offstage the brothers kill each other; the bodies of both are brought back. Honorable burial is decreed to one corpse, disgraceful exposure to the other. Their sisters mourn them; one sister accepts the city's decree concerning the bodies. The other sister, Antigone, chooses to defy authority; in her heart family ties trump civic ones. The chorus, divided in recognition that each woman is acting righteously, follows the two sisters off to their varied fates.

This climactic dividing of the chorus against itself may be profoundly significant. It is almost unique in the surviving tragedies. Would it be considering too curiously to say that that parting foreshadows a rift which was just then opening in the social fabric of Athens? From where we stand in this divisive twenty-first century, the rift feels familiar. New thoughts, new philosophy clash against traditions; economic and social conflicts as old as those Solon wrestled with assume new, angry forms under the influences of new kinds of skepticisms and aspirations. The chorus divides, and, since choruses by nature speak with one mind, a chorus divided against itself is striking. The arts are astonishingly often prophetic of social change. Aeschylus was writing this play before the conflicts we call the Peloponnesian Wars were to divide Athenian from Athenian so deeply; he cannot consciously have known the huge tensions building in the bed rock of his society — but then, animals cannot consciously know when an earthquake is coming, yet they do know, through senses as subtle to them as our arts are to us.

The German philosopher Hegel writes of tragedy at a length and intricacy I have never followed. I hope it's a fair reduction to say that he sees tragedy as coming from the irreconcilable conflict between two mutually exclusive moral imperatives. That idea is more wieldy among polytheists than among monotheists — fundamentalist Muslims, Christians or Jews can't comfortably admit that moral imperatives can exclude one another, since all that is moral proceeds from one God. But that bind, that cosmic catch-22, was a recurrent theme among Athenian writers of tragedy. What Aeschylus made of the moral dilemma in his trilogy about Thebes can't be guessed at from the one play. We can only feel sure, on the basis of the rest of his work, that he dealt with the problem intricately and head-on.

If some papyrus-stuffed mummy one day gives back to us Aeschylus' two lost dramas on Oedipus's family, they'll not only enrich *The Seven Against Thebes*, but also shed fascinating light on Sophocles' *Oedipus Rex* and *The Antigone*, two of the most famous plays from the ancient world.

An anecdote remembered from the performance of *The Seven* shows an audience quick to think in terms of current events, even when watching a mythic story. As a herald describes the menace of the seven attackers, he praises one, the prophet among them. Calling him "a man of moderation and the best in strength," the Herald goes on to say,

> He does not wish to seem best, but to be,
> Reaping the harvest of deep-furrowed thought,
> Where his good council grows.
> [*The Seven against Thebes*, David Grene translation,
> Univ. of Chicago Press, 1956]

At that line, someone recalled, every head in the theater turned to look at Aristides. An audience that reacts that way is listening for what an author may hint at about its own world. These plays were not just rituals. The Athenians were listening hard. If we do not listen hard for what plays say about our own world, we are a lesser audience than they were.

To underline the respect we owe good translators, I'll lift a passage out of *The Art of Aeschylus*, by Thomas G. Rosenmeyer. He doesn't feel Aeschylus' writing is as dense as some claim, but he admits that at times, in choruses, grammar dissolves. I condense his comments (using his own words) but leave his literal translation intact. He says that in lyrics "the sentence leads a shadowy existence. An extreme case is an ode [from The Seven against Thebes] which voices the confusion and disorientation of battle ..."

> Rumblings throughout the city, the turret-net
> Close, by man man is speared,
> Bloodied shrieks
> Newly born
> Of [infants] at-the-breast howl.
> Snatchings, blood-brothers of random-running.
> Plunderer contracts with plunderer
> And calls [him] empty [himself] empty,
> Wishing to have a partner ...

The impressionistic arrangement of wailing infants — not as infants but as wailings made up of blood and cries ... — of roaming plunderers and of leaning battlements ... is untranslatable. It is a mosaic of words ... violently removed from grammatical agreement [Rosenmeyer, *The Art of Aeschylus*].

This wild high-handedness with language made some people say that Aeschylus composed while drunk. If Aeschylus heard that, he would have grunted to recognize a poetic truth in it. The drink in question was spirit of Bacchos, promised to him in childhood dream under the vines and dipped from some deep cellar in himself. David Grene manages to be both poet and fairly literal translator, but he imposes more order on the words then the original has. He gives the same passage this way:

> There is a tumult through the town.
> Against her comes a towering net.
> Man stands against man with the spear and is killed.
> Young mothers, blood-boltered,
> cry bitterly for the babes at their breast.
> The roving bands of pillagers are all brothers;
> he that has plunder meets with another;
> he that is empty calls him that is empty,
> wishing to have a partner ...
> [*The Seven against Thebes*, Grene translation]

The Seven is murky, problematic and stiff, but a fiery horror of war flickers through it like Hell in a Bosch painting.

The Persians too takes place at a shrine, the tomb of deified Darius. I had the luck to savor a rare professional performance of *The Persians* at the Pearl Theater in New York City in 2002; war in the Middle East resonated in it. The play is a proud exultation at the victory off Salamis, but it is also an extraordinary recognition, by a victor, of the sufferings of the defeated. Homer had set the example: his Trojans are more likeable and humane than his quarrelsome Greeks. But Homer never fought against Trojans or lost kindred to them. Aeschylus is generous in the Homeric way. Could anyone in Britain or the United States in 1952 have written a publicly financed play empathetic to the agonies of German or Japanese citizens of 1945, or (to find an image more vivid to us at the moment) to the despair of defeated Taliban* fighters seven years after New York lost the World Trade Towers? I think not. It asks an order of generosity and a hugeness of imagination our heightened nationalisms exclude us from.

I won't over-glorify Athenian magnanimity. Its literature was too rarely reflected in its politics. We make our commitment to their political innovation because on the whole democracies do usually treat their own enfranchised citizens better than other governments do. However, in foreign policy democracies may be as savage and shortsighted as dictatorships. Before the brilliant century had run its course, many smaller city-states preferred submission to Persia or Sparta over alliance with Athens. Monarchy at least was consistent, whereas Athens was a loose cannon to its neighbors.

One of the many towns destined to suffer eventually from the paradox of Athens was Eretria. It had paid dearly for a pro-Athens stance in the days that led up to Marathon and was eventually to pay just as dearly for an anti-Athenian stance! The play *The Persians* calls Eretria to mind for a tangential reason remote from politics, a question of staging, trivial perhaps but intriguing.

The main visuals in *The Persians* are three. There is a first arrival of Queen Atossa with great splendor, "in ample folds adorned" and in a chariot. The more elaborate her panoply, the better it counters the final coming home of Xerxes, battered and in rags. Between these two

---

*I don't suggest the Afghan Taliban were responsible for the plane crash bombings in New York and Washington. They were not; they offered to arrest the perpetrators. U.S. authorities preferred to invade Afghanistan. But since the U.S. citizenry tends to blame the Taliban for evils they opposed as well as for the very real evils they actually do, they make as extreme a parallel as I can conjure up.

visuals there's a third, a raising of the ghost of Darius. Costume might make him ghostly and grand, but there is greater effect in his literally rising from his tomb. A vase from about 490 B.C. shows a parallel scene (though the chorus is not of Persians), with a figure rising from the center of a shrine while soldiers pray in a theatrical unison salute to it. Darius' almost first words to the chorus are

> ...you lamented, standing
> Near my tomb with cries of resurrection
> Calling piteously. Ascent is not easy.
> The chthonic deities more readily
> Receive than give;
> [*The Persians*, Bernardete translation]

Chthonic means underground. A vase from southern Italy a century later shows a moment from Aeschylus' *Oresteia* when the ghost of Clytemnestra tries to rouse the sleeping furies; she is literally half out of the ground. *The Persians* and many other plays could profit from a stage trap door.

Was there such a thing? Eretria suggests yes.

Due north from Athens, passing west of Marathon, you come to the strait between Attica and the long island of Euboea. A strong rower could cross to Eretria in a small boat. The Persians, before anchoring at Marathon, had burnt it; its citizens who did not flee into the Euboean forest had been killed or enslaved. (Surviving Eretrian children were to see Pericles repeat that destruction.) During Aeschylus' career Eretria was rebuilding itself with energy and pride. It had a theater modeled on this Theater of Dionysos. The remains seen there now are from long after the great century, but archaeology had revealed its earlier shape and size.

Like this theater in Athens, the Eretrian older layout had a round orchestra considerably bigger than its later one. Also, like Athenians, Eretrians eventually dug out their hillslope to lay out more comfortable and symmetrical seating, at which time the orchestra was made smaller although the theater and its town as a whole were growing.

In that older theater an underground vault extended in under the orchestra from off upstage center; when the theater was remodeled and the dancing floor was lowered, a new, deeper understage passageway was dug; clearly presenters valued the uses of that earlier passage and kept it. It emerged into the orchestra, I presume behind the central altar. It was the equivalent of our "stage trap." Such passages are found, rarely, at other theaters and the name given them, "Charon's steps," hints at their use for ghosts and apparitions; Charon was ferryman to the dead.

Didn't this Theater of Dionysos once have its Charon's steps? The era's approach to staging is at issue, not just the use or nonuse of one particular stage device. Was ritual tragedy at this time already circumscribed in traditions or restlessly open to experiment? Openness to the new was the essence of the time. I can't believe ancient drama emerged with rigid, Noh-like formalities immediately in place; its bones grew stiff with time, but in its youth it was limber. If ever such a passage was dug at Athens, it would have been in those early years.

No one has found any Charon's steps here. An underground passage, shored up with wood, not masonry, would leave hardly a trace once it fell in from neglect. This site now is a national monument not lightly dug into in quest of a passageway that might be chimerical. The big digging here was done by a German named Dörpfeld in the late 1800s. Dörpfeld was meticulous by his era's standards, but he worked with pick and spade, whereas today archaeologists would scarcely stir gravel with a whisk, even if bureaucracy let them. The scholar A. Pickard-Cambridge wrote an exhaustive book titled *The Theater of Dionysos at Athens*. He states his conviction that there was no underground passage here, and his word should be nearly law to someone like me. But he goes on to say that "at various times there were [ancient] excavations under the orchestra subsequently filled up, the date and purpose of which are quite unknown; some of them may go back to the Fourth Century and there are traces of a prehistoric spring...." No provable sign of any Charon's steps here is apt to be found now.

Nonetheless Athens was the great maker of fashion, and other cities built their theaters to stage Athenian plays. Would such an effective theatrical device be found in lesser theaters if there was none at Athens? If developed elsewhere, wouldn't the Athenians have appropriated it? They were not shy to learn from others and to better the instruction. So much of theater work is theft or, less ironically, inspired borrowing; when we are directors, we are as alert as pickpockets to what has done well in other's productions. Like pickpockets, we are careful not to appropriate too obviously, but we appropriate. There would be no such thing as a style in any era if we did not. (Now, into the thick cypress down where Dionysos' temple once stood, a black-

and-white magpie flies with something in its beak. I recognize its furtive pride of prize; I have sometimes felt the same.) In Aeschylus the ghosts of Darius and, later, Clytemnestra cry out for that entrance from underground. Later in one of Euripides' plays, *The Suppliant Women*, a grief-maddened widow throws herself into her husband's blazing pyre. I cannot imagine that scene done effectively without a Charon's steps. (Some suppose that Evadne's self-immolation must happen offstage, but the script reads as though she destroys herself before our eyes.)

In fairness, given the dramatic power of a mid-stage entrance from below, one might ask how it could ever have lapsed into neglect. Later classical theaters seldom had Charon's steps. That is a puzzle and there is yet another.

Why, both here at the Theater of Dionysos and over in Eretria, did the orchestra shrink rather than expand when the theaters were rebuilt? With growing populations and the growing popularity of theater, you'd think Eretrians and Athenians would have enlarged their dancing place. In the next centuries theaters and their orchestras did enlarge — astonishingly huge ones were built. What was going on here to explain the contraction?

To both questions there are answers that pretty much satisfy me. One is pleased by one's own notions; the goose thinks its goslings good. I'll propose an answer to the second question first.

Edith Hamilton's essay *Fifteen or Fifty*, which I recommended earlier, points out that the question of the number of chorus members is vexed (scholars love calling gaps in their mosaic "vexed"). No one from the playwrights' era cites a number; a Roman encyclopedist named Pollux, 600 years in their future, is the first to be specific! Here is Edith Hamilton:

> In the day of our oldest authority, Pollux, there was a tradition of an original chorus of fifty superseded by a smaller chorus ... [at the time of Aeschylus' Oresteia]. There was good reason for Pollux number of fifty in the early chorus. Long before Aeschylus' day the Athenians had watched contests between choruses of fifty. At [the first day of the Dionysia] ten such choruses, five of men and five of boys, competed for a prize. Athens was used to the spectacle... [*The Ever-Present Past*].

When the chorus was reduced by about three-quarters, it makes sense that the dancing place shrank. In the new, smaller orchestra the newly shrunken chorus did not look lost — also it had more elbowroom for dramatic choreography.

In 468, after *The Persians* had been produced and won its honors, the younger playwright, Sophocles, defeated the master for the first time. Two years later Aeschylus took the crown back with his *Seven against Thebes*. In 465 the Theater of Dionysos underwent one of its reshapings, and I suspect it was at that time that the orchestra shrank. I also suspect Aeschylus was among those who had a crucial voice in that conversion.

You have seen how dense a poet Aeschylus was, how he liked to pursue his thoughts into the thicketed, poetic shadows language can cast. Some good poets seem not to care to be generally understood; some, not so good, pull a sequined veil of unintelligibles over the vacuous face of what they have to say. But their poetry is written to be read in private. Plays — and all Greek poetry — are a public art. Aeschylus, like every genuine playwright who ever lived, must have wished his audience to hear and grasp his words.

Even if singing is spare and slow, it is next to impossible for a huge chorus to make unique, unexpected phrases intelligible. Our own choral music has always understood this. Our oratorios drew texts from scripture that could (at the time of composition) be relied on as known. Lyrics in operas and musical comedies are typically repeated, sometimes over and over. Furthermore our librettists and songwriters are forever being told, "be simple, leave room for the music." Aeschylus certainly did not do that.

I am not going to guess about Greek theater music. Without harmony it was less dense than ours, but at frenzied moments in the plays it must have been rapid. Church fathers from late classical times anathematized all but one or two musical modes; they felt that most of the music their flock knew roused either crazed, licentious passions or languorous, unseemly lassitudes and lusts. The musical extravagances they banned will have been the essentials of drama. Whatever Greek music really was, it sounded in ears of its day at times as frenetic as acid rock or as furious as rap or as plangent and narcotic as country-western.

The strophe/antistrophe tradition in choric verse, which goes back to Arion and before, may, I've suggested, have aided the diction by dividing the bigger chorus into twenty-five answering twenty-five. My guess is that the competing poets (sometime in Aeschylus' career and with his hearty consent or initiative) chose to reduce the number of the chorus in order to be better understood. I can imagine the producing *choregoi* dismayed and needing reassurance that there would still be opportunity for great display. Let me fantasize the argument:

"My dear Aeschylus, you know what our fellow citizens are! Every index finger in Athens will be pointing at me and snickering that I was too cheap to pay for a chorus of fifty!"

AESCHYLUS: "But, by Heracles, a chorus of fifty might as well be fifty bullfrogs in a crock! Can't you..."

PRODUCER: "You were happy with fifty before, so why..."

AESCHYLUS: "I was *never* happy with fifty! Never! I used fifty because fifty were there! *We were used to the spectacle!* You want to throw money to the crowd? Get together with the other producing *choregoi* and build a solid *skene* shed!—or put in new seating that doesn't leave splinters in the backs of everyone's knees! Peacock with something that doesn't make verse sound like a gutter gargling rain!"

PRODUCER (*half to himself*): "If your Muse gave you verses that were just a *little* plainer... Nothing. Nothing. It doesn't matter."

The first permanent *skene* came soon enough, though not immediately, I think.

That bit of dialogue has probably frayed any last tatters of readers' faith in my seriousness. Before the century's close Aristophanes would be writing things much like it, though funnier. He made Aeschylus a cranky character in *The Frogs*.

The shrinking chorus may be an answer to the puzzle of the shrunken orchestra. The puzzle about why Charon's steps fell into disuse must twist in the wind a bit longer; I'll propose some possible causes for it in time. Settle now for the fact that chorus and dancing place both grew smaller and that Darius' ghost, at least at Eretria, loomed up from underground behind the altar and sank back down out of sight again.

When its theater was reshaped in 465, Athens had other news to talk of. Aristides was dead. The less well recorded Ephialtes headed the democratic movement, but reactionary leadership held many major offices in Athens, in part thanks to Themistocles' disgrace. Hounded from city to city, Themistocles was actually now in Persia, living up to what he had been accused of. Would he repeat Hippias' role and guide yet another Persian fleet against his own people? Fear of that is the only pale excuse for the turn Athenian foreign policy was to take. A line from *Macbeth* cuts deep (and both ways):

III. First Plays and Other Newness

> You all know, security
> Is mortals' chiefest enemy.

We are at our absolute worst when we are afraid.

A first crack in the League of Delos had opened and closed when Naxos, one island with enough timber to build its own ships, tried to withdraw from the pact. It was invaded and reduced to a subject state by the general-politician Cimon. Athens had showed its teeth to it allies and had started on its way toward an unstable, toxic paradox: a democracy-empire. A nasty little war abroad, if not prolonged, may make its instigator briefly popular at home. Cimon was oligarch of the hour once his mission was accomplished.

Word arrived from across the Aegean that Xerxes had been murdered, along with a son. Persia's greatness seemed moving into eclipse, but there was no way to be sure.

Aeschylus had met a worthy rival, Sophocles, who was soon either bending a rule or stepping beyond assumed convention by using a third speaking actor. Aeschylus followed suit in his final plays.

IV

Prometheus, Then Orestes

FORETHOUGHT

Of Aeschylus' surviving plays the last four, *Prometheus Bound* and the *Oresteia* trilogy, stand the best chance of intriguing an audience now. Though the chorus is still intrinsic, individual characters loom more strikingly into the foreground. Lyric tragedy with choral song at its core gives way to drama of individuals, a drama we understand better.

Until modern times, *Prometheus Bound* was held high as Aeschylus' next-to-final masterpiece. Now some scholars question whether it is by Aeschylus at all. Their doubts recognize that the writing is very different from that in other plays. I don't know enough Greek to argue. However, suppose that only *Julius Caesar, Antony and Cleopatra* and *Pericles, Prince of Tyre* had survived of Shakespeare's work, plus *Henrys* enough to make seven plays in all. Could we believe that the same poet wrote the spare rhetoric of *Julius Caesar* and the fluid, odd, word-lovely music of *Antony and Cleopatra*? Or that either play was by the job-lot playwright who hacked out or rehashed *Pericles*? We have enough of Shakespeare's work to see bridges between one style and another, but he certainly does not have one consistent style. Should we think Aeschylus did?

Doubters note that the *Prometheus* chorus of sea maids has untypically little dance (though that little could be spectacular, since they must seem to dance in air). That raises one point that I really can speak to from experience. A life treasure of mine was an opportunity to stage *The Oresteia* trilogy with adequate rehearsal time and a supportive young company. Among myriad discoveries during that process, we found what gifts Aeschylus made to his chorus. In the first play they are old men, in the second frightened and wishfully vengeful slave women, in the third maddened Furies who transform at last into benevolent, protective demons of Athens. How often do actors get to run through a range like that? Whether or not an audience encounters Aristotles' cathartic healing in the play, the performers of that chorus certainly do!

The work made us realize that one cannot judge a chorus's potential, either for performers or spectators, without knowing all three plays of a trilogy. Remember that (*The Persians* perhaps excepted) each of the surviving pre-*Oresteia* plays of Aeschylus is a one-act excerpt from what amounts to a huge three-act play. Among other things, experiencing the *Oresteia* convinced me that the same chorus *did* perform in all three plays of a trilogy. Acting (outside the confines of realism) is not about typecasting; it is about conquest of type, and the varying character of the chorus from play to play is part of the bravura of performance. A fragment of the lost *Prometheus Unbound* lets us know that the last play had a chorus of Titans. I'm sure that whatever they were in the first play contrasted with both hovering sea maids and archaic giants. If a chorus had a bit less in one play, it had more in another.

Aeschylus, by the way, is credited with (blamed for?) inventing thick-soled elevator boots called cothurnoi that became traditional to all tragedy in a later, more stylized era. He did not use them often; Agamemnon, who takes off footwear on stage, was not suddenly six inches shorter for doing so! Those cothurnoi would make sense for a chorus of Titans and might have made their debut in *Prometheus Unbound*. Getting down to the simplest level of practicality, if I were rehearsing a performance where there was to be a lot of movement on high-soled boots, I'd shorten some other aspects of the production to ensure rehearsal time for that footwear. Unpracticed performers on cothurnoi loom and wobble ludicrously.

The Prometheus myth touches on one of the haunting ideas of primitive religion: that there were gods before the gods and others even before that, a divine evolution, cosmos from within cosmos from within cosmos. Sky and Earth emerge from the Gape (the *Chaos*), make love and beget a multitude of vast Titans. These beings are phenomena like Okeanos, monsters like Typhon or couples like Kronos and Rhea who are heavenly and earthly avatars of their father and mother. Kronos and Rhea revolt, put Earth and Sky in their places, one might say, and rule, begetting children in turn. They foresee that it is their fate to be done to by their children as they have done to their parents. Kronos therefore consumes each child as it is born, immortal but imprisoned in his belly. (Goya has an unforgettably hideous painting of that.) Rhea saves one son, Zeus, by giving Kronos a wrapped stone instead of the divine child. Zeus grows, castrates his father and forces the vomiting forth of his brothers and sisters, who marry one another and take over the universe from the heights of Olympos.

There was no one version of all this; I sketch what the dour and literal-minded poet Hesiod patched together and what an unreflective Greek would nod at and say, "That's probably so. In my city some tell a bit differently..."

Is the myth a dim recall of invaders supplanting local divinities with their own imported gods? When Apollo kills old Earth's Python at Delphi and takes over her shrine, it sounds like a new tribal priesthood usurping an elder one of priestesses. Or is it some shadow-picture of inevitable familial struggle? To survive a harsher world, the helpless old must be abandoned and the malformed or superfluous young exposed. A folktale of war between the generations could make that cruel reality more bearable. The name Kronos does not mean Time (*chronos*), but it does seem to mean Old One, linked across the wilds of Europe to the Irish word *crone*.

Yet in Kronos' ancient golden age food was had by humans for the eating and springtime was perpetual. (Greek myths about where humans came from were so vague that a philosopher could suggest we descended from fish without sounding blasphemous. Athens' "monkey trial" occurred later over whether Anaxagoras thought the sun was a stone or a god.) Kronos, however grimly he treated his own children, was remembered as making life good for humanity.

Zeus started his reign with an unkindlier view of us. Little, brutish caricatures of gods, "creatures of a day" he reckoned humans. He first intended to wipe us out in a flood. But one Titan, Prometheus (Forethought), prompted a man and his wife to build an ark and saved them. Beyond keeping base life afoot, Prometheus taught us skill after skill and at last brought us the creative gift that Zeus had flatly forbidden to us, fire. Cookery, metallurgy, warmth for surviving winter and for smoking meats and fish to last through the lean months ... Greek culture was not so advanced that it had forgotten what the basics are and how to value them. For a scantly furred creature with small teeth, nothing is more need-answering than fire.

Prometheus is so different a figure from the other Titans that he seems grafted from another stock of myth. His name means both prediction and intelligent concern for results. Intelligent foresightedness, on the occasions when we use it, is humanity's friend.

Prometheus, being foresighted, had sided with Zeus and the Olympians in their great revolt, though almost all his brother and sister Titans had fought ferociously against them. The Titans were now either locked down like emasculated Kronos or assigned unending tasks like Atlas, whose giant shoulders kept Earth and Sky apart (perhaps to prevent their begetting more Titans). Others, like Ocean, surrendered themselves, sullen and oath-bound, to a vast subservience or, like the Cyclopes, herded sheep and fueled the forges of volcanoes.

This titanic world is what Aeschylus chose to bring on stage in a trilogy. Aeschylus once said, with something like modesty, that all he did was "serve collops cut from the great feast of Homer." He was speaking not only of *The Iliad* and *The Odyssey*; many other vast epics that the rhapsodes chanted were credited to Homer, and one of them was a *Battle of Titans*. Some version of the Promethean story was embedded in that. The first play of Aeschylus' cycle was probably called *Prometheus Firebringer*, the last was *Prometheus Unbound*, the middle play is the one we have, *Prometheus Bound*. I say "probably" of *The Firebringer* because there is speculation. Other overall structures have been suggested for the trilogy. There's a fragment of the presumed satyr play *The Firekindler*. Could Aeschylus' first play of the trilogy have opened so zestfully that later it was mistaken for a satyr play? Intriguing if unlikely. It is most plausible that *The Firekindler* was the satyr play that followed the trilogy. We'll never know. So many times the barbarians have burned the libraries; fire is not always a gift, and smoke gets in our eyes. At any rate, whatever the title, the first play involved Prometheus' heroic trespass against orders from the new master god of heaven and earth.

The play we have, *Prometheus Bound*, as second of three, is in a sense the pause between actions. Zeus had Prometheus arrested for treason and dragged off to the cliffs to be chained forever. Might and Force make the unwilling, limping smith Hephaestos hammer Prometheus' bonds through his very chest into the rock and leave him.

The Daughters of Ocean, the chorus, gather in sympathy; old Ocean himself comes to offer submissive advice that almost seems one more attempt of Zeus to get at his rebel prisoner. Then another victim of Zeus wanders by, hapless Io, now cursed with cow's horns and frenzied with a gadfly because she yielded to Zeus' lovemaking. Hera hates her and Zeus will not protect her. To her Prometheus can offer remote comfort. Prophetic with suffering, he knows her wandering will bring her at last to Egypt, where she will finally bear the child of Zeus she has long and wretchedly carried. As horned Isis she will be exalted there. And Prometheus tells her his own secret hope. Zeus is fated to suffer as first Sky and then Kronos each suffered: Zeus will beget a son greater than himself and be overthrown — unless he learns the name of the one woman he must refrain from fathering a child by. That woman will be a descendent of this Io in the thirteenth generation to come. Prometheus knows her name, and he will keep that secret, through all tortures, unless Zeus relents. Io wanders away, she doomed to centuries of unpausing flight, he to centuries of motionless torture. A final messenger from Zeus, Hermes, arrives to demand that secret; Prometheus hurls back steadfast mockery and there is an ultimate, stormy deadlock.

In his nearly last speech Hermes describes what is about to befall Prometheus:

> ...no escape for you. First this rough crag
> with thunder and the lightning bolt the Father
> shall cleave asunder and shall hide your body
> wrapped in a rocky clasp within its depth....

Prometheus' last speech confirms the cataclysm:

> Now it is words no longer, now in very truth
> the earth is staggered; in its depth the thunder
> bellows resoundingly, the fiery tendrils
> of the lightning flash light up and whirling clouds
> carry the dust along: all the winds blasts
> dance in a fury one against the other
> in violent confusion: earth and sea
> are one....
>   [*Prometheus Bound*, Grene translation]

IV. Prometheus, Then Orestes

Prometheus Bound involves staging challenges as great as any a playwright ever set a director — or, in this case, set himself. Its whole action is tortured inaction. The protagonist, Prometheus, is brought on, the staples of his chains are hammered into rock, he stands or hangs through the entire play.

Some suggest a dummy was used, from behind which a performer stood to chant Prometheus' speeches; I can't feel that idea solves much. As for the stake Hephaestus drives through Prometheus' chest, a village conjurer can manage that effect without a dummy. The dummy supposedly avoids having a third speaking actor on stage — but an actor as a voice behind a stage rock is still a third actor. Those who wrote of theater's development felt the addition of a third actor was noteworthy, and Sophocles is credited with having first done it. By the time of the Prometheus cycle Sophocles was already staging plays and winning; Aeschylus uses his innovation here, though sparingly.

The custom of having few onstage speakers at a given time emerges out of a practicality of masked performance. The problem must have been noticed as soon as two actors wore masks. In a space as big as the Theater of Dionysos, only ears in the front rows can tell for certain who among masked figures is speaking when they stand near each other. Masks obscure the added cues the eye picks up. A puppeteer understands: the speaker must move, the spoken to must stand still. Yet if the speaker jerks his head too much, the effect grows grotesque. The more characters on stage, the trickier that compromise. So, for clarity, few principal players are brought on at once. Evidently Sophocles' troupe cultivated the emphatic gesture, the motionlessness, the turning of nonspeakers upstage, techniques that clarify talk among three masked personae. By the time of *Prometheus Bound* and certainly of *The Oresteia* a few years later, Aeschylus had picked up from his younger rival how to make triologue work smoothly in this performance space.

A more difficult staging puzzle in *Prometheus Bound* is how, on a curtainless, day-lit stage, did one avoid killing the final effect of Prometheus' doom? You either stage that end with an event vivid enough not to undercut the awesome, cosmic words or you rely wholly on the words and close with them — which leaves Prometheus on stage. Often I am all for relying on words, but with that choice made, does the actor hang there till all spectators have gone? Does he slip out of whatever it is that has looked like a stake through his chest and stalk off? Does he stay during the long wait till the next play begins?

There has been much throwing about of brains over that, and over a yet more puzzling effect. The chorus arrives on wings. They are the Daughters of Ocean, apparently sea nymphs in some kind of winged car or else sea birds. People speculate about the famous *mechene*, which, in later plays, lowered a God to the stage. The text seems to demand that the entire chorus be flown in! Considering the weight of fifty or even twelve young dancers hoisted in at once, the derricks needed would tower over the stage like a dockyard; the play would be about machinery. Derricks set up and taken down overnight? Or there throughout the festival? There was no *skene* façade to mask hoists or cranes.

The Prometheus cycle profited from an empty playing area. That blank space had great virtues. An architect wants a striking building; a play maker wants flexible neutrality. The farmer wants fences, the cattleman open range. Architects tend to win the inevitable shootout because those who put up the money also want big structures that will earn them their kudos. So medium buries message, *skenes* grow to loom over dancing spaces, opulence elbows in upon openness. Currently an anti-decor of ducts and girders may pretend to simplify our theaters, but is usually as obtrusive as rococo plasterwork without even rococo's shallow charm.

I rant but my convictions hesitate. Right now at the Acropolis, restoration work is going on in the Propylae; marble column drums are being hoisted from cliff bottom to the top. Kim and I earlier today peered down from the north ramparts and saw, behind hoardings far below, the winches that would send up the next huge loads. In Aeschylus' time oxen and human muscle were doing the feat motors do now. Multiton blocks of marble were dragged from Mt. Pentelicon, and somehow timber cranes and flax cables got them from the cliff base up the rock! We humans are as amazing as ants. Just when the Prometheus cycle was staged, Athens' main construction effort was going into more walls around Piraeus, but if the face of the Acropolis was being made shear with masonry here as well, hoists could have been in place around this theater for pragmatic purposes. One principle of the artist is: use what is at hand; it can serve more magically than what your patron pays for. Technique to fly that chorus could have been ready.

The flesh was willing, but wouldn't spirit have rebelled? The director in a person may revel in overproduction, but the poet in a person hates it. Why reduce a chorus from fifty to twelve so they can be better understood if you then bury your words in an avalanche of creaking visual effect? One thinks of our brilliant Julie Taymor's *Lion King* or of *Cirque du Soleil*. Spectacles like those are wonders in their own right, but in mounting them Taymor and the *Cirque* directors are not working with any verbal excellence they must defend; there are no compelling ideas to clarify. Aeschylus was his own writer. He would not have cut his throat just for some red spectacle. The huge derricks dissolve from my imagination.

There remains the drop-off, which in those days fell away at the back of the dancing circle. It hints at a staging solution, manageable and effective without overwhelming the actors. Over at the upstage edge of the space, the drop-off down out of sight is at least five or six feet, maybe more in places. The first entry of Daughters of Ocean is solvable: yes, they are arriving winged, but they are arriving from the sea *up* onto a mountaintop. Their journey is upward from below, not down from above, whatever the mechanics of the up-levered winged "chariot" or chariots they speak of may have been. They sweep up over the edge of the lip. "Winged chariots" could even possibly be Aeschylean for wings they wore; sometimes his metaphors are that unusual. If ships' oars can be their "feet" or their sails "wings"—as they are in *The Persians*—can't worn wings be chariots? One early vase painting shows a chorus (usually taken to be from a comedy) with arms fitted with bird wings.

Once the upstage drop-off is imagined, the effective exit of Prometheus also suggests itself. In thought-experiment, set up some suggestion of cliff top there on that edge. Since the audience is to see this as the very peak of a mountain, it need not be vast; even an eight- or nine-foot set piece looms effectively over an actor. Only a central upright where Prometheus will be chained absolutely needs to be solid plank. That plank is trigged or hinged to drop back over the stage lip at the finale—this, after all, is Aeschylus himself on stage. Forethought can come up with rope nets or whatever to control that drop so the chained actor does not break his back. Laurence Olivier, as Coriolanus, did a backwards fall from a platform and hung, slain, by his heels night after night. The salute "break a leg" was not coined without cause. It took our multimillion-dollar medical lawsuits to curb actors from athletic risk. Producers' accountants now restrain our dafter impulses.

And fume, lightning and thunder? "Greek fire," the ancient naval warfare's napalm, may have been in the future in Aeschylus' day, but caulking pitch was a commonplace of a fleet-building city. Smoke, dust and fire are natural; the whirling, choreographed wings of the Okeanides themselves can flash and spiral to the thunder of beaten bronze or a bull-hide kettledrum. Big can come from small — watch Japanese Kabuki. Theater may be bounded in a nutshell and think itself king of infinite space.

Bold effects in this play counter its central figure's immobility. Father Okeanos probably arrives by the *parodos* on a winged horse, animal or artifact. He needs the support of the spectacular. To shift attention from visuals to characterization, Okeanos is an interesting character, paradoxically, because he's dull. Every translation seems to agree that his language feels either fussy, costive or slightly foolish in its formality, a kind of Polonius-speak. Some find grounds in that for thinking Aeschylus did not write Okeanos, that he is an interpolation. The advice he gives — that one is wise to yield to a power one cannot oppose — is unheroic but not silly. Like Polonius' advice in *Hamlet*, it is good counsel from a flawed source. The uninspired apparent practicality of what he has to say seems to caricature a functionary, some Olympian secretary of defense with too small a mind and cramped a heart for his position. One recognizes the type.

Some serious scholars, if I understand them, argue that *character*, as we think of the word (a consistent set of psychological traits that make an individual unique), was not a thing Greek playwrights attempted to portray. True, Greek plays don't have the range of idiosyncratic personalities met in Elizabethan theater, but the lack is of degree, not of kind. Okeanos is a character, and the grave respect Prometheus uses in refuting him and sending him off — contrary to the contempt we would expect for such a personage from a sufferer — makes Prometheus a character too. Prometheus is rebel god, tortured and wrathful; yet, in dealing with this fatuous oldster, he is also what a later age would call gentlemanly. In his forbearance we glimpse someone capable of loving flawed humankind as truly as he says he does.

The figure of Okeanos pushes the Titanic world toward our own. On the verge of comedy, he suggests a political dimension in the play, as though Zeus' tyranny were an allegory and some actual dictator were being mocked or warned against. Hiero of Syracuse, who had been Aeschylus' patron, would fit the bill, or some would-be dictator closer to home. Political uproar over the oligarchic leanings of the successful general, Cimon, and over the assassination of the radical leader,

Ephialtes (though they no longer make headlines in anyone's overview of history) disturbed Athens furiously in 462, and that approximate date fits with when the Prometheus plays were likely to have been entered in the festival.

Zeus is unsparingly denounced for cruelty and shown engaging in torture of a good, generous kinsman; he is accused of abuse of newfound power; he is represented as surrounded by sycophants and fearful henchmen. In short he is an archetypal dictator. Even wedge-bearded Hermes, friendliest of gods to men, comes off as a tyrant's thug.

Athenians could look about or back into their past to know that democracy was vulnerable and its security insubstantial. They had not grown, as we have, complacent in a long tradition of self-rule; the older folk had lived under Hippias and knew that if circumstances turned bad, a cabal of malcontents might on any day appeal to fear, greed or national security and bring a new tyrant in. Police states in the ancient world lacked the horrible efficiency of ours, but they were fully as ruthless, while the mindsets that would oppose them were even less ingrained. The Athenian citizenry could not miss the image Aeschylus called up and must have reacted uneasily.

However, it is not politics in this play that has seized so many imaginations. What is? *Prometheus* is static and to follow it, you need more background than most arm themselves with. Still, it tantalizes, fascinates and evokes awe. Its substance is mythic, theological and philosophical. Zeus was Father of Gods and Men. Elsewhere in Aeschylus Zeus sternly administers justice, delaying but unforgetting, pulling down the wrongdoer and propping up the right. His name embodied almost all the virtues monotheists attach to the word God, loving kindness perhaps excepted. In *Prometheus Bound* it is as though Aeschylus had dared to look at the sun until the disk went black. One thinks of the response to those who talk now of an "intelligent designer" (a benign cosmic intellect that planned organisms): a designer of rabies bacilli and botflies would be a sadist. Evils do exist; belief in an absolute deity has to account for that deity's countenancing of evils or at best the turning of a blind eye. The common, least complex-minded explanation proposes some fallen angel, some rebel resistance who spoils perfection and misleads humanity. That is Zoroaster's answer, and it is still with us. The rebel in *Prometheus Bound* is sympathetic hero, saving prophet and outcast demon all in one.

Surely there was, in the finished trilogy, a resolution. The myth (and the next play) told that long, long later the man-god Heracles, Zeus' favorite son, unbound Prometheus. The trilogy's final chorus of Titans saw the arrival of some new covenant among the powers that be. Certain daringly minded theologians in our times have posited an evolution in which God (or at least the relationship between Creator and created) grows through the eons. Can the All Wise become wiser? The thought is either outrageous or profound in paradox. Aeschylus walked some such path of thought, suggesting a Zeus who at last changes for the better.

Anaxagoras' free market of ideas is open for business here. We are in a unique land where questions as well as answers are legal tender. Much has been thought and written about *Prometheus Bound*. I only point at it as a testament to daring supposition hung on the cliffs of bafflement. To start somewhere in dealing with this play, you might look up the poet Paul Roche's introduction to his translation.

The Athenians did not exile Aeschylus, not that they necessarily liked what he wrote about Prometheus and Zeus. The cycle did not win at the Dionysia. Some suggest it was produced in Sicily; I doubt this play would have found welcome at the court of Heiro of Syracuse. Tyrants do not look willingly into mirrors; both Stalin and Imelda Marcos banned stagings of *Macbeth*, and in the 1970s the brutal generals who ran Greece banned *Prometheus Bound*. There is a story of an Aeschylus play inciting such furor that he had to take refuge at the altar of Dionysos mid-stage. Some outraged moralist then arraigned him on the charge that his play had revealed mysteries from Eleusis. I don't know if anyone has suggested the play at issue was from the Prometheus cycle, but that would be plausible.

If that trial happened, it would have been as much a mockery as, say, trials among us that involve national security. A trial has to be a mockery when the evidence turns on secrets no one is allowed to say. To the credit of Athens, the case against Aeschylus was thrown out when the court was reminded that here was a veteran of Marathon and Salamis.

Before leaving *Prometheus Bound* and its near-blasphemy—a last coincidence. Scholarship can't settle when most of the Old Testament was written, but *Job*, one of its later pieces, seems roughly contemporary with Aeschylus. Of all ancient Hebrew literature it reads most like a play and least like other writing from its time and place. It is in verse dialogue; its theme is a righteous sufferer afflicted by God. Athens lived by trade. Who knows what scrolls some voyager brought along with wares from Pireus to Joppa, or, if not written word, then discussion? Hebrew lifestyle, so different from Greek, shared with it a deep fondness for discussing, and the *Book of Job's* author had a daring mind and a masterful poetic gift. Phrases like "bind the sweet influences of the Pliades" are worthy of the music of an Aeschylean chorus. The *Book of Job* responds to the enigma of injustice in the universe more humbly than Aeschylus does. Fundamentalists, for whom *Job*'s author is the Holy Ghost, might assume that the Ghost knew what Aeschylus was writing and paid him the compliment of an answering polemic.

Flippant ghost story aside, the possible literary cross-pollination is worth pondering.

The Cry on the House of Atreus

Ara, a word translated as "curse," was a term for extemporized, vengeful prayer (as opposed, I think, to ritual). Aeschylus uses the word in *The Seven against Thebes* and elsewhere. It means the outraged cry of a sufferer, passionate enough to ring down through time and demand retribution. In the Greek folk view, great wrongs conferred that hapless power on victims. Their outcry cracks the bedrock of social life till it must quake at last. The curse on Oedipus and his family was of that kind. Its origin may have been a child-sacrifice committed by Oedipus' grandfather. (Sophocles in *Oedipus the King* for his own reasons does not trace the evil that far back.) Human sacrifice was so rare in Greek life and so unforgivingly disastrous in Aeschylus' plays that I circle back to the guess that at Salamis the night before battle, he saw the mob-led priest cut the throats of those captured Persian women and children.

When all folktale strands are braided together, the *ara* against the House of Atreus, central to the *Oresteia* trilogy, goes back to a human sacrifice that parallels the Abraham and Isaac story. It makes the same point: gods once liked human blood offerings but now hate them; one should sacrifice cattle, not kin. In the Greek variant, Tantalus (a human so archaic his parents may have been Titans) serves his son Pelops to divine guests. The revolted gods restore the boy to life and damn the father to eternal tantalization in Hades. The son migrates eventually to Greece and confers his name upon the Peloponnese ("Isle of Pelops") by cheating his way to marriage with a native princess. One victim of Pelops's murderous tricks cries a curse on him as well.

Pelops's sons, Atreus and Thyestes, are cursed and curse in turn. Atreus, avenging his wife's seduction, serves two of Thyestes' sons to their father at a supposed meal of reconciliation: Thyestes cries out an *ara* against Atreus and flees with a remaining son, Aegisthus. There is a blur of traditional versions about which of the many bad ends Atreus comes to. One version has Atreus killed by the boy Aegisthus, but that does not quite fit with Aeschylus' telling.

Citizens of Argos in Aeschylus' day (and ours) could point out to travelers the round tomb of Atreus; he was as tangible a figure in their history as were his sons, the Atridae, Menelaus and Agamemnon. Those two, as it happened, did *not* quarrel. They divided rule of the Peloponnese, Agamemnon as a High King at Argos and Menelaus as his ally at Sparta, where, with questionable luck, he took to wife the miraculously beautiful Helen. Atreus, even less lucky, married Helen's sister, tough-minded Clytemnestra. Helen's abduction to Troy and King Agamemnon's sacrifice of a daughter to the winds while launching a retaliatory ten-year war are redundant to retell. Those happenings form the immediate background to *The Oresteia*, another "collop from the feast of Homer."

The Oresteia builds on Homer. Its contemporary relevance to Athens would not have struck its first audience until the third play, when with unexpected logic a current significance emerged from the drama like an Athena from the head of Zeus. A major and divisive city institution, the court of the Areopagus, revealed itself as the triology's central concern. Like *The Suppliants* (and no doubt like many of the plays if we could find the keys to them), *The Oresteia* is about both the timeless and the timely.

The ancient court of the Areopagus had fairly recently been appropriating powers to supervise all state functions, punish all officials and even inquire into private lives. Its judges were by custom of aristocratic descent, and its leanings were conservative. However, eight years before *The Oresteia* was presented, earthquake struck Sparta, and that, by a train of events, triggered a constitutional upheaval in Athens. That quake devastated Sparta. Her subject towns rebelled, and by 461 Athenians were assuming Sparta's very existence was threatened. As has been said, Athenian conservatives favored Sparta, and the current hero-general, Cimon, led out an expeditionary force to help the Spartans put down the revolt. His band included many influential conservatives, and while they were away, democrats led by Ephialtes passed laws to limit the Areopagus's scope, leaving it only its ancient jurisdiction over cases of murder and arson.

Cimon's pro–Spartan campaign ended ignominiously. Even in a desperate hour Spartan paranoia could not trust Athenian self-interest. Cimon and his forces were sent home again embarrassed, unthanked and discredited. Loyalties unraveled. When Cimon tried to get the Areopagus' powers reinstated, he found himself charged as friend of Sparta and enemy of the people and was ostracized.

Passions had run so high over this that, in one of Athens's rare political assassinations, conservative hirelings beat Ephialtes to death. In history violence comes more often from the self-righteous right, more fiercely from the hungry left. The shock created a popular martyr and compounded the disgrace of Cimon's party. Into the power vacuum young Pericles was able to step. Holding one office or another, he was to be a principal leader in Athens (though certainly not unchallenged) for thirty-two years till his death.

So, in 458 the Areopagus was still sorely on everyone's mind. I try to watch both *The Oresteia* and its audience at that first performance.

There is no knowing whether *The Agamemnon* was staged in the first season of the new, solid *skene* building, but it is the first play we have that takes advantage of it. Certainly that building was relatively novel to this audience. It was one-storied, flat roofed with perhaps a bit of battlement to make it imposing, and it had the closemouthed look that wide, shut, central doors give a façade. For this morning several altars, set pieces with kindling ready on them, ringed the orchestra.

Pre-play ceremonies were less time consuming than they would become — there were not yet the rousing dumb shows of war-driven patriotism, the parading of war orphans nor the prolonged display of ingots. For now Athens was still just a democracy, not a democracy with an empire to awe.

The Agamemnon takes advantage of the gray hour and the new *skene* building right from the first surprise: the action opens on the roof. A royal watchman complains to the real fading stars overhead. From the top of Atreus' house he is on dog-watch for a signal gleam to tell his man-hearted Queen Clytemnestra, here in Argos, that Troy across the seas has fallen. Think out the scenic resources of this place. Did a timed signal fire gleam from the conical Museon, that black hill-shape off to the predawn right of the *skene*? Why not? That would be manageable with a signal lantern from the back of the *skene* house alerting watchers on the distant hill to light a bonfire. It would be awe-provoking. The watchman points, prances, whoops and descends out of sight.

The chorus enters. They are slowed, brooding elders, embodiments of a burdened past and bleak present. They mutter of the bitterness of being left behind for ten years while the young away at war are earning brief glories and sudden deaths. These elders summarize remembered wrongs and murky forebodings; a known plotline can be touched on obliquely and metaphorically — what the audience remembers and knows is dipped into and stirred.

Since we are in Argos and Agamemnon has not yet returned, everyone will expect Aegisthus to be talked of and to appear — the King's exiled cousin who has slipped back and become the Queen's lover. Homer tells of his killing the returned Agamemnon; that has to seem to be what is about to happen. The old townsmen make only veiled reference to things not right in the palace, and out through the doors comes not the lover but the Queen. With either womanly reticence or aristocratic arrogance, she at first ignores the old men. Unspeaking, she goes about kindling altar after altar, making a ring of small fires.

At last she does speak. She says Troy has fallen and describes the rape of the city — not from second sight but from knowing life: post-siege atrocities are a predictable ritual. When the elders doubt her, she tells them how she has learned of this; she names each crag and peak in turn from which signal fires she had ordained have tonight passed the gleam of news north across the Bosphorus and on around the vast mountain rim of the Aegean, west, then south, over the heads of peoples after peoples. When she is done, one senses that this woman has flung a web over her entire world. She goes in.

Aeschylus in this pre-sunrise dim has played with actual fire to conjure for us burning Troy and make us sense the crackle of danger and smell primal smoke. All his audience over the age of thirty-five had seen their own city in flames. The Chorus is left to reminisce, half hopeful yet still bent down with premonition.

Here one of those covert phenomena of drama happens: present tense becomes timeless. To explain, I briefly jump ahead eighty or more years to the world's first theater critic, Aristotle. Mouse fetus, measurement of time and motion, the function of government, why mountain rocks have sea shells ... Aristotle looks at *everything*, including how plays are written. His incomplete lecture notes on drama, devoutly collected by students, form the still-influential *Poetics*. It is as astute a collection of observations as if he'd devoted his study single-mindedly to tragedies. Still, now and then one glimpses him as more audience member than theater man, slightly an outsider to the art and disoriented in the way a good audience member should be disoriented between belief and disbelief in what he is watching.

Saying the best plots seem to unfold "within one revolution of the sun," he asks, as I've mentioned, for some proportion between the real time passing as one sits at a drama and the imaginary time portrayed. Plays play by different rules from those that govern epics and other storytelling. Aristotle overlooks a paradox that an audience member *should* overlook (and that dramatists should talk of very little) — the way in which a play has no objective time at all.

A dream dissatisfies and usually dissolves the moment we realize it is a dream. Not knowing it is dream is part of its essence. Just as there is no real clock in a dream, there is none in a play; things on a stage take however long they seem to take. This is true even in relative realism. Ask quick readers of *The Glass Menagerie* how long a time span the story covers and they'll say a few days, a couple weeks at most. Actually midwinter passes into late spring for Tom, Amanda and Laura, yet to sense a condensed brevity is not to read carelessly; Williams contrived the piece to seem both short and long. The time is long so that characters can endure and develop; it is short so we can feel event triggering event.

A notion persists since Aristotle that Greek playwrights *tried* to fit plays to a twenty-four-hour time frame — and sometimes failed. They didn't. What they and all playwrights *do* try for one way or another is a domino sequence. This makes the microcosm of the play a coherent apparatus, what Cocteau called an "Infernal Machine." It is what Aristotle asked for when he praised "unity of action." So, here, enemy city falls, surviving soldiers come home: domino sequence. A first returnee from captured Troy enters as the real sun of the performance day is rising. While the Chorus was chanting, time has lapsed, not definite time but dream time. Queen Clytemnestra, telling the messenger why she is not more demonstratively joyful at his news, says

> I raised my cry of joy, and it was long ago
> when the first beacon flair of message came by night ...
> [*Oresteia*, Lattimore translation,
> Univ. of Chicago Press, 1953]

The story has moved ahead, dreamlike, some uncounted number of days.

The play's turns and counterturns never quite lead where expected: there is not an overt word about plotting against Agamemnon, and where is the king killer Homer tells of? Slowly the audience would begin to wonder if this Clytemnestra had no lover. Might she be going to kill her husband on her own? There is a dynamic tension, unrecoverable for us, between what must have been looked for and what happens.

Real aficionados noticed a pattern unfolding here like one they had seen in *The Persians:* oldsters fret, Queen prays, messenger describes battle woes, King arrives. Agamemnon comes charioted; the very opposite of the defeated Xerxes. He is glossed with victory, rich with booty and bringing an unacknowledged insult for his wife. In his chariot stands a new concubine, the Princess Cassandra. She is mad with an unwanted gift of prophesy that no one will heed. For the time being her famed oracular voice is mute; one only knows her by knowing the story. However, when a man arrives home to a wife with a beautiful woman at his side, the unspeaking speaks.

Now there unrolls a famous business. Clytemnestra has a red-purple carpet spread from the door to Agamemnon's chariot, a blood path for her doomed man to enter his home upon. Agamemnon hesitates, saying that to tread on a thing so finely woven is wasteful, almost arrogance. That carpet has been pointed to numberless times as an example of symbolism in staging, a tangible object electrified with idea*: the arrogant path leads to doom. Still, for those of us not primed by commentary, Agamemnon's compunction seems oddly finicky. Does a treader down of cities scruple to step on a rug?

I've a notion about that carpet. Were rugs still at this point foreign luxuries from despised Persia, so that Aeschylus was reflecting cur-

---

The poet T. S. Eliot coined a very handy term, objective correlative, for this type of image.

IV. Prometheus, Then Orestes

rent Athenian prejudice? Granted the spread cloth is called "weaving," "tissue," or "textile"—its value and rarity are stressed, rather than its function. Still, in idea it's a rug. When Homer speaks of a rug, he may mean a "throw" to spread on a seat. A floor was more often strewn with sweet grass. A word for rug, *tapes,* is Near Eastern, kin to the Persian for weaving. The mingling of Greek and Near Eastern ways at the Mediterranean rim flowed in both directions. Another word for rug, *eima,* basically means something worn. At the time of *The Agamemnon* I suspect that floor rugs were alien imports and smacked of amoral opulence as snow leopard coats and shark fin soup do for us. (Staging the scene, I used banners pulled down at a gesture from Clytemnestra; treading on a thing like a flag might give us the frisson that treading on that carpet had for Aeschylus.)

Whatever we make of the rich carpeting, the whole *Oresteia* is wound and knitted through with imagery of woven stuffs, webs, wefts, nets, veils and knotted entanglements so that we feel the snare of the *ara* itself. Even the final peak that fire signal flashed from was Spider Mountain.

Agamemnon strides through the palace doors; Clytemnesta orders an unresponding Cassandra to follow and goes in as well. The end of the scene can be very eerie if this ground cloth is what Clytemnestra uses to entangle Agamemnon in offstage and will later display bloodied. That's dubious realism but powerful imagery. If so then, when Clytemnestra has followed Agamemnon, we watch the cloth pulled in after her, a tongue of red drawn into a closing mouth.

Does Cassandra keep still so long because of some contest rule about how many actors could be had? Long-gone scholars suggested that, motionless among the plunder, a dummy represented her and that a live actor took its place only when Agamemnon and then Clytemnestra had gone in. That's even less feasible than a dummy in *Prometheus Bound.* Cassandra's silence is dramatic and needs no two-actor rule.

Once Cassandra speaks, Aeschylus is in his lyric element. She is mad and divinely inspired (with an Asian accent?) Her words hover on the tantalizing border between sense and sound. In that no-man's-land poetry is most powerful, eradicating separations between rational and irrational, conjuring up x-ray visions of experience as felt from within. Oh, for a muse of fire, a Dylan Thomas or a Hart Crane to translate her!

> The pain and flame that lick me over, Lord
> Apollo, ah, O litch king of appalling pain!
> Yonder woman lioness, she bedrolls with a wary
> Wolfman while her maned mate prowls for prey,
> She'll cut me up and down as housewife whets
> Her knife to chop the zest of herbs and serve
> Him right for bragging this poor baggage home...
>> [very free trans-adaptation, off the mark but
>> with some of the wild word-savoring]

She babbles of slaughter, of Thyestes' murdered children and of monstrous traps, she frantically reproaches Apollo for the gift of second sight that must speak the unspeakable in vain. She sees though the palace walls until we see through them as well, bringing the murder out to us. Greek theater learned early what horror film makers know and keep forgetting: we can shut our eyes to the monster in plain view but not to the monster imagined. The mind's eye has no lids. Through Cassandra the playwright has his caked blood offstage and eats it with us too!

> ...and I too, with brain ablaze in fever, shall go down ...
> ...No longer shall my prophesies, like some young girl
> new married glance from under veils, but bright and strong
> as winds blow into morning and the sun's uprise
> shall wax along the swell like some great wave, to burst
> at last upon the shining of this agony.
>> [*Oresteia*, Lattimore translation]

By now the rising sun slants a sidelight stage right to left into the bowl of the theater and casts long shadows on the marble flagstones. Aeschylus uses that.

> ...Yet once more will I speak, and not this time my own
> death's threnody. I call upon the Sun in prayer
> against that ultimate shining when the avengers strike
> these monsters down in blood, that they avenge as well
> one simple slave who died, a small thing, lightly killed.
>
> Alas, poor men, their destiny. When all goes well
> a shadow will overthrow it. If it be unkind
> one stroke of a wet sponge wipes all the picture out;
> and that is far the most unhappy thing of all.
>> [*Oresteia*, Lattimore translation]

Her exit into the house feels not just fated and compelled but deliberate, suicidal.

Cries come from the house (Lattimore's translation is odd: his Agamemnon shouts, "*They* struck me ..." though Clytemnestra later boasts she struck alone). Each of the twelve chorus members has his own two-line reaction; they mill, too disunited in panic for effective action, and the doors open. The Queen stands over the corpses of Agamemnon and Cassandra entangled in cloths "as in a net," she says, as she vaunts her killing.

One famous stage machine may have made its debut at this moment. Given the sharp bright and dark of daylight and the acute sight line angles of those seated at the sides of the theater, even very wide doors couldn't satisfactorily reveal an interior. An "outroller," a sliding platform, moved forward, bringing what lay inside out into the light.

Eventually this outrolling *eccyclema* became a stage convention; when a bed or a throne slid out, the audience accepted that they watched interior events. At the outroller's first use no convention would have yet been at work. The circumstances of this scene help the audience accept its introduction to the device. For them that outroller might be yet another of Clytemnestra's elaborate preparations, a strange superbier she had readied to display the fallen monarch and cow the citizens. Even the noise of its trundling forward was a sound effect, supportive to the action rather than undermining it.

Clytemnestra justifies herself fiercely to the outraged Argives. Agamemnon had sacrificed her daughter Iphigenia; dare they challenge what has been done? At last the lover, Aegisthus, does appear. He swaggers, bragging of his share in the plot though acknowledging that the woman carried it out. Agamemnon's father killed his brothers; he claims blood-right to vengeance. When threatened, he calls out thuggish bodyguards. The couple and the Chorus fling furious warnings at each other, and then Queen and lover turn their backs and go in, closing the palace doors and the play.

A Son Comes Home

The Libation Bearers is a theme-and-variation recapitulation of *The Agamemnon*, and its last scene reechoes and extends *The Agamem-*

non's close. Again a prior crime drives its central character to an avenging slaughter; however, this time the protagonist's motive is not concealed. The heirs of the house, Orestes and Electra, and the Chorus share with one another their impassioned will to punish Clytemnestra and Aegisthus. These slave women of the House of Atreus have no shadowy, half-prophetic forebodings and memories like the first chorus; a willful energy animates them and the play.

Exiled Orestes, with his foster-friend, Pylades, starts events by furtively offering a lock of hair at his father's grave. The two hide as house women approach, bearing a libation offering sent by their hated mistress Clytemnestra. She, prodded by nightmare of giving birth to a snake that nursed and bit, seeks to appease Agamemnon's ghost, but she does not come herself. With these bearers she has sent her daughter, the faithful Electra, who as a child contrived to get young Orestes away to safety. The women pray, but not to appease the ghost. They rouse it. Electra is shaken to find a lock of hair and then a footprint that matches her own. Her intensity lures Orestes from hiding, and she throws herself into his arms, questioning yet frenzied, eager to share in the slaughter he plans. The servants too yearn to see violent justice. Brother and sister pray fiercely, plot and set off.

Here a choral song bridges not time, as in the first play, but place: we move from grave mound to palace doors. Was Aeschylus assuming Agamemnon was buried in the palace dooryard? That is not how the scene feels; at its close Orestes says specifically that he is going to the palace gates, yet he leaves the stage rather than walking up to the *skene* doors. Electra, who is to carry false news of Orestes' death, goes off a separate way. If she goes in through those doors, establishing them as the palace, can watchers help wondering why Orestes has gone elsewhere?

For *The Libation Bearers* in itself those would not be momentous questions; they have various plausible solutions. A play can have a dream's fluid space as well a dream's timing. Still, in relation to staging in general here at the festival of Dionysos, the questions enlarge. How much setting did these plays rely on, and how inconsistent a locale would the audience accept?

The orchestra of the Theater of Dionysos is not as huge as the later theaters of Epidaurus or Ephesus. Here it is uncomfortable to picture, say, in the first half of *The Libation Bearers*, a gravemound downstage, which was focal, while the upstage doors were ignored, and then action in the second half around the upstage door area with the downstage grave ignored. Was the gravemound left in place, removed while the Chorus chanted or removed in an interval after the chant, or was the grave marked simply by the low permanent altar present in all plays? That altar, a familiar part of the space, would have been conventionally all but invisible when not referred to. It might do service here. On the other hand, in *The Eumenides* there will be three, if not four locales, and Aeschylus must have indicated them somehow in the staging. Since he had to deal with those shifts, wouldn't he deal with the locale change here as well? I have not read or come up with a fully satisfying answer. Of course there was some answer. Aeschylus wrought his play with his own production solutions in mind.

Sophocles is supposed to have first used scene-painting. *Periactoi*, three-sided, free-standing flats that could present different faces, were probably invented later by Sophocles or his contemporaries. For this trilogy they do not seem necessary, even with the three or four locale changes to come in *The Eumenides*.

Clearly, in Greece scene change never felt wholly satisfactory. Ingenious and committed as the Athenian theater community was and superb though some realistic painters of their day may have been, I doubt that either Aeschylus or Sophocles really solved scene change to his own complete content. What can't be doubted is that they tried it. Let's say that, in the choral interlude between Orestes and Pylades' exit and their return, some décor was added to the doors or to the roof to signify the palace.

Orestes knocks at the gate, intending to kill Aegisthus first. A porter comes out, then not Aegisthus but Clytemnestra herself. Orestes, pretending not to realize who she is, claims that he and Pylades are travelers and tells blunt news of Orestes' death. Clytmenestra's pain seems genuine, self-controlled and underplayed; she acts with the stiff reserve to male strangers that fits a well-behaved Greek wife. That restraint seems more hypocritical to us than to Athenians. Orestes and Pylades are sent off to the men's quarters of the palace, guided by the porter. Do they all, men and woman together, go in via the one door asking us to believe that they part company inside? That would be awkward and set up a real staging puzzle a little later.

The Chorus hovers in the courtyard, expecting (as the audience must) a cry from within. Instead, out comes an aged nurse, Cilissa, weeping for Orestes. She is half-comic in her mistaken grief and reminiscences. She recalls tending Orestes and how a baby wets itself, its "little insides being a law to themselves." She has been told off by Clytemnestra to fetch Aegisthus and his bodyguard, who are somewhere outside.

Cilissa has seen what we could not see in Clytemnestra: she says the Queen

> ...puts a sad face on
> Before the servants, to hide the smile inside her eyes ...
> [*Oresteia*, Lattimore translation]

The Chorus women do not trust Cilissa's old wits enough to tell her Orestes is alive, they let her go on mourning and just urge her to get Aegisthus to come alone. She totters off, a down-to-earth touch to the story.

Aegisthus wastes no time. He does arrive alone, pauses only to claim to the Chorus that he takes no joy in hearing of a kinsman's death and goes in. Once more the Chorus waits; there is a cry. It is either Aegisthus or Orestes. We know Orestes has done his work when a follower loyal to the current rulers stumbles out, crying a choked alarm. His shouts bring Clytemnestra on. She grasps his unclear stammer and her one unforgettable line defines her:

> Bring me an ax. An ax to kill a man.
> [*Oresteia*, Lattimore translation]

The follower dashes off; and Orestes, bloodied sword in hand, comes out.

For a reader the play rides its current of tension. When one stages it, a scenic question of doors emerges: Clytemnestra cannot come out the same door as the follower; they enter only seconds apart. Whenever on a stage two come from the same entrance within a tight span of time, they come, for us, from the same imaginary offstage place. How could Clytemnestra not have seen what that follower has seen? It would help to have a central palace door and two side doors, one to the male guests' quarters and one to the women's quarters. The puzzle is not about this one play but about all staging at this time. If the *skene* already had three doors at this early date, why does not even one other tragedy rely on them? A few tragedies can be made to use multiple doors, but only here are they truly needed. Three doorways became standard in later centuries, but here? Is it conceivable, if those doors stood there, that no other dramatists in quest of variety took clear advantage of them? The *skene* was rebuilt several times over the coming years; side doors, once added and used, would not be left out of following renovations.

The first *skene* building, I think, did not flank the entire playing area like later ones. *The Libation Bearers'* climatic scene plays smoothly if Clytemnestra can come and go to her women's quarter from around the corner of the building. Later, the *skene* was widened, and entrances around its sides would have been indistinguishable from entering by the *parodos*. Probably later in the evolution of playing space layout the comedians first used the three doorways, simultaneous popping in and out being a staple of comic business. Best guesses on the doorways are flimsy.

Doors or no doors, Clytemnestra pleads fiercely for her life; she cajoles Orestes, and for one redeeming moment he is shaken and asks Pylades what he should do. Pylades reminds him they are acting on commands from Apollo himself— they had visited Delphi before coming here — and Orestes recovers purpose.

Clytemnestra's unresolved call for the ax suggests tempting business. She's not a woman whose commands get ignored. A return of the follower with that ax, stopped in fright by the drawn swords, would strikingly motivate Orestes' recovered determination. He would see, wordlessly, what his mother intended. With no stage directions, there is no scrap of evidence for or against that or similar moments. I don't say Aeschylus used the bit; I do say he and his actors did things we can only imagine by leaps of unfounded guesswork.

Orestes drives Clytemnestra in to be slain where she slew. The doors open on a visual repeat of the disclosure in *The Agamemnon*, an avenger over two corpses, male and female. To complete the déjà vu, Orestes holds up the same net robe his mother showed the crowd after snaring Agamemnon. Orestes displays it now to justify what he had done. The *ara* has reiterated itself, the visual underlines in red that this is a reduplication. It is a damning statement about blood-feud: the progression of revenge for revenge can be endless. But this time around the Chorus responds jubilantly while this avenger, unlike Clytemnestra, is not self-assured. The more Orestes says to explain his act, the more uncertain he sounds. The curse long ago cried against this house has still, he senses, not said its last. He'd had in mind to undergo ritual purifications at Delphi, an absolution available to justifiable bloodshed; but his speech becomes wilder, the babble of a frightened man, and suddenly he sees the Furies, embodiments of his guilt as a matricide.

> ...they come like gorgons,
> they wear black robes, and they are wreathed in a tangle
> of snakes....
> ...real, and here; the bloodhounds of my mother's hate...
> ...you cannot see them, but I see them. I am driven
> from this place.
> [*Oresteia*, Lattimore translation]

He dashes away pursued by his visions. The stunned chorus sings briefly:

> Here on this house of kings the third
> storm has broken, with wind
> from the inward race, and gone its course.
> The children were eaten ...
> ...Next came the royal death ...
> ...Where shall the fury of fate
> be stilled to sleep, be done with?
> [*Oresteia*, Lattimore translation]

Just as in the close of *The Agamemnon*, a baffled Chorus slinks away in silence.

Thoughtful Athenian viewers, as they rise and exchange comments to a son, a wife or a friend, note that Aeschylus has followed a lesser bypath. Some few won't like that. "Orestes killed Aegisthus, not his mother," they may mutter. They don't yet realize that what they have just seen, interwoven with what Sophocles and Euripides are going to write under influence of this play, will become forever how Orestes' story is told. The sensitive prince, maddened by obligation to avenge his father's death upon mother and unkind kinsman, will crop up again in theater.

THE GODS COME TO ATHENS

It is *The Oresteia* that lures me into a stubborn heresy that the three plays of a day (at least in these years) were staged at dawn, midday and dusk. Better scholars doubt that. There is no question that *The Agamemnon* uses the dimness of dawn and the sunrise. It is less demonstrable that *The Libation Bearers* (*Bringers of Offering*) must have the full glare of midday, but the visual climax of *The Eumenides* (*The Furies*) is a torchlight processional. Those torches echo the altar fires Clytemnestra lit at the opening and would profit from deep dusk's natural closure.

The Eumenides opens with a scene at Delphi. The dramatic content is wild, and the staging puzzles tantalize. First the Pythia, the aged priestess, serenely praises the site and then enters the shrine; immediately she reels outs again, so debilitated by terror that she crawls on the ground. She has seen Furies sleeping in foul unease inside the holy of holies. They surround a desperate supplicant who clings to the sacred stone that marks Earth's midpoint. The Pythia totters off.

Now we are in the shrine itself and see the Furies asleep, Orestes at the navel-stone and the god Apollo standing over him. Hermes too is a silent presence.

How is this staged? It matters that the Furies are disclosed asleep. It is always assumed that there is a full chorus of twelve to fourteen of them. Yet surely they do not walk out and lie down. That might be bearable before the play, but within performance it would not only disrupt but also be confusing, unless we're to believe they walk in their sleep. They were certainly not onstage when Pythia first entered. Are they rolled out on the *eccyclema*? With Orestes, Apollo, and perhaps Hermes, some seventeen people as well as whatever represents the navel-stone would have to ride on one rolling platform! That is as hard to credit as the whole chorus hoisted to hover in air in *Prometheus Bound*. Even at the huge later theaters whose doorways still stand (those are from Roman times), none has an opening wide enough for so huge a platform to trundle through. Probably I'm not the first to wonder if Aeschylus worked with just three Furies. Euripides, decades later, first speaks specifically of three. Homer usually mentions just one. However, the Furies are an overwhelming presence in this play, its driving, tempestuous force, and are, after all, its chorus. No one could imagine Aeschylus surrendering the effect of a swarm to the convenience of one moment's staging. But what about three at first, twelve or thirteen later in the scene?

I suggest the solution not with conviction but to show that solutions can be found. We know the *eccyclemas* carried four. Suppose

Orestes and three sleeping Furies are rolled out. Three makes a mystical number, like the three Gorgons, the three Graiae, the three Fates and other triple goddesses. The *skene* roof has already been a playing space; it works well for this scene to have Apollo loom up there. Hermes — if we imagine that he is shown and not merely spoken of — could appropriately step out into the shadowed doorway, waiting to lead Orestes off at his brother god's command. That gives the *eccyclema* a plausible load.

Orestes, still clutching his sword with bloody hands unwashed, huddles at the Earth's navel. The audience would have known what the Delphic navel-stone looked like — picture a half-egg as big as an armchair and covered with a tasseled net. It's an odd thing to focus reverence upon, but a Christmas tree or a Buddhist shrine looks bizarre to anyone outside the tradition. Wherever objects stand for spiritual intangibles, a showy clutter accumulates. Among religions, only imageless Islam keeps a tidy house.

Apollo gleams, like the statues we all know but richly robed. Was there ever nakedness on stage in tragedies? Nudity and mask contradict each other, and probably nudity was too ordinary to have theatricality. In vase paintings naked figures stand among others who are clearly in theatrical costumes; however, I suspect the nudity is a painting tradition, not a theatrical one, and others seem to have thought so too.

Hermes had a traditional stage image: broad traveling hat, cloak and a unique pointed beard that gives him a foxy look; he is a god not only for travelers and merchants but also for thieves and tricksters. His snake-looped wand designates him at a glance. The doorway shadow would lend him phantasmagorical presence-with-absence.

Apollo promises he will not give Orestes up:

> ...through to the end standing
> your guardian, whether by your side or far away.
> [*Oresteia*, Lattimore translation]

Spoken from aloft, "by your side or far," fits well. With contemptuous disgust Apollo boasts of casting sleep upon the Furies; he is helping Orestes escape to Athens and Athena's ancient idol. Orestes gets away under Hermes safe conduct, and once he has gone and Apollo has withdrawn, the ghost of Clytemnestra rises. What better entry for her than up Charon's steps, emerging from the ground as she does in a vase painting?

In that painting the Furies are not ugly; they have the conventional good looks standard on vases. I've seen just one vase on which a fury or harpy has a grotesque, hooked aquiline beak and knitted brows. She looks more like a Thai or Balinese demon than anything typically Greek. Aeschylus is specific. His Furies dress in black, they are enormously old though vigorous, their eyes ooze blood, and they are as ugly as gorgons and as filthy as harpies. Even calmly unshakable Athena, when she sees them, will marvel at such things not "stamped in the likeness of a human form." They sprawl and snore here, diseased and drunken with blood-rage.

Has death changed Clytemnestra? Very little, I think, but her wounds are visible. "Look at these gashes!" she cries. She is a nightmare the Furies are having as much as the Furies are her nightmare: she rages to rouse them in pursuit of the escaping Orestes, reproaching their sleep till they mutter, "Catch him, catch him, catch him ..." (*Oresteia*, Lattimore translation).

Clytemnestra vanishes as they pull themselves awake. Her descent is their uprise; her outrage has become theirs, and from here on they are her terrible surrogates. Could something in their costuming echo her, or could each have a gashed neck like her? They halloo wake-up cries to one another. I suggest that it is here, as they writhe and haul one another erect, that more and more of them emerge from the shadow, three turning into thrice three and then a swarm. Watching the Furies multiply themselves seems chilling and appropriate.

> The hunted beast has slipped clean from our nets and gone,
> Sleep won me and I lost my capture.
> Shame, son of Zeus, robber is all you are.
> A young god, you have ridden down powers gray with age,
> Taken the suppliant, though a godless man who hurt
> The mother who gave him birth...
>   [*Oresteia*, Lattimore translation]

The conflict is no longer mere self-perpetuating feud between wronged humans and human wrongers. It is now also between elder gods and younger ones and is about what powers shall hold sway in the cosmos. It also becomes about female versus male, the two possibilities of what we can be are pitted relentlessly against each other.

Apollo reappears or perhaps has stood still on the roof watching the Furies awaken and now responds to their outcry against him. He is as vituperative as they are and spurns them out of his sanctuary. They whirl off in baying pursuit of their quarry.

An immediate and challenging scene change here jumps over times without benefit of chorus and brings us to Athens. Orestes has vainly sought blood-purifications at mortal hearths and now crawls to Athena's shrine. He is, in terms of story, up there some eighty vertical feet above and behind us in the old temple on the Acropolis. The great Parthenon is still an aspiring architect's sketched dream at the time of this performance. A temporary wooden "House of the Maiden" stands on the site. Orestes is understood to have come to the temple the Persians burned, and the statue is the one the Persians hacked and threw down twenty-two years ago. In the devout memories of most adults a vivid reality underlies the laminate of myth and performance.

Once more let's hazard a guess about a scenic solution, one to get us from Delphi to the Acropolis. It would be clumsy to close the previous scene by trundling the *eccyclema* off with the navel-stone on it, closing the doors and then, after a backstage scurry of stagehands, reopening and trundling it forward immediately with the statue of Athena. Still, somehow that exchange needs to be made. Folk plays have always accepted theatrical awkwardness — unspoiled audiences are generous. But this is not folk art, and Athenians were spoiled. This play's elaborate poetry of word and poetry of action demand a bewitched focus, and each time attention is drawn to the machinery, a spiderweb of verbal and visual imagery is torn.

It would help if the *eccyclema* withdrew and the doors banged shut at Apollo's first commands that the Furies leave his shrine. The motion and noise then would emphasize his powers rather than those of the stage mechanic. There follows an angry exchange of over thirty-five lines with Apollo above and them below before the scene is over, long enough to create a dramatic bridge. Then the stage empties and the statue of Athena emerges. If it is recognizably like the old lost statue that was this city's pride, a ripple of recognition shivers through the audience and deep civic nostalgia overrides any other feeling.

Human rites have not helped Orestes; this ingrown curse must be healed by means beyond the human. The blood may be washed from him, if we are being literal, but he must look haggard, more driven, clutching that olive wood statue of Athena. The Furies overtake him in this House of the Maiden. Horrors are often best offstage, but nothing so truly eerie in the way of onstage verbal dark magic was to be written again until Shakespeare conjured up his witches to harry Macbeth. I have loved the play *Macbeth* almost to idolatry (as a boy I could recite it end to end), but the creepy music of these Furies is more powerful than the Weird Sisters' chants. Nightmare fantasy works by corresponding to a truth in our psychies. Our murder entertainment calluses imagination, but real murders are monstrous for not only killing victims; they kill the humanity in the killers and eat out the lives of families and friends of victims and perpetrators. As long as any live to remember, the vile resonance excruciates. In *The Eumenides* the Furies are an image of that. They chant a shrill binding song and tie Orestes as they wreathe around him. They are not monotheist conscience; they are the inexorable, clamorous interconnectedness of things, the wiry sinews of being. Inflict wrong at one point in the cosmos, and the whole organism flinches; reflex inflicts new pain in turn.

Now abruptly Athene herself arrives, summoned by Orestes' agonized appeal. It is she, and not Apollo, who in this play will at last produce resolving chords; hers is the first serene voice we have heard all day. I think she is not on the roof but on or near a level with her visitants. Perhaps thick-soled boots make her preternaturally tall.

> I see, upon this land, a novel company
> which, though it brings no terror to my eyes, brings still
> wonder. Who are you? I address you all alike,
> Both you the stranger kneeling at my image here
> and you who are like no seed ever begotten ...
>   [*Oresteia*, Lattimore translation]

At first her dispassion seems like divine indifference. She listens to Orestes, and in the sharp light of her impartiality his protest that he acted as Apollo commanded sounds like Eve's "The serpent made me eat," in the Genesis myth. She listens to the Furies too, giving fair hearing and respect to both sides. She tells Orestes,

> The matter is too big for any mortal man
> who thinks he can judge it. Even I have not the right ...
> ...You bring no harm to my city; I respect your right
> but these, too,
>   [she gestures to the Furies]
>   have their work. We cannot brush them aside.
> And if this action so runs that they fail to win,
> the venom of their resolution will return
> to infect the soil and sicken all my land to death.

> Here is dilemma. Whether I let them stay or drive
> them off, it is a hard course and will hurt. Then, since
> the burden of this case is here, and rests on me,
> I will select judges of manslaughter and swear
> them in, establish a court into all time to come.
> [*Oresteia*, Lattimore translation]

There's a gradual stir through the audience. The trilogy reveals at last what it has been pointed toward from the first. It is about the founding of the Areopagus, the ancient court just now such a source of political dissention. A whole new kind of uneasy interest effervesces in the bowl of the theater.

A jury of Athenian citizens is convened, and Orestes' trial begins.

Is there one more scene change? The Areopagus ("War God's Crag") is a holy outcropping of hard ledge just down along and around the corner of the cliff walls here, near the gated stairways to the Acropolis. Along with other tourists, I climbed on it this morning; its old, irregular steps are so worn with the bare soles, sandals and shoes of centuries that the wrinkled rock is slick like ice, as perilous as the slippery hardness of trial at law. Eventually Athena will specify "this rock." In some imaginative way Aeschylus let the viewers know they are now moved down to it from Athena's temple. In a modern production the shift does not matter, but to this first audience for *The Orestia* the two locales are very specific and near at hand; the change of locale could not be ignored.

Excavators found, over to the west side of the fan of the theater, an outcropping boulder that once had intruded up a few rows into the concentric arcs of seating and also out a little into the orchestra dance floor. There is no telling just when, in the many reconfigurations of the site, this big rock was finally chipped down and flattened. If that intrusion of real into imaginary stood here at the time of *The Oresteia*, simply stepping up onto it could have suggested the Areopagus; what had been ignored before became a part of the playing area. That would have simultaneously solved a secondary visual issue: Athena and Apollo on the rock would be slightly "outside the frame"—not too removed to touch humans and Furies yet neither literally nor figuratively level with them—and specially lit. As sundown shadow creeps into the playing area from the west, the east side of the theater bowl where that outcrop stood glows with light while the main playing area dims. Writing for a known theater space, one uses what is at hand.

The trial is in two parts. The first contention is between Orestes and the Furies. His cleansing rites versus their cursing spells having come to stalemate, so the struggle is waged here through impassioned legalistic argument. We, at our best, exclude religious issues from our courts, but separation of church and state was not a possible concept in Aeschylus' world — and especially not with gods in court!

Apollo functions as a defense lawyer. At the Areopagus, accuser and defendant were to speak for themselves. But it was already customary to hire a "friend" skilled in argument and law. Teachers of rhetoric earned income and prestige in trials and began a profession. Our lawyers too often embarrass us with their obligation to obscure all unserviceable truths and confuse witnesses, but our most highly paid and corrupt lawyer is no worse than a typical orator in a classical trial. That lawyers might be sworn to speak the whole truth just as witnesses are — and be held as perjurers if they break that oath — never crossed the minds of the ingenious Greeks. We cannot despise them: it has not yet seriously crossed our minds either; on that score two and a half millennia have gone for naught. Many of our own bright best start out in law careers with a sincere thirst for righteousness, only to have the profession jade them into cynics. It's no surprise then that Apollo, god of truth and light, pulls out all stops on Orestes' behalf. He argues that killing a mother is not really murder of kin: the woman, he says, is merely soil in which the father planted his seed; paternal kinship trumps maternal. The Furies are just as unyielding (in our view just as sexist); they hound Orestes but did not hound Clytemnestra because "The man she killed was not of blood congenital" (*Oresteia*, Lattimore translation, Univ. of Chicago Press, 1953). They also point out that Zeus (whose power backs up Apollo and all the younger gods) attacked and overthrew his own father. How sacrosanct then is fatherhood?

The gender quarrel looms big for us, and for us it should. Our greater knowledge of biology can make us smug; for some it invalidates the whole *Oresteia*. For Aeschylus and for a world that had not yet undertaken to restore or create equality between the sexes, gender was only a part of the issue. When Apollo presents that argument, most likely to make us (and the Furies) hiss or laugh, Athena intervenes in the debate — in a contemporary production she seems embarrassed by her half-brother's line of reasoning.

Can gods talk back and forth this way without being comic? Moments like this expose imponderables in polytheism. The many gods are most convincing when they appear one at a time, as they typically do when they intervene in tragedies. These plays, after all, are from the moment when belief in the many literal gods was beginning to crack and were, like our own plays, aimed at a divided audience of the devout and the skeptical. Tony Kushner's *Angels in America* plays get away, straight-faced, with divine conversations somewhat as Aeschylus does. In them our two-mindedness about whether existence has a spiritual dimension is toyed with or relied on.

In an Athenian court the jury functions as judge; nonetheless Athena has de facto authority here because this city is her holy ground. She umpires the argument, calls for a vote and instructs the empanelled free Athenians that a precedent for all time is being set. Their city is being launched on its future course, one they must steer between "anarchy and the rule of a single man," achieving a collective rule "nowhere else found among men." It is not only the fate of Orestes that is worked out here, nor even what happens to the house of Atreus and the many *aras* cried against it through past ages. Rule of law, stabilized by collective consent and made just by collective reason, is to replace blood feud and halt the endless avenging of acts of vengeance.

When the jury vote is a tie, Athena sets another precedent familiar to the audience. She casts a deciding vote for acquittal, and henceforward whenever a jury is evenly divided, the gods will be assumed to throw in a ballot to free the accused. Orestes gives brief thanks, and he and Apollo leave the stage.

But the conflict is not over. Athena has said earlier that the venom of the baffled Furies will infect the soil; they are defeated but unappeased; the old and new order are still at odds.

Very patiently Athena talks them out of their anger, reason assuaging passion, elder forces and younger coming to a compromise. As maiden without mother, totally virginal and harnessed for defensive battle, Athena is as nearly impartial an arbitrator between male and female as a two-gender world can picture. She agrees that dread of crime has a valuable function in society; she offers the Furies a status in Athenian civil ritual: a holy shrine in a cave under the Areopagus itself. They will have new names, the Semnai ("honorable") and the Eumenides ("kindly minded"). Little by little Athena weans them from their outrage until they accept their new place and begin to sing a new kind of music. It is new to the play, that music; it feels new to the world. It is a serene charm of blessing upon this land.

> Let there blow no wind that wrecks the trees.
> I pronounce words of grace.
> No blaze of heat blind the blossoms of grown plants ...

and further on

> ...let
> not the dry dust that drinks
> the black blood of citizens
> through passion of revenge
> and bloodshed for bloodshed
> be given our state to prey upon ...
> [*Oresteia*, Lattimore translation]

A torchlight procession is formed.

The Furies, "Eumenides" now, even change their appearance in the shadows, layering red robes over their black so as not to vanish in the gathering night. The whole audience knows that this procession, going out via the stage left *parodos*, is headed toward the actual shrine of the Eumenides a short quarter mile off under the real Areopagus. If my guess is right, the moon has risen now; those torches glimmer off through trees and between low house walls into the city they have spread peace upon. Real and imaginary merge, reconciled and sharing in the charismatic spell.

Only one other moment I can think of is like it in all of theater. In rare, superb productions of *A Midsummer Night's Dream,* when actors and directors have the luck to get it right, Titania and Oberon's blessing of the house concludes the play with tones of this same therapeutic harmony — blessing our own inner and outer house, not just the house of Theseus. The serious subsoil of comedy is tapped and our lives replenished. As *The Oresteia* closes, a jovial subsoil underlying dark tragedy is tapped; it is the *city* of Theseus that is blessed, and all who have assembled here.

Afterthoughts

The audience rises and stretches with much to ponder. Different minds will savor the eerie serenity differently and be dogged and nipped at by different queries as they stroll home or linger to watch the scenic servants mutely setting up for the coming satyr play in the darkening orchestra.

One might be asking himself about Apollo's role. Apollo stands by Orestes, but he does not come off well in *The Oresteia*. He is truth incarnate yet seems, in human terms, mean-spirited, dishonest. One gropes for some distinction between truth and honesty. During the Persian Wars, Delphi had foretold ruin to the Greeks; this generation's faith in prophesy from Apollo's Delphic shrine had been shaken. One more rift was opening in society. That rift will have been very like our own: the pious people dreaded sharing in bad fate brought on by impious neighbors; the skeptical people grew cynical in contempt of the pious. A midground of less active minds gravitated toward piety for the comfort that certainty gives and uncertainty takes away.

Another watcher might notice in this telling an indifference to humans. Electra seems vivid, yet she vanishes halfway through *The Libation Bearers*. Orestes' friend Pylades has only one line. Cassandra has her great scene and is not so much as mentioned again, forgotten as she had foretold. In the last twenty minutes of the play neither Orestes nor any human characters except the mute jurymen remain on stage. Of all poets, should a *dramatic* poet be so high-handed about persons? That question would have crossed minds only because of what some newer playwrights were doing.

One audience member, Sophocles, has to have thought that way — while recognizing with grudging respect that today he had lost first place in this year's Dionysia. He had a right to suspect what he would never stoop to saying aloud: that he may have taught the old boy something. Sophocles' forte was as much in showing individual people's wills and passions as in exploring the ideas they embodied. Along with other skills, Aeschylus had belatedly begun giving attention to that.

Harold Bloom near the end of his wonderful, idiosyncratic book on Shakespeare says, "Most of us, I am persuaded, read and attend theater in search of other selves. In search of one's own self one prays, or meditates, or recites a lyric poem, or despairs in solitude." Aeschylus came fairly late to furthering that aspect of theater's service, the search for other selves. He was surely never a conscious follower of others, but no writer is completely immune to the influence of contemporaries, especially younger, successful ones. *The Oresteia* could be thought to owe something to what Sophocles' plays had begun revealing.

It would strike this thinker, this Sophocles I am imagining, that one figure does move through all three plays of *The Oresteia*, unifying them in a person as strongly as they are unified in idea. The central self here is Clytemnestra. She embodies, one after the other, the three essential dramatis personae of any blood feud, first the killer, then the victim, then the ghost demanding vengeance. In a sense, alive in the Furies, she is on stage to the last, and if so then, through them she ends appeased. Up to the closing moment she seems the least likely candidate for our empathy, but at the finale she is given a place among us.

Fellow playwrights, as twinges of jealousy mingled with admiration, might wrestle with the difference between plays like this, the solemn goat songs offered to torn Dionysos and the exuberant "country plays," *komoidai*, that celebrate laughing Dionysos. Which, really, was this triumphant ending? Was it still fitting to straddle the two in this way, as goat song had straddled in the past? Evidently a deciding majority of playwrights came to the conclusion that it was not — or else they had not the requisite stride for planting a foot in each territory at once. Such people would certainly be among the many who lingered in the cool to see the satyr play. Knowing it was called *The Proteus*, they'd be wondering what tenuous link Aeschylus would have found between that beach-haunting shape-shifter and the House of Atreus. They might guess the play would deal with the storm-tossed home voyage of Orestes' uncle, Menelaus, how he met Proteus on the muddy Egyptian shore and wrestled a prophesy from him. Since *The Proteus* is long lost, we too can only stand in the moonlight and guess.

Probably many citizens who rethought what they had watched were trying to work out where Aeschylus stood on the issue of the Areopagus court and its recently pruned powers. Aristocratic conservatives would have felt they had witnessed a reaffirmation of that court as the immemorial pivot of all Athenian government. Democrats, human too, probably heard reaffirmed that the Areopagus had been founded specifically to mete out justice in cases of murder and blood-guilt, not to be some all-encompassing Department of Homeland Security run by an old guard. And what *did* Aeschylus mean? Well, he was from close-lipped Eleusis. Furthermore a poem should not mean but be. I'd venture that what the Athenians had to thank Aeschylus for was not a constitutional analysis but a sense of reconciliation and a praise of healing. At this juncture they needed that. In the years that followed they were to come to need it as direly as we do.

Should we think of these plays at all in terms of their day's politics? Such delving now helps any production only indirectly. But yes, we should delve that way for understanding. We think of the plays as written for all times (any good play is), but they were also a specific year's entries. There was no promise that they would be produced again, so it did not trivialize them to address current affairs as well as ageless matters of myth. That gives us an insight, among other things, into the sheer number of plays these authors wrote. Composing three tragedies and a satyr play was a way of summing up a given year, the keeping of an annual holiday.

What became of the writing of trilogies from here on? Aeschylus had invented the three-act play. Sometimes *The Agamemnon* or *The Libation Bearers* or *The Eumenides* is anthologized alone and everyone speaks of each as a separate play. I can never understand that. To me it is as if one act of *The Masterbuilder* or *The Death of a Salesman* were printed or performed alone. Neither *tragoedia* nor *drama* necessarily meant a complete work; for Aeschylus I'm sure both words meant a part of a whole. *The Persians* perhaps excepted, Aeschylus' other plays are wonderful yet inconclusive like parts of long plays because that is exactly what they are. As each good act of a multi-act play does, they move toward climax and end with something accomplished, but like first acts they also end with much left to resolve, or else like last acts they leave much unsaid because it had been stated earlier. Whence came the courage of the faithful sister in *The Seven against Thebes*? How will the daughters of Danaus confront their suitors? Will Zeus or Prometheus prevail? A job of the craft is to set up questions and then to answer them. *The Oresteia* shows how masterfully Aeschylus can do that when we have all three of his plays.

Sophocles and Euripides made a choice. They do not write three-act plays but complete one-acts. I understand not always choosing to write interlocked and coherent trilogies — often a concept must have presented itself in the compass of a single event. But with Aeschylus' examples before them, did they never paint on the bigger canvas?

I can't think they were daunted. Each tried a hand at bettering Aeschylus' version of many myths. If they wrote trilogies that do not survive, even that says something about the general taste. Looking at the titles and fragments of the lost works, it seem as though Aeschylus and his contemporaries had left such a legacy of sketched subjects that a main preoccupation of playwrights in the second half of the dazzling century was in variations on themes. Complete originality was not much a goal. The range of folk myth was vast but not infinite, and Sophocles, Euripides and their fellow playwrights seem interested in looking closely at variant possibilities in specific moments picked out of the huge parade of prior stagings.

My final guess about the turn away from trilogy is simpleminded. I doubt that one could count on having the same audience at all three plays. Real lovers of theater would see each one, but there would always have been turnover. If even a minority is not following the story, they cool and they rustle, ask each other things or lose interest. A playwright can feel that and has to hate it. Oscar Wilde may have been the only author with the gall ever to say, "My play was a success; the audience failed," but others have felt that way. In *The Poetics* Aristotle has a whimsical moment thinking about how an animal several miles long cannot be beautiful — at least to us. We cannot take it in. Did trilogies suffocate like beached whales from sheer size? It's not an appealing idea; we like thinking the Athenians capable of any breadth. However, especially if the three tragedies were performed hours apart at dawn, noon and dusk, trilogy may have proven unwieldy. South Asians enjoy still larger epic dramas, but those plays shift mood and story line with kaleidoscopic variety; they don't hold to the compressed, unified idea Greek tragedians pursue. It was wonderful that the Athenian audience kept getting huger and more varied, but that must have brought its own constraints.

The Oresteia was very likely Aeschylus' last gift to Athens. It's tempting to think of him as conscious of that, like Shakespeare aware of *The Tempest's* implicit farewell. Soon after staging it he went out to Sicily, and it happens he never came back.

Spiteful rumor claimed he left in disgust with some turn of Athenian politics. An excursion against Corinth in 459, just before *The Oresteia* was staged, was a prelude skirmish to what would become the prolonged, ruinous war with Sparta that would drag down the next fifty-five years, but Aeschylus, no matter how farsighted, could not have foreseen that. When Sparta entered the Corinth war, Cimon, on whose behalf Ephialtes had been beaten to death, was recalled from exile. Would that drive Aeschylus away? Some said he left because another poet's epitaph was chosen to be engraved on a monument honoring those buried at Marathon. With his brother in that mass grave, the rejection might have stung, but Aeschylus won and wore the proud crown of Dionysos too often to feel undervalued. More likely he went out to Sicily because a city there had commissioned something. He had written for Sicilian theaters before (and describes erupting Etna in *Prometheus Bound*). He stayed for three years. The Sicilians must have treated him well.

Soon Athens was to break with one of the traditions of the Dionysia. It voted city money to reimburse any producing choragos who would mount an Aeschylean play. This suggests there were plays of his, probably written out in Sicily, that the city had not seen and wanted to see. At Gela, where the Carthaginian invasion had been turned back in the days of Salamis, Aeschylus died.

Eagles learn to crack open turtles by dropping them from a height. At Athens it was told, grotesque joke or truth, that a Sicilian eagle dropped a turtle on Aeschylus' bald skull and killed him. It is hard to make anything of that, either as symbol or fact. Was it someone's veiled and inept jibe about Sicilian high-flown aristocracy having turned the man's head? On the other hand it is so banal an accident that it just may have happened.

Poetry is a solitary business with us, but in the past it has been a family trade. Aeschylus' son Euphorion (named for a grandfather) also was a tragedian, as was Aeschylus' sister's son Philocles and Philocles' descendants for generations. Only the families of Sophocles and the Bachs passed on so much of their genius with their genes.

Euphorion the Younger would have sailed out to see that his father's burial had been properly done. No one names the site of his own accidental death: Euphorion must have at least retouched the famous epitaph sometimes credited to Aeschylus himself. Like Shakespeare's epitaph, it says no word about the man as poet or playwright.

> Aeschylus the Athenian, Euphorion's son, is dead;
> this tomb in Gela's cornlands covers him.
> His shining courage hallowed Marathon could tell,
> and the long-haired Persians knew of it.
> [Edith Hamilton's translation, no doubt
> paraphrased a bit, since I quote from memory
> and no longer know just where she cites it.]

Knowledgeable fellow playwrights respected and savored Aeschylus but did not imitate him in everything. Among other things they did not write wide-hearted blessings of cities like those upon Argos in *The Suppliants* and on Athens in *The Eumenides*. Political benedictions on any but one's own immediate neighborhood were to be less at home in the next half century.

V

Sophocles and Euripides — Worse War News

An Unpleasant Few Minutes

Political benedictions are not at home in our times either.

Some three years after Aeschylus' death Pericles backed and got a law through the assembly that closed the gates of Athenian citizenship. Only sons of Athenian mothers could participate in choosing their political fate in Athens. That law was narrow-hearted but popular. Athens was growing very fast; one hardly knew one's neighbors any more. Swarms of foreign resident aliens daily insulted the community by not even speaking Attic Greek! The time was over when an outlying town could be welcomingly incorporated into Athens.

A man as sophisticated as Pericles, who welcomed foreigners at his table and profited from their knowledge and views, knew better than to promote such a law. But a man as eager as he to see major plans put into actions wins the popularity that empowers him by supporting less than admirable measures. A gesture to motherhood and the Athenian equivalent of the flag may have seemed to him a small compromise, a tactical coup to help leverage the assembly into accepting a five-year armistice with Sparta. (We will see later the extraordinary personal revenge fate took on him for that law.)

Was it with that bit of legislation in 451 B.C. that a tide turned in

Attica? The turning can be pegged earlier or later, but there was a turning, and it was not a constructive one for democracy. "Us" had come close to meaning all Greeks, and "them" the *barbaroi*, the non-Greeks. From now on, more and more, "us" in Attica was to mean Athenians, and "them" everybody else. Pericles' party was under pressure. A grandiose, five-year expedition to support Egypt's latest anti-Persian revolt had failed miserably, with great cost of young lives. For the moment the new Great King of Persia looked formidable. The treasury of the League of Delos was removed from Delos to Athens itself—supposedly for safety from Persian capture—a move that fueled distrust and ill will among non-Athenians, who were feeling more and more like subjects.

That kind of ill will is not remote.

There has been just one unwelcoming moment, an unpleasant few minutes in Kim's and my stay here in Athens. We played a shabby role in the trivial incident, but it thrummed of huge things at distance as a guitar string will quiver in response to an explosion or thunderclap miles away. Strolling at dusk, we found ourselves hungry in one of the poorer districts. We pictured some wine shop where an oven and a few tables share space with a worn gameboard, walls with local notices, family photos, the genial smells of olive oil, of cooking rice and pita. We would be oddities, perhaps brief diversions to the proprietors, covertly watched and nodded to by regulars, and we would eat. We turned many shabby corners in the labyrinth, and the gray light grew grayer before an open door more or less of the kind we pictured looked out at us sidelong. We went in.

The place was narrow. At the far end there were four or five people, all men. They stared.

They did not want custom, not from us. They looked at us as we might look at a pair of foxes or raccoons that walked into our kitchen — no, we would be disconcerted, these men just disapproved. They and we both knew instantly that we did not belong there. Still, the door was open, there were tables, we were hungry. In old, big cities, I told myself (without any real cosmopolitan savvy to back up my assurance), strangers do eat, pay and go; human friendliness is not a requisite of that basic, ageless transaction.

These men were not Greeks. I'm not attuned enough to the Eastern Mediterranean to tell whether they were Turkish, Lebanese, Syrians or Palestinians, but their sensibilities were Islamic. Still, we were not wearing shorts, not bare armed nor hung with cameras, jewelry crucifixes or those frontal money pouches that look like Elizabethan codpieces. How obnoxious could we be? We sat when a man walked toward us with a sheaf of something. He set it in front of me as though it were a menu. It was the folded front page of a long-kept newspaper in Turkish. The lead picture was of a hooded man, cruciform, with electrical wires attached, an Abu Ghraib photo.

We tried to leave without gestural comment, as one leaves a stage when a careless playwright has given you an exit in the middle of someone else's key speech.

My main theme here is the work and lives of tragedians in ancient Athens, yet my own presence in modern Athens is part of the subject. I am alive in 2005 A.D., one more of the billions of neurons in the world's present nervous system. To look back in time, I watch what, before digital cameras, we called double or even triple exposure — as in a brook one may see sky, water surface and gravel bottom at once. I fail at unlayered, imaginative entrance into the old Athens. Too much is subtly too different. Slaves, women deprived of selfhood, people who define themselves as fixtures of some one city or quarter — these are findable here and now in Brooklyn or Keramikos. But to try to conjure up those who lived with the Attic tragedians is to be monolingual among many languages. Talk lapses unpredictably into noise, into Cassandra's "speech incomprehensible, wild as swallow song" — and less friendly. To focus on things I *can* enter into in the Greek plays, I oversimplify or over-complexify and so, groping for honesty, I reiterate that all here is fiction.

Fiction as a protective habit is my hedgehog trick. After leaving that unwelcoming table for an uneasy street, my imagination did one of its absurd plunges oblique to the discomfortable now. (Small help to Kim, who walked beside me, silent and equally shaken.) Some small-time Roman from the era of a late pagan emperor has allowed himself the Grecian tour. He will see the city where they say all the good stuff began. He strolls to find the Tower of Demosthenes he has read of in Polybius' travel memoir. Instead he finds, abruptly, a Christian Quarter. He has heard of those neo-Jews and their fabled hospitality; supposedly their religion enjoins them to treat all strangers as they would treat family members. He knows they make reliable slaves who rarely embezzle or seduce wives or sons. But here in sophisticated Athens, of all places, he finds a shop of them staring at his Romanness, not so much with hatred as with physical revulsion. He is terribly disconcerted. He is recalling how a Christian mob tore apart the woman philosopher Hypatia in an Alexandrian agora. They are recalling how his emperor illuminates gardens with the hanging bodies of live Christians smeared with pitch and set alight.

Back in his lodging, this Roman returns to the pamphlet he is scribbling (for private circulation) about the Latin Lucretius' debt to the Greek atomist Democritus.

Did remoter Euripides walk home in this mind frame from some evening stroll through one of the resident alien quarters? Did he retreat to imagine Troy? Story has it his habit of solitary walks in a far land was at last to turn fatal for him.

THEATER LIFE AFTER AESCHYLUS

From here on down my own pamphlet should flow brisker. Athenian democracy has shaped itself. With *The Oresteia* all elements of Greek tragedy are at last assembled ready for younger writers and stagers to use. Chorus has yielded captaincy in the play to individual characters. Focused plotting is preferred though not a rule. The chorus and orchestra floor have shrunk to manageable size. The wall of the *skene* house works as a sounding board to throw voices to an ever-increasing audience. The number of speakers on stage, still limited by the nature of masked performance, has enlarged to three and rarely four or five. Also goat song, *"tragoedia"* defines itself by its seriousness, as opposed to the *"comoedia,"* which has rowdily entertained market places here and in other cities and is now let to compete in the Dionysia. The notion that a tragedy always portrays unmitigated disaster is not yet firm and won't be absolute until after the famous tragedians are all dead. However, the rictus of dramatic irony will now be the nearest thing to the grin of comedy that Greek tragedy typically allows itself.

What of that other half, comedy, from which tragedy separated? Comedy evolved in rural Sicily, some said, or in Crete or Italy, a natural outgrowth of celebratory misrule in many places. It formalizes the informal, flinging off of taboos against open insult or displays of sex as one throws off a shirt after working up a sweat. It is young. It began by and for yokel stand-up comics, drunk after planting or harvest, then was carried here and there by semi-vagabonds like Susarion. But once settled into Attica, comedy became a zany voice for social comment in a city grown too big for more direct communication among its people. For those with an agenda, comedy could be a raucous political tool.

At the close of Plato's dialogue, *The Symposium*, the still sober Socrates argues to the comic poet Aristophanes and the tragedian Agathon that the spirit of comedy and tragedy is one. Was he suggesting that, like comedy, tragedy shared the spirit of its times, had a social consciousness? The two poets have drunk too much to disagree effectively or even listen. Whatever point Socrates was making had to wait in abeyance almost two thousand years. Under monotheism, playwrights dramatizing Bible stories set Shakespeare and us the example by again mingling comic with solemn. However in Athens the two split into distinct irreconcilables still symbolized by theater's trite icon, the paired masks. The second half of the century was aware of things at which it could not bring itself to laugh.

That split may owe something as well to a provincialism of urbanity. Comedy was not of pure Athenian stock. Tragedy *was* Athenian, *autochthonous*. That fine, odd word, "sprung from this earth" expresses our reverence for whatever grows from the same dirt we happen to grow from. U.S. Americans truly believe they hate snobbery, yet they are as snobbish about their nationality as Chinese, Israelis, Saudis or anybody else. Alpha dog or underdog, with humans the pack is to be loved or left. Athenians were the same. Milton called ambition the last infirmity of noble minds, but nobility has many infirmities — and one is passionate patriotism. Athenian patriotism was noble and became fatal. Comedy, being everywhere's bastard child, is a great burner of flags. It could toss self-respect to the winds and even often get away with mocking Athens itself. When tragedy began with Euripides to mock its own home city, it became courageously suicidal and contributed to the end of its own creativity.

The theater life that follows Aeschylus begins as prosperously as a goat's beard. Our first glimpse of Sophocles is as that boy, leading the dance of victory after Salamis. He is not the only artist to have had every advantage dropped in his lap by nature and opportunity, but most have squandered those goods in one careless way or another. Sophocles survived his good luck throughout a varied, enormously productive and very long life. He was a master citharist; one early success was in the role he wrote for himself of the bard Thamyris, blinded by envy of the gods for his playing and singing. Sophocles was well-to-do. His aristocratic father owned a sword factory, and business never turns really bad in the arms trade. He grew up in the suburb of Colonos near the then-still-clean brook Cephisus, and into old age he reverberated with its beauty. A chorus from his posthumous *Oedipus at Colonos* testifies:

> Who comes into this country and has come
> Where golden crocus and narcissus bloom,
> Where the Great Mother, mourning for her daughter
> And beauty-drunken by the water
> Glittering among the grey-leaved olive trees,
> Has plucked a flower and sung her loss;
> Who finds abounding Cephisus
> Has found the loveliest spectacle there is.
> [*Oedipus Rex*, translated with the shameless freedom of genius by W. B. Yeats, Macmillan, 1934]

One of the loveliest things there is, surely, is a good childhood in a place where nature is beautiful. Poets come in two kinds, those who learn the beautiful before they learn the terrible and those who learn in the opposite order.

It is told that Sophocles "studied with Aeschylus." It seems wildly unlikely that Aeschylus ever gave formal courses or lectures in any theory of writing tragedies or even took on a private apprentice. In the old bardic tradition, the "sons of Homer," there was that kind of learning through discipleship, but the drive of competition in the Dionysia was strong. Leading contenders in any sport are bent on extending their own powers, not on cultivating the powers of others. The nucleus of that story of Sophocles as pupil to Aeschylus will have been that the playwright as director of a chorus was called the *chorodidaskalos*, the "chorus teacher." Of course young Sophocles would have taken part in the most exciting of the theatrical events available — given his gifts, playwrights must have vied to include him in their casts. He learned in the best possible way, by doing, and he learned from the best.

Sophocles was rewardingly connected. Pericles liked him, and the table of Pericles was becoming a heady meeting place. Here Anaxagoras, Phidias the sculptor, Ictinus (soon-to-be architect of the Parthenon), the grand old musician Damon and any from a wide roster of poets, painters, generals, rhetoricians and officials might sit or lie. They would meet there a few at a time; Pericles was not one to host a name-dropping galaxy where illuminati speak fast to get in their five seconds of liquored wit. In his house eventually the hostess would be Aspasia, a lovely foreign woman so well educated and deep minded that people whispered she wrote Pericles' best speeches for him. Perhaps she did.

Sophocles handled occasional public office, even a brief generalship, well enough to escape sharp criticism. He never seemed to accrue envy, though Pericles did say of him that as a general he was a fine playwright. Good fortune became him, and it does that only to the unassumingly genial. He founded and maintained a shrine to the healer, Asclepios, functioning as its priest, which means in our terms he financed a small public clinic. Therefore it is probable that he hosted Hippocrates, who was his junior and visited Athens often.

Sophocles had already won prizes from Dionysos before Aeschylus died; after Aeschylus he was for over forty years the foremost figure in Athenian theater. Every time he entered the contest, he won either first or second place, never third. He must have entered most years, since he wrote well over a hundred tragedies and satyr plays. By a meaningless coincidence we have seven plays from Aeschylus and seven from Sophocles: *The Ajax, The Women of Trachis, The Antigone, Electra, The Oedipus the King, The Philoctetes* and *The Oedipus at Colonos.*

Trying to fathom Sophocles and those plays makes one think that some people's inner and outer lives must be reciprocal opposites the way a mold is the negative space of the statue cast in it. The comfortable, handsome exterior and urbane flare for changeable loves that never seemed to leave an enemy, enclosed an imagination that understood furious jealousy, singeing shame, unrelenting anger, flinty stubbornness, every misery a soul can inflict on itself. Imagination wavers between two pictures of him. One makes him internally the easy child of fortune that he seemed, with money, looks, connections, intelligence and, just as importantly, charm — someone with an objective flare for comprehending others' passions all the more shrewdly for not himself suffering from them. The other and more haunting image is of a man concealing his pains with a success only intelligence could achieve and only pride would demand. That second Sophocles knows his outward fortune sets him apart from the usual quiet desperations of fellow humans, so that any complaint from him, any hint of personal suffering is going to seem absurd weakness. For such a person writing tragedies could be an enormous relief.

A truth and witticism that digs deep with me, by a now forgotten writer, Hugh Walpole, goes: "Life is a tragedy to those who feel, a comedy to those who think." If humor is detached intellect, while gravity demands emotional involvement, what are we to make of thinking tragedians? To generalize, I'll call Aeschylus' tragic gift philosophical; he fixes his attention on the ideas a dire situation evokes. Sophocles' most unique gift is psychological, a fascination more with impassioned hearts than with what their writing may finally mean. It is significant that gods appear on stage only twice in the Sophoclean plays we have. Athena hovers briefly at the beginning of his earliest play, *The Ajax*. At the visionary final moment of his next-to-last (and last he was to stage), *The Philoctetes*, Heracles looms up, recalling his own days as a suffering mortal to soften an old companion's miseries. Those two epiphanies bracket an opening and close of Sophocles' works; everything that lies between is human.

To make another much-flawed generalization, it is Sophocles who deals most clearly in figures who draw down disasters on their own heads with a maddening mix of grandeur and shortsightedness. His protagonists are less often the gods' chess pieces that Aeschylus sees and less the random victims Euripides sees. Their fates are their own characters. That hews close to our commonest notion of what a tragedy should be. No surprise: we get that notion from Aristotle, and he got it by watching Sophocles. Sophocles lived his active public life while Athens was arbitrarily making grandiose, shortsighted policy choices that were to pull down disaster on all heads at once. He even participated in some of those policies. Athens' character became its fate. By instinct or by insight authors express their times.

Of Ajax and of Heracles' Wife

We can't date all of Sophocles plays, which is frustrating. The politics, social life and campaigns of Sophocles' era got well recorded, and it would be revealing to peg the plays to definite years. *The Ajax* may be earliest. It is the awkward one of the family, like its lumbering hero (whom Homer pictures half humorously). In it the element of conscious choice I just spoke of plays a shabby role. The war prince, Ajax, barred from his claim to the armor of dead Achilles, broods over his wrongs till he rushes out to trap, torture and kill his fellow captains. Athena deludes him; he drags sheep and cattle to his tent to mutilate and slaughter, imagining them to be Odysseus, Agamemnon and their peers.

Returning to his senses among the heap of maimed, bound, dead animals, Ajax is crushed with shame. Could there be a more vivid, repulsive stage visual of a man who has ruined his life and fouled his own nest? As he, in bleak sanity, confronts his terrified wife and child, our empathy with his disgrace cancels out our visceral disgust. At least I think it does — I've never seen or worked on a production; few have. Awful though it is, the myth does not drag us beyond the bounds of human experience. Many an alcoholic or disturbed person has awakened after fury to the accusing wreckage of a smashed and defaced home. As we now begin to awaken to the despoiled trash heap we have made of the planet in pursuit of spoils, all of us are, in a sense, Ajaxes. Ajax, though it means abandoning wife and little son, kills himself.

Over the detestable Agamemnon's objections, Ajax's archenemy, Odysseus, joins with Teucer, a faithful half-brother, to arrange for Ajax the burial rites that were so much more important to Greeks than we (or I, at least) can appreciate.

There are public rituals I exempt myself from judging: ball games, weddings, funerals. I cool to ceremonies in church, mosque, stadium or cemetery, but since I'll expend energy on ceremonies of theater, I don't mock. In Greek tragedy burial is hugely at issue because it was so in Greek life. Ajax falls on his sword halfway through the play, and I was about to say that it is as though Sophocles, under the influence of Aeschylus' multi-play approach, made two dramas, one on how Ajax died and a second on how Odysseus honored his enemy. It may be truer to say that Ajax has not fully died until those who knew him have paid him his due of insults, tears and honorable rites.

A minimal pinch of dust on a corpse prophylactically kept the dead from roving to harm the living. For the more sophisticated the gesture, like democracy and like theater, "made moment of individuals" (I re-echo Whitman's phrase). It signaled that others, helpless now to do anything for this person, still recognized that a person had been here. Nothing felt more irresponsible than denying funeral rites to relative or stranger. Those who were philosophically indifferent to formalities were still weighed upon by the opinion of their whole society.

Burial mattered especially for a hero. That Greek word has meanings remote from what we hear in it. A hero was half divine for having been singled out by the gods. Divine notice does not do a mortal an unalloyed favor — heroes often suffer terribly for being the focus of that blazing attention. Think of Danae, Perseus' mother, or, further afield, of the Greco-Judean idea of the Virgin Mary. (Yes, a hero might be feminine; Helen of Troy was one.) Burial sites of heroes become shrines. Offerings were made there not just by kin on yearly days of the dead but by whole communities. The hero's spirit was looked to for healings, miracles and prophetic dreams.

In both *The Ajax* and *The Antigone* rites of burial loom large. Later in Sophocles' long life, as the fighting of Greek against Greek grew more savage, the subject was to seem prophetically admonitory.

It may be that *The Ajax* shows Aeschylus' influence in demanding two stage sets, three if exterior and interior of a tent are two. Sophocles could have plotted the events he tells so that it would unfold in one place. He chose to emphasize the play's halves and possibly to utilize the recently invented *periactoi*. We start outside a tent, then it opens, and we see the slaughtered animals and the self-loathing Ajax. The heap of dead animals must be removed before the locale can shift. The smoothest solution would use an *eccyclema* for them, rolling it forward perhaps as the *periactoi* turn to bring us from outside to within.

Periactoi were big prisms whose three sides were painted with different scenes and were turned to shift locale. It is uncomfortable to picture *periactoi* freestanding in front of a *skene* façade. It takes a very postmodern sensibility to accept two backgrounds conflicting with one another in that abrupt way. There is one stage layout that makes them less awkward — at least to me — and more in keeping with Greek artistry. Here or there outside of Athens, at Delphi and at Oropus on the Attic shore opposite Eretria, there are ruins of a type of stage layout not yet mentioned. It is a colonnade, a row of pillars that background the playing space with a *skene* façade behind them. *Periactoi* could be set effectively into the spaces between the pillars. Framed in that way the panels would be of manageable size and suggest vistas beyond the line of columns, with the added advantage that stagehands could turn them unseen. The pillars at Oropus are unusual: they have no swell or tapering of girth and no bases. *Periactoi* would fit between them snugly, with no gaps. In that arrangement the opening between the two middle pillars would serve for the central entryway most tragedies need.

Reconstructions and modifications left no trace here in the Theater of Dionysos of any phase with a colonnade layout like that. However, this space was much reworked over the decades of the 400s; a time when there was a colonnade is just possible.

However scenic problems are managed, Ajax goes off to die at the seashore: let's say the tent rolls in and *periactoi* reveal painted coastal rocks, or the scene is changed by some other device. After his suicide, Ajax's body must lie unnoticed by the searching chorus till Ajax's wife finds it. The John Moore translation awkwardly suggests a bush be brought on; others make other suggestions. Simpler would be to let the permanent altar mask the sprawling corpse while the chorus is hunting for it. The conviction that Ajax's body must be somehow hidden from us as well as from his friends comes, I think, out of two misconceptions. One is that the play *must* be done with only three actors — somehow the actor doing Ajax slipped away unnoticed and the body was replaced by a dummy. Another is that screening Ajax's final moments fulfills in token a ban against onstage violence. Use of a dummy here is not as implausible as in *The Agamemnon* or in *Prometheus Bound*. The body is soon covered with a mantle, and if the Charon's steps mouth was just upstage of the altar — the most logical place for it — the substitution of a dummy is possible. It can have been no joy to the actor to lie there so very long as Ajax's corpse.

Onstage suicide? Yes. Greek tragedy did not always keep violence offstage. The restraints against it seem strong but cannot have been rigid until later. The driving of a stake through Prometheus' chest is certainly violent, and in one of Euripides' plays, *The Suppliant Women*, a widow throws herself into a blazing pyre (a hard effect without access to Charon's steps). During Sophocles' creative life it is certainly false to think of stage movement as formalized and minimal. Japanese traditional theater may offer starting points toward imagining what these tragedies were like, but Japanese lifestyle evolved to make an insular, over-packed society function. That is profoundly different from the elbowroom the Greeks allowed themselves. Surely exuberant Kabuki is closer to Greek tragedy in style than is the trembling, stilled energy of Noh. A notion of static performance persisted long about Shakespearean plays too. A reader looks at a column of verses flowing in a placid river down a page and assumes that it expresses all there is. As a young performer in his own lost play, *Nausicaa*, Sophocles wowed his audience with a danced ball game! Choreography with things thrown in the air demands nerve and the active freedom of a Twyla Tharp.

I find myself writing as though I did not believe at all in the restraints and rules generally assumed in Greek tragedy. That's my twenty-first century mindset. Yes, there was a reluctance to indulge in much violence, to throng the stage either with numerous characters or with a flurry of quick, aggressive events. I try to understand the double nature in these performances. They were fictions yet at the same time rituals, recreations of a magic reality. Ritual has to be symbolic, not literal, because it is an act that pictures the intangible. It is not *the thing* but a reflecting *likeness* in this world of a thing from a deeply different world. If participants in a Christian mass (for extreme example) received actual hunks of Jesus' human flesh and cups of his blood, only wildly ecstatic, disturbed communicants could bear it. That is what made Mel Gibson's recent film of the passion of Christ and the gory, explicit passion plays of the Middle Ages so futile. They rouse berserk furies and blood lusts but little more. If an event really happened, any spiritual content it had is different from the solids and fluids; the devils are in the gruesome details, but the god is elsewhere. See this emerging art, tragedy, as the savage, back-country rites of Dionysos Destroyer transformed by that whatever-it-was that I've called the Ethical Revolution.

Technology abets and increases our taste for realism — and blunts our appreciation of symbol and ritual. In the Theater of Dionysos, the choral dance and the dance-expansive gestures of characters must have reinforced the sense of ritual in the midst of suspended disbelief. The music must have added yet another separation. Here was Ajax living his last; here also was a ceremony commemorating that event. Drawing a contemporary audience into that double vision is the hardest thing I know about presenting these plays. Perhaps we can only know that side of Attic tragedy as Helen Keller knew of landscape. But even of that her reaching imagination knew somewhat.

A man who has thought very deeply about all these plays (and Greece in general) is H. D. F. Kitto. Before working on any Greek play I would read what he has to say about it in his *Greek Tragedy, a Literary Study*. He suspects that at the opening of this play Athena, when she seems to boast to Odysseus of how she has hoodwinked Ajax, is tempting and testing Odysseus, probing him for mean-spiritedness, not exhibiting her own. As the play draws to its conclusion, Odysseus passes her test. He insists that Ajax have full burial rites. This makes a neat dramatic whole and Odysseus a central character. When I read

Kitto, I feel as one can feel listening to Bach, devout as long as the music lasts. I believe what Kitto says while he is saying it. When I try the test of mentally acting out ideas Kitto has read into a play, sometimes either I or the ideas fail. Still, the ideas are useful.

Like *The Ajax*, *The Women of Trachis* deals by way of myth with a recognizable life dilemma: love that poisons with much cherishing. In it, Heracles' wife, Deianeira, fearing to lose him, sends him a supposed love charm that kills him. Like *The Ajax*, *The Women of Trachis* divides into two halves. The wife is the center of the first. She dies. Then we watch Heracles, poisoned yet unable to die, forcing his followers to burn him on a pyre. No rationalizing gets round it: halves with characters who never overlap on stage dissatisfy our sense of story as chain. But our taste for comprehensible human dilemma is fed. Sophocles keeps to the humanity. In the myth, the burning of Heracles clears the way for his apotheosis as the only mortal ever fully to become a god. This play does not even mention that. We watch an agonized woman who wants to keep her husband's love, and then we watch a man who feels fatally betrayed by a loved one. How Deianeira came by that poison, why she thought it a love potion and what fatally induced her to use it make the play a tale.

In this play the Trachian chorus women have a neighborly care for what is happening to Deianeira but their fates are not deeply entwined with hers and certainly not with those of Heracles. This can't be carelessness; Sophocles wrote an essay on the uses of the chorus. It is lost but proves he gave the choruses craftsmanly thought. The usual guess is that he dealt with rhythms, poetic patterns and modes that separate choral song from dialogue and individual outburst; there were very elaborate traditions to be hewed to or varied from. Whatever he theorized about in that essay, in his practice of playwriting he explored some idea as radical (and theatrically perverse) in its way as Brecht's "alienation effect"—a deliberate push of the chorus *away* from the direct involvement most of us would call a deep goal of theater. He would not have been making any Brechtian attempt at shaking the audience awake to social reality, but maybe his goal was to allow the chorus a freer lyricism by drawing it further back from the immediate event.

The weakened emotional links between chorus and individual characters did not happen through one artistic choice. It has to have been parcel with exploration going on among dramatists in Athens in those years. Focus was being turned on the individuals and away from the community. Individualism can pass beyond an enrichment of society and become a new stage of enlightened savagery, the sheer solipsism an Ayn Rand theorizes and the rest of us fall into with no help from theory at all. The shift reflects a flaw of human nature, one that makes political decency difficult, in old Athens and in new. Our strongest empathy is always more available to the individual than to the group. Call it "the mouse-mice paradox": one mouse is charming, ten mice unappealing, a thousand mice a plague. In war, hundreds of thousands die in a hideous blur we can turn away from; one burnt child screaming naked on a napalmed road is an image that at least briefly reaches the heart of us comfortable, housebroken Muslims, Christians or Jews. That was as true of Athenians as of us. The lone character trumps the chorus. We will be better creatures when we can extend to the many the compassion we expend on the one. In the meantime, there is theater.

A ONE AGAINST A MANY

The structural shell of *The Antigone* is bivalve, like *The Ajax* and *The Women of Trachis*: a key character dies two-thirds of the way through the play, which then becomes about the antagonist. Somehow this time there are more pearls in its two shell-halves. It stays in one locale, though a shift to the mouth of the cave where Antigone is walled in alive might serve the action better than the shift to the seaside serves *The Ajax*. Experiment must have convinced Sophocles that one scene was better than two for his purposes; after *The Ajax* none of his surviving plays moves about.

It's a puzzle then that Sophocles was remembered as an innovator in stage sets. The famous Agatharchus from Samos was recruited into scene painting for him (and for the aging Aeschylus too). Art's first awkward description of linear perspective is in an account of Agatharchus' technique. Yet only the last two Sophoclean plays offer scene design much scope. *The Oedipus at Colonos* has a grove instead of central doors (and somehow one can walk into it); *The Philoctetes* has a double cave mouth raised a bit above the stage floor.

I perhaps pay too much attention to settings, props and visual poetry of actions. On that theme everything is guesswork except for the theme itself: event and visuals matter. If not, there's no point in staging a play. Why is Sophocles the one most credited with innovations of setting although, after *The Ajax,* he makes few demands in that line? Perhaps the paradox had to do with an expanding of backstage professions. Sophocles was soon no longer his own actor. In his creative lifetime scene painter and technician came into prominence. We hear of choreographers. We don't hear of costume designers, but vase paintings let us glimpse their unique work. A theater event was becoming less a creation of a single personality. Teamwork is wonderful; however, even from my own minor experience I know that when one can rely on good designers, the scope of one's own imagination shrinks a little. It refines, one hopes, and does its narrowed work all the better, but it no longer scours the wide field. It may be that Sophocles is recalled as a scenic initiator because he wasn't one — meaning that he came to rely on others more than Aeschylus' generation had. His imagination's center of buoyancy was therefore less visual. The strongest links in his plays are more in the plot and the characters, which is where we nowadays think we prefer them to be.

I no longer know which poet, John Crowe Ransom or T. S. Eliot, wrote my absolutely favorite critical insight: "a work of art, unlike a chain, is as strong as its *strongest* link." It is certainly true of *The Antigone.* Sophocles picks up the story Aeschylus touched on in *The Seven against Thebes,* how Oedipus' daughter buried her brother at cost of her life. Did Athenian playwrights expect the audience to remember and compare earlier versions? *The Seven* had been staged twenty-five busy years before. After a quarter century how hotly does what we saw in any play still smolder in memory? But *The Seven* did get remembered for its unusual close: its chorus divided and left the stage in two directions, a visual tearing of the social fabric. Antigone and Creon are the torn halves. *The Antigone* felt the richer for Aeschylus. Sophocles picks up the trail of a human dilemma from the Aeschylean trilogy, and he tracks it to its dark conclusion.

The story is for all eras. Brecht wrote a 1948 version, and Anouilh wrote his in Nazi-occupied France, an impassioned praise of individual against state, spirit against letter of law, one against many. Versions are staged whenever there is fiber among us to resist unbridled government. Ignoring it we date ourselves, not the play.

Yet Sophocles is far more evenhanded in *The Antigone* than we would be apt to be; he gives Creon and the state a strong case. His audience, men and women both, would be much more uneasy than we to see a young woman making her own choices against the grand alliance of received opinions. The play's first chorus almost summarizes *The Seven against Thebes*, reminding themselves and us of the terrible war Thebes has just survived and the appalling assault that Antigone's disgraced brother committed on his home city. One understands why he is denied burial even though it may be an affront to the gods. Sophocles was himself a participating member of a ruling class and knew that the powerful too can feel the pinch of dilemma. The situation is a case of two rights making a wrong, the inescapable bind humans can find themselves in. Still Creon, as the one with the most choices, is the most culpable one in the play.

We are now arriving among plays that anyone will have had a chance to see or read or at least hear of, and many good critics have excavated them down to clay. It feels impertinent to retell plots. There are good screen versions. The BBC production of *The Oedipus the King*, *The Oedipus at Colonos* and *The Antigone*, with Juliet Stevenson and other fine performers, is hard for me to warm to, but I respect it. Stevenson is a wonderful Antigone. In *The Oedipus the King*, John Gielgud as blind prophet makes stylization eerie and eeriness authentic, a shamanist power. At his best Gielgud had performerly incontrovertibility. (Hitler, Billy Graham and probably Eva Peron had that: you could go to laugh but might stay to believe. Performerly gift, like courage, is amoral, and great actors can be as saintly, vile or blandly middling as anyone else.)

Rather than synopsize *The Antigone,* I'll look around at the year of its production. If we sit here in the middle of the Theater of Dionysos in 442 to watch *The Antigone*, we see to our left the cornices of a new building, huge, crowding the theater and untypically square. It's part of Pericles' policy of civic building for display. Public works are employing thousands of stonemasons, carpenters, tilers, skilled and semiskilled citizens (one is a homely, talkative twenty-seven-year-old Socrates — thought harmlessly mad or oddly comic by some who meet him at that age). That square building has four triangular roof slopes like an immense tent, and it is intended to look like one. Years back at Plataea, where the last of the Persian army surrendered, Xerxes' pavilion was part of the city's spoils. It has been erected and displayed often enough to have begun to tatter. Pericles has had it copied in stone as a public concert hall, the Odeon ("hearing place" just as "theatron" is "seeing place"). No need to call it "The Great King's Tent"— everyone remembers.

The Odeon's footprint does not intrude (as it will later) on the symmetry of the rungs of seating. The layout of spectators' benches is not as large as it will later grow—many watchers still stand or squat on the higher irregularities of the slope. A newer Odeon that a distant generation will wander through at the far end of the Acropolis wall will be a Roman replacement and of conventional design.

Pericles' presence in the front row is much felt here in these bleachers. Last year he was reelected one of the ten generals whose wine-offering to Dionysos is by now part of the inaugural ceremony here. And his presence is more than personal. By a law that he sponsored, any poor citizen now who finds public service or public entertainment beyond his means receives two obols per annum to recompense his service on a jury or to pay for his ticket to plays and contests. That generosity of the public treasury colors the makeup of the audience and affects its attitude. Shoemakers and sail makers sit here as proprietorially as the families of the great producing *choregoi*. (That feeling will fill American ball parks twenty-three hundred years later; then ticket price will filter out the truly poor and turn those games into displays of means—or of a willingness to live beyond them.)

It is just four years since the traveler Herodotus, at Pericles' invitation, publicly read parts of his *Inquiry into the War with the Medes and Persians*, in this theater. It won him a huge award and, since Greek for "inquiry" is *historia,* it brought into use a new word for the written remembrance of things past.

It is also just four years since the Euboeans declared themselves no longer members of the Delian League. Pericles, following Cimon's example at Naxos, led an expeditionary force against them, rushed back when a Spartan-led counterthrust got as far into Attica as Eleusis, worked out a treaty to turn away that incursion from the south and then marched back north to crush the Euboeans, who were now in Athenian eyes both rebellious and treacherous. Among the athletic citizenry some few have scars or amputations. There are widows present

Eager fans settling in here are aware that Sophocles himself has given up performance. He had every other skill but too quiet a voice for the tiers of benches that each few years have ascended higher toward the cliff wall. Attendance, like the city itself, kept on growing. His favorite actor, Tlepolemos, will play the central roles. A performer who is neither poet nor director/choreographer is a new enough trade not to have its own word. *Hypocrites,* an "answerer" or "expounder," is used for what we call an actor. In a couple generations the word will also mean (at first slangily) someone who acts a role in real life.

Actors have their own enthusiastic followings, one more testimony to how sharpened the ears of the hearers have become. In masked plays they know their favorites by voice. Gesture and mannerism matter, but the ultimate test is vocal, which makes those actors in a way like our radio performers or singers. For seven years now actors have competed for their own victor's wreath, and this year, for the first time, comic actors will also be judged as distinct from the comic poets.

It might have been at this play, if not earlier, that Sophocles sat for the first time with his audience. He was too polished, too instinctively good-mannered to pace uneasily behind it; he would have looked serene, aware of eyes upon him. Still, he must have felt uneasy not to be onstage. He was undergoing something new, a playwright's and director's helplessness once performance begins. The child in one is abruptly shut out of the game. But once the play is under way the author/director really *is* back onstage, mentally performing everything that's performed, reinventing each line, often with a pang of longing to rephrase, to add or wipe away.

Rephrasing a moment or radically reshaping a whole scene had now become possible. Athenian plays were being regularly performed elsewhere — plays of Aeschylus were even being revived for performances here in Athens. This gave new dimension to the occupation of an author who sat in his audience instead of playing onstage. He had a vantage from which to observe things he had only sensed uneasily as a poet-player. A plausibly authentic copy of a statue of Sophocles shows him at midlife, vigorous, sharp nosed, with a mass of curls, and a little bucket beside his ankle. It is full of scrolls, a portable bookcase. Winning authors' plays were now circulated and read as poems, becoming not only events but literature. I've said writing freeze-dries poetry; there is an irretrievable loss of immediate heat, but there are gains too. To put stylus to wax or tap a keyboard is to do something unique — to talk to the future. The readers will be hours, perhaps centuries, off. Of course in a sense poets always talk to a future. They shape their words sculpturally because they want them to last, but for Sophocles and his fellow dramatists a road forked here. In one way they dealt as always with a thing so wholly of the moment that vanishingness was one of its essences. In another way, their work was now more like bronze casting. A written play can be *finished* as a live play or ball game never can — one can polish a final draft that respectful future generations may take for inviolable. That inviolability is an illusion (one some writers — Beckett, for example — have clung to fiercely), but in the processes of art as well as in its products, illusion matters.

If play*wrighting* was discovered by Thespis and his followers down to Aeschylus, play*writing* was discovered by Aeschylus and his followers Sophocles, Euripides and the many others whose names we forget. A wrought play *is* its costumes and masks, its music, choreography and business as much as its words; it is event. A written play can be read as if apart from performance — it is a book.

I puzzle over this. How plays were to be written down was settled in Sophocles' time: of all actions, only the act of speaking was recorded. Who conceded such total pride of place to the verse of a play? Did failure of imagination simply accept what had worked for epics and lyric poems? Surely Clytemnestra's carpet or Ajax on his heap of mangled animals belies that. What of those painted shields that, I believe, carried symbolic voltage in *The Seven against Thebes*? All such powerful effects and gestures are lost unless the spoken words hint at them. This surrender of the visual has to relate in part to the new distribution of theatrical jobs. When he is no longer designer, director and actor, the poet is more isolatably a poet.

Directors and actors can now be wryly grateful to the playwrights for what was left out; the survival of the plays may actually owe a lot to those gaps. Having only dialogue to work with leaves us tempting blanks that invention and interpretation will always be eager to fill in. But surely no playwrights planned to offer posterity that pleasure. In Elizabethan scripts spareness — besides following Greco-Roman precedent — guarded trade secrets. Those plays, once in the public's hands, were fair game for any troupe of rascals, so playmakers with livelihoods to protect relucted to publish a handbook of what their toil and stagecraft had breathed life into. But London's commercial theater conditions didn't apply in Athens. The competition here was not monetary.

Flight of theory about stage directions circles back to practicality: performers had to learn speeches by heart, and written script saved the poet hours of repetitive teaching. Actions, on the other hand, are absorbed in rehearsal by doing; hardly anyone learns a dance or blocking from a page. Besides, sheer simplicity of taste said something like this to a Greek: the play, complete and fugitive, is an artwork elaborate to the point of clutter. Let its lasting relic be a littler thing — and that well done. Sophocles had detached, sparse taste. He could let some things slip through the cracks.

Things do slip through cracks. That they do is perhaps theater's deepest lesson to its practitioners. Many feel this but few of us speak of it because outside the theatrical experience it is misunderstood as morbid. Over and over one is involved in some unique, miniature world; over and over the bubble bursts and leaves not a wrack behind. To temperaments appropriate to the trade, that is not at last depressing. In absurd small scale some Brahma breathes out intricate universe after universe and then inhales them into nothingness again. Like the epitaphs in Gray's *Elegy Written in a Country Churchyard*, theater "teaches the rustic moralist to die." Every strike (not a work stoppage but theater's jargon for the putting away of the mortal remains of a play) is an antiritual about the interlockage of being and nonbeing. It is a pity that our actors' unions, with all the crucial good they do, bar members from the strike. Like refusing to let family members go to a funeral, it is unhealthy. Instead of sharing some therapeutic hard work, at the close of a run most of us amble off somewhere and drink. If this idea of theater as a memento mori or a Sarah Bernhardt's coffin strikes you as repellant, forget it. If it resonates, you understand one private quirk about being an actor. Also about being within history. Individuals of a generation dissolve, but their genes may persist. Words are genes.

Given that advent of the little bucket of written scripts at Sophocles' heels, a few in the Athenian audience who settle now to watch the first performance of *The Antigone* may have actually read it beforehand. If so, those people will be observing in a wholly new and double way, pitting preconceptions of a reader's inner eye against the passing outer vision.

After ceremonies the music begins, a reed pipe like an oboe. *The Antigone* calls the chorus "Theban Elders," or words to that effect. They file in. Will they be stately and unathletic? Perhaps? Old men do Tai Chi, and other peoples have been more willing to watch elders appreciatively than we have been. But one effect of the depersonalization of the chorus after Aeschylus is that sometimes they seem stylized beyond being any particular age, class or sex. In some plays (and *The Antigone* is one), they seem defined only as chorus; their behavior and movement need not be much bound by type. Speech and choreography take on in them a life apart from realism. They seem to be humankind in general.

PROBLEMATICS

A person who talks about any art should notice how fine museum docents or good forest guides do their work. They point (at times wordlessly) to things that are beautiful or to oddities that may slip off through the undergrowth, but they are shy of saying, "This is bad" or "That's clumsy." People quickly enough find out faults on their own. So, I hesitate to mention my stumbling blocks. If no one else barks a shin on them, why break out the iodine? However, I do know things in the tragedies Greeks loved that feel awkward to many now — myself included. Our likings and theirs aren't always reconcilable.

One problem is the use of the messenger. No advice is more commonplace in critiquing playwriting than "Show me, don't tell me." Our films are *about* the visual, about "moving pictures." In film, image was the medium before sound was. On bus rides I watch movies without the headset and often follow them well enough. Athenians called this site laid out for their dramas "the seeing place." So, when in these plays a narrator comes onstage to tell some crucial event, we feel cheated. In *The Antigone*, a messenger describes Antigone and Haemon dead in the prison cave, and we wish the *eccyclema* would roll them into view.

The original dithyrambs were as much narrative as dramatic; event was told as well as mimed. So, the messenger was an inheritance; he came with the farm. Real messengers were part of Greek life. Heralds were professionals with memory trained to repeat word for word what they'd heard and with a flare for the spirit of the news — their society's equivalent to our television anchor people. They were traditionally sacrosanct, immune from assault; some even had their fifteen hundred heartbeats of fame.

Greeks had no newspapers, no reportage; from childhood to age they were telling and hearing things told across the gap between stranger and stranger and between generations. We seldom feel a teller of a long story is doing us a favor, especially a story from remote space or time. Few fourteen-year-olds listen spellbound or even duty-bound to a story from an elder, nor elders to one from a teenager. We grin at the idea. Part of our selective deafness to such things comes from how our money is made — from styles, songs and prejudices bought by one demographic or one age group. To sell inessentials, our economy fosters illusory separations that becomes a divisive reality, a feudalism based on age-peerage or socioethnics. Communication breaks down; the live telling of events does not happen. We throw the shuttle of narration too skimpily in weaving our social fabric, and the flimsy fabric falls apart. We don't even sense that this is atypical in humanity; it seems natural unless the arts alert us to how tightly woven a society can be.

Does recognizing all that make messengers in these plays more satisfactory to us? Not much. It does remind us that they were not a mere expedient. They were organic to a way in which Greek life differed from ours. Part of theater is about how like us others are, part about how different. Messenger sequences now become weaker links, challenging to perform or at times to abridge, possibly even to illustrate.

A second problem is trickier to shed light on. Greeks almost had a word for it, *stichomythia*. "Line-of-verse-talk" is poets' jargon for a rhythmic crackling of dialogue; two people counter one another, metric line for metric line. "These swords have all a length?" Hamlet asks. One-liner athwart one-liner, cut and thrust, is dueling. Bold actors can make sparks fly from it. At its best stichomythia conveyed the sustained tension of argument; its stylized pattern intensified the heaving deadlock of matched wills. In high mountains the all-but-musical concussion of bighorn sheep clashing head to head in their rutting season, gives some sense of how dramatic stichomythic argument can be between hot wills trained, as we never are trained, to talk.

That training was much a part of Athenian life. Along with the more theoretical philosophers, like Anaxagoras, whom Athens drew in, there came a kind who brought a pragmatic skill — persuasion, the ugly stepsister of reason. "Persuasion" was a word on everyone's lips in Athens. It was a noun you could speak of as a goddess and set up an altar to. In Greek the verb *I persuade* in its *I-persuade-myself* form, means *I obey, I do as told*. Recognition of persuasion's power was built into the language.

Part of our own nation's current dilemma is that none of us makes nor hears reasoned argument very clearly. The ability to put one's case forward was a necessity of democracy at its best. At worst, persuasive skills became life or death weapons of aggression and defense. Lawsuit-addicted Athenians had a court system that made each man his own attorney. Teachers of the powerful skill of persuasion were called sophists, which is "wise man" or "wiseguy" depending on your tone of voice. Among the most striking, or monstrous, of the crew were followers (exploiters) of a Sicilian, Gorgias. They came and went, training learners briefly and brightly and moving on before the glitter wore thin. They said they were not sophists, only rhetoricians. They said nothing existed. They said if anything existed, it could not be known. They said if it did exist and could be known, it could not be communicated. What *could* be known was how to persuade others that things could be known. They argued subtly and with a winner's grin; for them words were what the cape is to a bullfighter. Their art was to reduce the opponent, whichever side he took, to the condition of a bull. If you truly believe that absolute truth is unattainable (and it is), it is a short misstep to decide that relative truth is invalid. From there the next step down is easy: when truth is not to be had, everything else can be had for the bold taking. That early in human history the moral vacuum pump was invented. It still functions in global business practices and in politics.

 A cynic could laugh that the ethical revolution had opened a whole new dimension to the scoundrel. Bad behavior that had once simply been done now needed to be rationalized, cloaked, "spun," as current jargon says it. Once the apple is eaten, the tailor's fig-leaf art is required. Spin paid; Gorgias' life style generated the adjective gorgeous!

 I am unfair to Gorgias — I could pick with more justice on several other of the era's teachers of persuasive art. He himself did not visit Athens until sent as an ambassador late in life, but his thought and method preceded him. One of Gorgias' paradoxes leads to intriguing ideas about watching a play: "Tragedy is a deception in which the deceiver is more in the right than the non-deceiver, and the deceived wiser than the undeceived." He had noted one essential of enjoying fiction: acceptance of deception, the willing suspension of disbelief.

 There was a fascination in Athens, even a fad, for argumentation as a formal skill. One of its techniques was to question and manipulate the meaning of each statement your opponent made, picking and shifting the sense of terms. That can be admirable for sorting out a truth when one applies it to one's own words as well as those of others, as Socrates did. But usually in life and in drama, each arguer has seized on a particular, partial truth before even beginning. Such debaters are not clarifying anything for themselves, only seeking to befuddle others.

 A patterning impulse of poetry merges with the techniques of sophistry to produce *stichomythia*. Young Haemon's argument with his father, Creon, in *The Antigone* will do for example. The life of

Antigone, the girl Haemon loves, is at issue; traditional respect for elders and for Creon's dictatorship barely restrain Haemon.

> H: I urge no wrong. I'm young but you should watch my actions not my years, to judge of me.
> C: A loyal action, to respect disorder?
> H: I wouldn't urge respect for wickedness.
> C: You don't think she is sick with that disease?
> H: Your fellow citizens maintain she's not.
> C: Is the town to tell me how I ought to rule?
> H: Now there you speak just like a boy yourself.
> C: Am I to rule by other minds than mine?
> H: No city is property of a single man.
> C: But custom gives possession to the ruler.
> H: You'd rule a desert beautifully alone.
> C: It seems you're firmly on the woman's side.
> H: If you're a woman. It is you I care for.
> C: Wicked! You try conclusions with your father?
> H: When you conclude unjustly so I must!

(And they fire this many more lines back and forth before Haemon strides out [Sophocles, *Antigone*, Elizabeth Wyckoff translation, Univ. of Chicago Press, 1954].)

For us stichomythic argument may seem like slow motion, the form feels stately and at odds with any rush of adrenalin. It is hard to believe the speakers are passionate, and an actor today must faith-leap broadly to commit to such lines. Still we can grasp that Sophocles was not sounding awkward to his audience. Many would have been listening for how the bout was being played. They would have picked up on Creon's line about "trying conclusions," rhetor's jargon for the ploy of challenging definitions. They'd savor the irony that it is Creon who is more playing the game of which he accuses Haemon. His hammering questions are pure sophistry. Athenians must have rarely talked in that way; the point is, they *wanted* to. An audience likes its entertainment not just to imitate lifestyle but to model it. We pick up clothing tips and mannerisms from films; others have learned from plays how to dress their thoughts.

As with accepting messengers, understanding may not help our audience accept long passages of stichomythia. Sometimes an adapter must be as splendidly false to a text as Hypermnestra was splendidly false to her fierce oath. Letting the play live one may have to break a promise to some of its lines.

Once, during the time Kim and I spent in the Theater of Dionysos, the place stood briefly empty except for ourselves, and she went down onto the orchestra floor to speak a few verses so that I could stand far up the slope and listen for the fabled acoustics.

> How happy some o'er other some can be.
> Through Athens I am thought as fair as she,
> But what of that? Demetrius thinks not so,
> He will not know what all but he do know...

(Kim has played Helena twice.) This place is too battered now for the sound to be as miraculous as at Epidaurus, but it is startlingly good.

Shakespeare's lilt and rhyme recall a baffling challenge: how to translate matched-line stichomythia or choral odes for people who have shut their lips to poetry? Greek poets heard rhyme only as a rare special case of alliteration, one to use sparingly. But with rhythm they were irreproducibly subtle. Most of our serious poets feel rhyme trivializes, and their convictions about rhythm are various and private, so we as audience have no idea what to listen for. Our untrained ears are indifferent. No game's fine points move the person who has never played or followed it. In the dialogue of a Greek play the intensity of situation can carry us along without a full flood of the poetry. In the choruses, however, we face a hard fact: patterned phrases do not much take our breath away.

Our taste in speech is for the quick-energy junk food of realism: ads and politics have made us cynics about intense language. Even our religions prefer banal translations of their holy books, as though rite and passion should sound like instructions for a washer-dryer! Here's a confession to make me a target of much disrespect: Twice, in staging *The Trojan Women*, I have turned to the outdated translation of Gilbert Murray. I adapted it in many places (his fondness for the—*th* verb ending to get rhymes for *breath* or for *death*, for example, can tire quickly), but that play obviously got to Murray and exalted him above his Edwardianism into what I take to be real poetry. The general agreement that English rhyme is inappropriate to Greek tragedy is for the most part right, I think, but rhyme does remind the ear that we are in the presence of something other than realism—and truly, rhyme no more breaks poetry than makes it, except for those who have been taught to discount rhyme where ever it is met.

The Antigone is not the best play to illustrate my gloom about getting at choral word music. Elizabeth Wyckoff's translation often proves the job can be done.

> Many the wonders but nothing walks stranger than man.
> This thing crosses the sea in the winter's storm,
> making his path through the roaring waves.
> And she, the greatest of gods, the earth —
> ageless she is and unwearied — he wears her away
> as the plows go up and down from year to year
> and his mules turn up the soil.
> [Sophocles, *Antigone*, Wyckoff translation,
> Univ. of Chicago Press, 1954]

A chorus could genuinely move and exult to those lines of Wyckoff's. But the content of that particular choral ode is close to our idea of poetry. Many choruses are webs of allusion to folktale and locale. Being tone-deaf, we find little to listen for in a song in a foreign language. When you sit, say, at a taverna table, talking with strangers in their own tongue, you have to relax and accept that they'll say some things you don't follow.

Two Electras, Sophocles' and Euripides'

After *The Antigone* Sophocles really says little more about politics than about the gods. The great powers he deals with are those within ourselves. That is one kind of wisdom — know thyself. For a citizen and a shareholder in democracy, however, it is also self-protection. There is something stubborn and dangerous in not looking at what one's class and city are doing.

One of the fine things about Sophocles was his generosity to a younger challenger who was his extreme personal opposite. Something in Sophocles himself opposed the outward man; that may have furthered his empathy for Euripides. Or maybe sheer geniality could let him bear no grudge against a serious rival. Democracy or no, Athenian society, even among its minority of male citizens, was not classless, and Euripides came from a stratum below Sophocles. Envious people chuckled that Euripides' father kept a tavern and his mother sold onions. A lesser writer would have adopted the aristocratic ring of a lofty style; Euripides could have done that very easily, but he did not stoop to it. He dared find his own kind of poetry. It was one so close to daily speech that his first surviving play, *The Alcestis*, gets used now as an introductory text. Since he uses that simplicity early on, clearly it is not something learned in the hard knocks of theatrical practice. It emerges from his own heart and mind.

They say he spent a boyhood on Salamis. In the postwar flush a hostel keeper's son could afford scrolls of verse and good tutors. For some, solitary reading feels like better company than they find among neighbors, and Euripides liked stealing away with books to a sea cave he had searched out for himself. There are natural sounds that teach poetry: brook rustle, wind in olives, wave break in a hollow of the rocks or the throaty hoof-rumble of a herd galloping in open pasture. Still, for all his lone bent, he grew into a writer startlingly in touch with the tangible world and with chafing human contact. The best Roman copy of a statue of him may have caught some truth. It shows the massive shoulders of a trained wrestler yet the reflective slump of a brooder.

If Euripides was born in the year some guess he was (485 B.C.), his two-year military stint fell in 463 and 464. He could have been led out as part of Cimon's unwelcomed excursion to aid Sparta. Certainly he knew young men who did march. If born as tradition has it during the Battle of Salamis, he soldiered when Athens sent out an expeditionary force to help a Pharaoh free his throne from Persian overlords. Nothing came of either venture to take pride in.

What does it mean that all the plays we have from the three tragedians come from mid and late in their careers? It might show how difficult a craft playwrighting is. Lyric poetry is about self; it can be a young man's game. Drama, being about selves, profits from a few more years.

When Euripides was probably in his thirties (448 to 446), Athens was ingloriously involved in fights in and around Delphi that are called the "Second Sacred War." Neighboring towns to Delphi had laid claim to the profits and honors of the Delphians perched up in their crags. Athens, where wealth was sacred, had sided with those neighbors; Sparta, where tradition was sacred, had sided with the Delphians. Under the surface, control of Greece north of the Isthmus was at issue. When dust settled, Spartans and status quo had won. Athens lost influence it had been building up over central Greece. The bitterness of that war helped doom Pericles' attempt to convene an All-Greece Congress. The residue of ill-feeling may also help explain an uneasy puzzle, blatant in Euripides, the undercurrent of disrespect for Apollo. Does it hark back to those pro-Persian Delphic prophesies of disaster? Does it have to do with a special Spartan reverence for Apollo? Does it crop up in plays because some opposition between Apollo and Dionysos was felt and plays were Dionysos speaking? For any or all of those reasons, Apollo more than other gods in the dramas is an unacknowledged target for skepticism.

In Euripides' *Ion*, Apollo's human bastard son, foisted on another man by Delphic prophesy, asks, "But mother, does Apollo tell truth, or is the oracle false?" When Ion is ready to walk straight into the Delphic temple and demand answer, Athena intervenes and unsatisfyingly smoothes things over between this mortal nephew and her divine half-brother. She explains that Apollo, to preserve dignity, will not show himself.

There are as many theories about what Euripides was up to at his oddest as there are readers. Sophocles said that he himself drew people as they ought to be while Euripides drew them as they are. That is not sneer but respectful, accurate observation. What people are is self-contradictory and often crazed under pressure.

Euripides was to become enormously popular almost the moment he was dead and the war with Sparta that had raged throughout his later life was finally over, at least for that generation. His dislike for that war and his disrespect for those who prolonged it were too obvious during his lifetime. In the generation that followed, even Aristotle, who definitely preferred Sophocles, called Euripides "the most tragic of the tragedians." In context Aristotle does not seem to mean the one with the saddest life, but that may have been true as well. He won at the festivals only four times. His plays got copied so often over the centuries that seventeen tragedies and a satyr play survive. That's more than we have from the elder two great ones put together.

There were innovations in the Theater of Dionysos between the 430s and the 'teens, the years when Sophocles and Euripides were most intensely at work. I'd pointed out how, back in Thespis' day, being surrounded by an audience gave way to an upstage and downstage, opening new movement possibilities. These were now being refined.

In our typical theaters the point of greatest advantage for an actorly moment is front and center, as close to the audience as possible. Here in the Theater of Dionysos, the seating encircles more than 180 degrees of the orchestra. When you move fully front-center, half your audience sees you in profile; to some you are almost back to. Your real point of advantage is upstage, close to the *skene* doors. You are further from your audience, but you have them all within your aim. There, however, when the chorus is onstage, you have twelve people between you and the front rows. Given the slope, that was no problem for the majority of your audience, but your judges were down front! Choruses often had to crouch or sit during intense scenes (though seated figures drain energy). That simple dynamic may have further diminished choral involvement.

Probably comedians first brought in a solution to this. In their streets and stubble-fields they had used carts, bales, anything to get their heads higher than the surrounding crowds, and no doubt some of their dearest rough-and-tumble bits came from scramblings up and fallings off.

Improvised scaffolding upstage near the *skene* got in the way of the doors and blocked the *eccyclema*. The eventual compromise was to build the *skene* and its doors higher, with what we think of as a stage permanently in front of it. That now looks absurdly obvious. To Forethought's brother, Afterthought, everything is obvious, which makes him a smug fellow. By the next century that raised stage was high and separated chorus from cast; almost all dramatic action was eventually done up there, and theatricality took on a greater remove. The stage was probably low at first, adding more fluidity than awkwardness.

A more noted addition of these decades, people believe, was that hoist to dangle an actor godlike in the air above a scene, the famous derrick of the *deus ex machina*. One term for it is *granion*, "crane," the counterweighted pole that unlades a ship and, like our word, also the long-necked water bird. Sophocles rarely if ever used the crane.

Talking of the flight of Aeschylus' Daughters of Ocean, I admitted my personal prejudice: that device disconcerts me to visualize. The side-to-side swing of the rope is one problem, the high, looming pole is a worse one. I'd rather picture the machine as a platform lowered by paired pulleys from the *skene* eaves a bit like window cleaners' stagings on the verticals of our high rises. That would at least never revolve; it would be within the capacity of Greek engineering, and most of the mechanism would be out of sight in the building. Actually, of course, no one knows what that *mechene* ("machine") was like; there were variants. What was it like *here* in the home theater of Dionysos during these formative years? Euripides is thought to have found that machine very much to his purpose. It puts his gods exactly where he seemed to want them, dangling between the miraculous and the absurd. Still, though much been said of his use of *deus ex machina*, none of the intruding divinities who close the surviving plays actually needs to descend to the stage. Speech from the rooftop would do, except in one very late play, his *Orestes*; in that a god looms above people on the roof. Perhaps by 410 the crane, in all its awkward ineptitude, was in use. I think the *mechene* was invented for comedy, and a later, spectacle-hungry era put it to use in tragedies after they'd grown accustomed to it.

I left off sketch-mapping Athenian current events at the time of Sophocles' *Antigone*, near the low end of the 440s. The Parthenon was being finished about then, and Phidias' fabled gold and ivory colossal Athena was arising within it, a triumphant replacement for that old olivewood goddess the Persians had burnt and Aeschyus had memorialized in *The Eumenides*. A first "Panhellenic" colony in Italy, Thurii, where Greeks from any city could be citizens, had been founded by Athens at Pericles' instigation and was now thriving in its third year. A so-called Thirty Years' Peace between Athens and Sparta was in a hopeful sixth year — Pericles had succeeded in escaping ostracism for supporting it. It really was the best of times.

The worst of times. A quarrel blew up between two Ionian members of the Delian League. Athens, for its own reasons, sided against the bigger, the island of Samos. Samos tried to withdraw from the League; Pericles followed Cimon's precedent with Naxos and his own with Euboea. The Athenian fleet attacked — and Sophocles was with Pericles among the elected generals.

A hideous tale is told of the defeated Samian leaders. Until recently I did not accept it; many lies attach themselves to a commander like Pericles. Supposedly the captured Samian leaders were left, tied to planks in the marketplace for days, then finally beaten to death with clubs. That was widely enough believed in Athens for one gutsy woman actually to reproach Pericles with it loudly in the agora. It would have been his style to listen gravely, then turn his back and walk away. As an American in 2005, who am I to say it did not happen? Quite possibly the torture was committed by Samians upon Samians, for Samos was savagely divided between its oligarchs and its democrats, but one thinks of what our own officials have nodded to and winked at in restive client nations, from Chile to Iraq. The pattern of torture by proxy behind screens of plausible denial is as familiar to us as it was to

Euripides. Torture inevitably turns angers into sacred causes. The distinction between a sacred cause and savagery is uncertain.

It was eight or ten years before the winged evils the Samian action let loose came home to roost in Athens itself, yet they came. The Peloponnesian Wars are often dated from 431, but the formality of declaring war was as sketchy then as it has lately again become. When it convenienced leaders to call attacks war, they called them war; otherwise the killings and burnings were defensive police actions, internal conflicts, exercises, preemptive strikes, what have you. Greeks were less apt to use euphemisms than we but just as quick to trade principles for opportunisms. The Thirty Years' Peace was soon a mere euphemism. Thucydides, an Athenian who lived through all but the very last catastrophe, saw the Spartans' turning away of Cimon's aid, way back in 462, as the moment when both combatants first showed their teeth. The Spartan rulers were very atypical oligarchs, empowered not by wealth but by hereditary status. They were a warrior class, a throwback in social evolution, living almost as roving chieftains had once lived, but in a settled world that had developed a new order. No wonder that, as Thucydides said, "Spartans were afraid of the boldness and innovative thinking of Athenians."

From our distance the Peloponnesian Wars seem a clear struggle between a Spartan collective way of life and an Athenian individualistic one. From close up it is messy, entangled and irrational. Throughout the century's thirties many Athenians thought now of Corinth, now of Thebes or some other city as the major enemy, and Athens struck often at her potential smaller allies. The deep problem was that most cities had a democratic faction who wanted popular rule and an oligarchic faction who wanted to see a small, tight senate of the privileged in charge. Dues to Athens' League of Delos (rapidly becoming Athens' "empire") weighed most obviously on oligarchs, whose gold and silver paid those dues. Naturally those men looked to alliance with Sparta. The democrats, people ground down to pay rents that created that gold and silver, usually looked (shortsightedly) to Athens. Those two factions kept town after town in revolutions and counter revolutions. "The Xians did this," almost always means, "The democrats (or oligarchs) in power at X did this although the oligarchs (or democrats) out of power opposed it." *Class war* is a feared, almost inadmissible term in English-speaking countries just now, but we might as well face it, class conflict is native to democracy. It is hope and greed at work;

only old feudalism or new totalitarianism can keep such impulses underground.

The eventual roster of alienated allies, atrocities, counter atrocities, deportations, slaughters, made and broken treaties tells of a foreign policy in both cities gone from dim-sighted to blind. There is reason to believe that the cutting of trees for huge fleet after fleet, built and sunk in the course of the Peloponnesian Wars, gradually deforested stretches of Greece, leaving the crags and wasted soil we find so picturesque today. Sheep and goats still thrive in their root-gnawing way, but this is no landscape to feed the herds of horses and proud horned cattle that once grazed or to sustain the deep groves of oak and beech whose mast fatted the boars and whose leafy shadows hid the lynxes and the bears. Even the shrewdest philosophers saw no connection between natural disasters and collective behavior.

All city dwellers must either go mad or walk unhalted every day past much misery — the beggar at the corner, the dog-in-office in high place, the veteran without eyes. Most of us at last turn away from the big evils into private concerns. But Sophocles? The big evils were his theme, so how did he live and share in what Athens was becoming? I ask not because the question is answerable but because it is apt. Such men as Sophocles take a pride in holding aloof from a descent into savage indignation. Angry pity risks appearing self-serving, though it serves the self badly. It seems wiser to face the pains of others with stoicism just as one faces one's own. Sophocles held on to equanimity. To achieve that aristocratic stance, you certainly don't have to be well-to-do, but the insulation helps. Sophocles' focus on the individual psyche is an excellence; it is also his limitation. Among moral imperatives he chose patriotism and clung to it. A person can be shortsighted and yet see at close range with wonderful sharpness.

From 432, when the war became undeniable and open, to almost the end of the century, Athenians lived in an off-and-on state of siege within their city walls each time invaders marauded and encamped.* Foresight had expanded those walls an implausible five miles to the seaport, and Pericles' unshakably imaginative faith in his city foresaw that it could survive without its countryside, a kind of navy beached on a rock — *if* it could hang on to its "allies," its empire of islands. But

---

*If you care to sort out further the situation in Athens at that time, the six pages of chapter five in Donald Kagan's The Peloponnesian War *(Viking, 2003)* explain with fine clarity how things stood in 431 B.C.

not enough of the dead were buried, nor enough privy pits dug. War, as it happened, was to bring plague and change all plans.

Euripides lacks Sophocles' equanimity. His protests are smoky torches, they don't always shed light, but the sparks from them burn. Inevitably, Euripides is the tragedian our films have the best luck with. *The Trojan Women* with Katherine Hepburn and Vanessa Redgrave is very fine (though it leaves out a crucial prologue of angered gods who tell how storm will drown these women along with their captors); *Iphigenia* with Irene Papas as Clytemnestra is superb, and Zoe Caldwell electrifies the video of a staged *Medea*. I won't compete on paper with things like that. No production is definitive, but a good one can be worth many thousand words, and each of those media versions has that worth.

The Medea, on stage, page or tube, gets to us as few other ancient plays do (except, I hope, *The Trojan Women*) and shows a Euripides as conscious of gender as of war policy. It gave him a reputation as a woman-hater, although it proves the opposite. The original, folkloric Medea was the bad witchwoman, the stepmother who tried to kill young Theseus, Athens' national hero. (Theseus' father, Aegeus, walks briefly and rather randomly into *The Medea*, a nod to the folktale or to another drama.) The play's Medea is an agonized, abandoned human, wronged to clear-eyed madness. At the close she does transform back into fairy tale's evil sorceress with a flying snake chariot (a snake doorway in the video). That display of magic in the finale contradicts the reality, her helpless lack of any recourse other than child-murder. Often it is Euripides' strategy to give us back our preconceptions about a story just before he leaves it. My private rationalization of that final moment is that in it we are seeing from inside Medea's madness: the flight and the snake chariot are a hideous illusion of righteous power that her murders have given her. A Sophoclean heroine would wake from madness to realize what she had done. Euripides is different.

The Medea segments of the Franca Rame/Dario Fo pieces known in the United States as *Orgasmo Adulto Escapes from the Zoo* amplify and contemporize but do not much distort the outraged essence of Euripides' play. The original still is contemporary.

From the first, but especially in later works, Euripides brings myths down to earth; at times he rolls them in mud. Is he being ironic; is he mocking the story he tells; is he being gory and melodramatic to please a debased audience or deliberately daring an over-refined one to be displeased? A writer who roves about in a deep, creative, personal unease may do many things. Euripides is not an easy writer. I think he is often not even a good one. Just great, incontrovertible.

Sophocles wrote an *Electra* (in the 420s?), and Euripides wrote his *Electra* around 413. So have many since. The story has intergenerational conflict, guilt, the quest for justice, the recurrence of evil, loyalty of kin, return of the outcast, divine ambiguity; there is room for almost any theme or portrait of type a writer could want. Richard Strauss's opera *Elektra* is from Hofmannsthal's vitriolic near-translation of Sophocles; Eugene O'Neill constructed a whole Civil War–era trilogy, *Mourning Becomes Electra,* on Aeschylus' outline. Giraudoux and Sartre each used the myth on which to hang philosophy. Aeschylus focused on the son; Sophocles and Euripides focus on the daughter. In *The Oresteia* Electra is driven and angry but vulnerable and uncertain. Her first exchange with the Chorus is full of questions; she leans on them for advice, and questions recur in her talk with Orestes till they become part of her character. When she vanishes from the play she leaves a sense of question behind. Sophocles and Euripides came up with strong answers.

Sophocles opens his *Electra* just before a sunrise (pre-play ceremonies now meant that first play of the day didn't start till almost sun up). The setting is the palace gate, Agamemnon's tomb is offstage. Orestes, with Pylades (silent) and the tutor whom Electra years ago sent him away with, enter even more warily than in Aeschylus. To gain an entry, they have brought an urn as proof of Orestes' death. At wails from within they retreat. Electra emerges. She, as the play's core, will be in tortured suspense about Orestes' return until almost the end. She has endured years of her mother's bad treatment and has given back still worse in insult and spite. A sympathetic chorus of Argive women share her grief but are frightened of her anger. We see her contrasted with a milder-natured sister; we see her under threat of burial alive for refusing to forget her father or let any in the household forget. We see her in confrontation with her mother. Clytemnestra justifies killing the man who sacrificed Iphigenia; Electra hurls back insults at Clytemnestra's taking her fellow murderer as lover. Clytemnestra cries her exasperation to the neighbor women.

C: There is nothing that she would not do!

Sophocles has Electra reply:

E: Let me tell you, though you'll not believe it, I am ashamed of
what I do. I hate it. But it is forced on me, despite myself, by your
malignity and wickedness.
[Sophocles, *Electra*, H. D. F. Kitto translation,
Oxford Univ. Press, 1994]

This Electra is intricate; she does hate herself and knows her self-righteous fury is a sickness. She actively seeks abuse; wrongs done her prove that her father was wronged. In this vision of the House of Atreus, passions are more ramified and moral issues more tangled. Clytemnestra seems a creature in the grip of circumstance and probably of Aegisthus, sinned against and sinning.

Sympathy is swung back to Electra when the tutor, ensuring that the urn-bearing young men will be let in, draws out his long account of Orestes' death in a chariot race. He spares no circumstance; his gruesome tale can seem tedious. I think Sophocles intends to let us watch Electra writhe at the story while Clytemnestra stands unmoved. Our Anglo-Saxon taste for the less demonstrative makes this a tricky scene for us. The broad reactions Electra needs to show here can feel pantomimic from any but a very great performer.

The Queen has heard that Orestes had talked of an avenging return, and she endures news of his death with grimly pursed lips.

C: What bitterness if I must lose a son to save my life!
There is strange power in motherhood; however terrible
her wrongs, a mother never hates her child.
[Sophocles, *Electra*, Kitto translation]

Electra is crushed and Sophocles continues to twist her, flashing glints from the many sides of her darkness as from a faceted jet bead. First her sister runs in, jubilant, having found a lock of offering hair on their father's tomb. Electra's despair will see no glimmer of hope, but the courage of her anger boils over. If a male heir to kill the killers is dead, she herself will do it. In a world where women should accept fate passively, she is her mother's daughter. Aegisthus is away; Electra determines to kill him with her own hands when he returns.

Beauty of sound not being our poetry's strong point, we can miss the juxtaposition of the terrible and the lovely that makes great tragedy disconcerting and mystifying. When Electra and Chrysothemis have quarreled stingingly, the Chorus, like family members quietly picking up shattered plates from a dinner table overthrown in rage, sings this, or words to this effect:

> When I observe
> The wise, small care of birds
> For fledglings that cry in the nest,
> How feeding and tending
> They hover and give,
> Why, I ask Heaven and Zeus,
> Is it hard for us to serve
> Our kin in love?
>
> Voice
> That sinks to the dead,
> Carry a bitter word
> To Atreus' son in the underworld
> Of wrongs new made.
>
> Tell him how ill his house,
> Tell him his own two children,
> Bickering, rancorous, sullen,
> As flickering heartaches rouse them,
> Make strife with one another,
> Old harmony forgotten.
> Tell him Electra, forsaken
> Is down in the waves and stricken,
> Ready to leave the light.
>   [my own very free adaptation]

Then the men bring the urn. Electra begs to hold it; she cradles it and weeps. She is so unwashed, wasted and poorly dressed that Orestes assumes she is some beggar. With slow shock he realizes this is his princess sister. She is shackled to misery, but the sight of their father's ring convinces her that Orestes is alive.

They exult and Orestes is let into the palace. The mother-son confrontation, huge in Aeschylus, here is just offstage voices. Electra is at the center of the picture; dramaturgically the Queen must be pushed to the side. Clytemnestra's death cry slashes the stillness, and Electra shows manic relief but unappeased rage. She has stayed out-of-doors for her final task, to delay Aegisthus if he returns too soon — and soon he does, lured by word that Orestes' remains have been brought. He sneers about the news to Electra.

> A: It will have special interest for you.
> E: I know. Of course I know. I loved my brother;
>   How then should I make little of his death?

A: Then tell me where these men are to be found.
E: In there. They've won their way to Clytemnestra's heart.
A: And is it true that they have brought this message?
E: More than the message. They brought Orestes too.
A: What, is the body to be seen?
E: It is; I do not envy you the sight.
A: You rarely meet me so pleasantly.
E: If this proves to your liking, you are welcome.
   [Sophocles, *Electra*, Kitto translation)

The palace doors open on Orestes, Pylades and a shrouded body. Still Aegisthus misunderstands.

A: Citizens of Argos, look!
   If there is any that had hopes in him,
   That hope lies shattered. Look upon this body
   And learn that I am master — or the weight
   Of my strong arm will make you learn the lesson.
E: I need no teaching; I have learned at last
   I'll have to live at peace with those that rule....
A: Call Clytemnestra, if she is at hand.
O: She is not far away....
   [Sophocles, *Electra*, Kitto translation]

Aegisthus lifts the cloth, and everything is over for him. And for us, with jolting abruptness. The Chorus briefly declares these descendants of Pelops winners of their own deliverance and leaves.

There was a shrine to the Furies out at Sophocles' beloved Colonos, but he does not summon them here to close his play. Fury has been internalized. Exchanges like that between Electra and Aegisthus taught the audience to savor dramatic irony, a moment when a chasm opens between what a line means to the speaker and what it means to the hearer. In grim contexts Sophocles sails that device close to the rocks of laughter, but the old world was not finicky about cruel humor. Irony was no more jagged than many other facts of their life, and a growled chuckle does not wreck a tragedy.

There can be dramatic irony of action as well as of speech. Sophocles' *Oedipus the King* is one long sustained irony; the King mocks the blind prophet while groping throughout the play with eyes wide open for what lies starkly before him. There is dramatic irony in almost everything Oedipus says.

The brilliant, ear-scraping harshness of Strauss's *Elektra* can seem as close as any modern version to the tone Sophocles strikes. Is dissonance (a chasm between what we feel two notes *should* do and what they do) to music what irony is to speech? Strauss's opera sticks close to Sophocles' plotline, and at its end Electra drops to the ground. We presume she has died — of exhaustion? — of extreme elation? — of having no further function in life? It's a fit closure. In the absence of stage directions, it almost might be what Sophocles intended. Certainly whoever played the role would want Electra to fall on the platform beside her half-shrouded mother and be drawn into the palace as the Chorus walks out. No plotline can show how vivid this tormented woman may seem onstage. Those who had the luck to see Fiona Shaw play her can testify.

Sophocles has here shaped a play that does not fall into halves, and none of his plays that follow will do that. He has come to value a very powerful unity of action.

Could *The Electra* have been a part of a trilogy? It does not feel like one, though that would explain the abrupt ending. To give a nod to a suggestion I don't accept, Electra does accuse her mother of sleeping with and *bearing children of* Aegisthus, and Aegisthus at point of death says,

> The house of Pelops must, it seems, behold
> Death upon death, those now and those to come.
> [Sophocles, *Electra*, Kitto translation]

Obscurer versions of that cursed family's tale gave Clytemnestra and Aegisthus a boy, Aletes, and a girl, Erigone. Lost plays by Sophocles had those names, so possibly talk of those children sets up further plays. A cycle? If there was a trilogy, then Electra's tortured inner life was not Sophocles' only theme. Still, it is the theme we have — and more than enough.

The play could have been written for any space. Give it a doorway, an *eccyclema* and an urn and it will ask for little else. *The Oedipus Rex* does not even need the *eccyclema*. Just maybe the gifted Agatharchos of Samos painted no more scenery for Sophocles after the Samian campaign.

Euripides, though he won seldom, was again and again among the three to compete. One half suspects the archons who kept granting him a chorus of using him as a quintain to be knocked over so Sophocles and others could triumph. Another guess is that he was included in the Dionysia in later years as a sop to a growing minority, the "Peace Party."

Euripides' music was not his own composition—yet another degree of drift from playwright to playwrite. He befriended a younger musician, the non-citizen Timotheus of Miletos. Timotheus' music "illustrated," people said, and he was so radical an inventor (of a lyre with an unheard-of eleven strings) that critics grew vituperative. Timotheus was seriously suicidal when Euripides first collaborated with him, encouraged him and foretold that Greece would one day hail him. The judgment proved right.

Euripides also counted Anaxagoras as a friend and a teacher. One of the causes thinking persons might have found for disillusion in Athens was the undercurrent of public animosity to Anaxagoras' adventuring mind. Mind was his God, a First Cause too remote to traffic in oracles or in Olympian intelligent design. General dislike of Anaxagoras' sort was at last to burst out in a set of trials after 432, when open war undermined the Periclean circle. The great leader's last two years were wretched, a struggle with political enemies and lawsuits. His friends were attacked. Anaxagoras had to leave the city to save his life. It is not surprising that Euripides held as aloof from public affairs as he could or that his most enigmatic plays were written after 432, when Anaxagoras had been driven away. Euripides himself was later twice harassed by indictments; the charge brought against him in 410 B.C. was impiety.

Euripides had quirks as playwright that don't endear themselves to us. He carried the separation of chorus from story line even further; his choral songs sometimes can seem mere intermezzi. (Did Timotheus' strange music link them to the event in subtle ways? The conscientious will puzzle over what the myths in those songs have to do with the unfolding story; the casual will lean back and let the verbal weaving happen.)

Euripides often relied on prologues. Critics bristle at a prologue as weak form, but launching a play by direct storytelling looks us frankly in the eye and says, "You are here for a tale, we are here to tell one." It is illusion *not* concealing illusion. But the magician who shows you how one trick is done has another up his sleeve. Euripides is high-handed with myths; when he chooses an unusual version, a prologue adjusts our preconceptions to his reimagining.

Euripides' own audience noticed his focus on women—too negative, some said; others thought him suspiciously sympathetic. That reaction may have been in part fashion: drama had always given women a voice unusual in Athens, but toward the end of the century comedians let them speak so bluntly that more people began to notice it and complain.

Once in a while Euripides let himself create a surprising sad sweetness, a retreat into a gentler world without apparent irony. We glimpse the universe he'd have preferred to the one he was given. *The Iphigenia in Tauris* is almost genial. It shows that its day's idea of tragedy was still open-ended. In it Iphigenia was not sacrificed at Aulis but spirited off to a foreign temple by Artemis. There she at last meets her brother, Orestes, saves him in his turn from sacrifice and they escape happily homeward. It is easy to tell any play's plot in a way that trivializes it. Goethe and many good minds since have thought highly of *Iphigenia in Tauris*. Perhaps it just does not sort well with our current moods. Euripides was omnivorous, with a taste for sweet as well as bitter. The play's characters have a nostalgic love for Greece, the good patriotism that is not proud but warmhearted, not exclusionary but embracing. I'd not know how to stage it without making it bland, but perhaps somebody would. Isadora Duncan wanted to dance it — she may have been silly at times, but nobody would call her bland!

That tenderness and positive patriotism merge with horror of war in Euripides' *Suppliants*. The story deals with the miseries of the bereft after the failed attack of the seven against Thebes. It is a play filled with the clamor of widows and orphans, and Theseus (that is, Athens) is drawn into the hapless fighting. The audience could not have missed what was aimed at. For us this is not as powerful an antiwar piece as it might have been, just because no *Iliad* casts a vivid side light on victims of the Theban War to give them extra depth. Hecuba in *The Trojan Women* is every refugee's grandmother; the widowed suppliant, Evadne, is a stranger. One minor staging puzzle of *The Suppliants* is that the chorus is specifically the mothers of the fallen seven. The tragedies were not labouredly literal, but it would be impossibly odd if there were the traditional twelve chorus members on stage. Is this one more hint that rules of competition were not rigid — or does it show a wartime scaling back of production?

When younger and wiser, I was impatient with Aristotle's definition of a tragic hero: an outstandingly fine person flawed, usually by *hybris*. *Hubris* (spell it as you will) is translated now as arrogance, overweening pride. In Athens *hybris* meant out-of-bounds behavior including assault, pillage and rape. Overweening pride *is* a vice of many male central characters in the tragedies, but it seems a stretch to apply it to most women other than perhaps Clytemnestra and Medea. Certainly it is inapplicable to the widows in *The Suppliants*. Some charge of pride can be laid against any self-respecting person. Aristotle makes it essential to the best tragedy, but if we fault Antigone, Iphigenia or even proud old Hecuba for hubris, the term must mean almost anything a human can do except be abjectly inert.

The dramatic heroines are to be wondered at. In Athens good women led lives that appall us in their restriction, yet the range of women in the comedies and tragedies is astonishing. They are courageous, wicked, blazingly honest, slyly subversive, gentle, bold, impulsive, persistent, frail, strong, stupid, very wise — in short, often more human than their menfolk. You would never guess the conditions of an Attic upper-class woman's family life from these plays. Sometimes theater is not about the surface of its audience's lives but about what flows under the soil. Although Roman women had greater freedom, Latin theater, such as it is, shows us only the shrew, the silly maidservant, the sweet, young thing (briefly and mutely) — and that's about all. Did Rome's ladies move about more freely because its men hardly saw them, even in plays?

Some contemporary scholars, weary of dead white males, point out that those characters in the Athenian tragedies are not women. They were written by men, it is argued, and played by men; they are male projections. But that objection challenges all imagination. Is Brontë's Heathcliff no man; is Austin's Darcy no man or, well, boy at least? If you feel authors are confined to their own gender, their own nationality, their own social class, their own direct experience, then for you fiction is only valid when it is veiled autobiography. Plato in his late work *The Republic* (like Solon in crotchety age) wants to exclude poets as liars. These contemporary theorists strike me as equally strict. They deny our imaginative capacity for empathy.

Athens was, for women, a special and bad case. In Ionian and Aolian islands (where Sappho had lived and where the love of Pericles' life, Aspasia, came from), conditions were freer. In Athens itself many lived outside the stiff codes of the old citizenry, and mental life profited from that elbowroom. Remember how Pericles as a younger politician back in 451 had pleased voters by promoting legislation to exclude from citizenship any whose mothers were not citizens. In 432 he learned to his bitter cost how mean-spirited isolation of the alien is. Aspasia had borne him a son, and the state would not accept the boy as one of its own! Instead, his enemies contrived to put Aspasia on trial, and Pericles, who had been so proud never to rely on emotional display, openly wept in court to save her. Given human migration, we are all immigrant strangers. No one is autochthonous.

It was in 430 that things had gone so badly that the country populace of Attica withdrew behind the walls the city had spent the last sixty years building. Filthy conditions followed; plague erupted. (Cholera, bubonic, malaria — the plague gets variously named. Twenty-five centuries of microbe evolution can alter diseases unknowably.) The death toll was horrific. Pericles died, noted even among the tens of thousands mourned.

Euripides' humane temperament is one we might expect love stories from. Love affairs play an unobsessive role in tragedies and even comedies of the dazzling century. Eros gets little time onstage. Haemon loves Antigone, and in Aeschylus' *Suppliants* Hypermnestra must love the bridegroom she spared. *The Women of Trachis* and *The Medea* show wreckage prior loves have left, but there are no Juliets and their Romeos. Love as theme in Euripides' *Hippolytus* is a ravaging sickness divinely sent to punish chastity. Sophocles in old age was asked if he still had affairs. He answered no, thank the gods, he had outlived that madness. Erotic love was seen as a seizure, profoundly sweet while it lasted but a thing to awaken from and get on with life. Homosexual couples are even rarer on stage than heterosexual ones, though love between men was accepted all round the Aegean. With no trace of it on the surface of the tragedies and only jokes in the comedies, Greek homosexuality, I used to suspect, was a private preserve of the literate. Theater, I supposed, excluded it because theater was an art for everyone. However, names and fragments of lost plays (Aeschylus' *Lovers of Achilles*, for instance) hint that the absence of homosexual and heterosexual lovers is due more to the Byzantine monks who copied the plays than to Athenian restraint. Many titles refer to myths that offer dramatic possibilities only if treated as love stories. Certainly the life of Electra is loveless, except for her love of a brother she knew only as a baby.

Of the parallel *Electras*, *The Electra* of Euripides is last and strangest. I've risked the generalization that Aeschylus was the philosophical tragedian and Sophocles the psychological one. To complete a triad of oversimplifications, call Euripides the bizarre tragedian. His *Electra* veers from the traditions. Playwrights were seeking out variations on a huge but finite number of myths. A young contemporary playwright, Agathon, actually had begun making up his own plots. But the wackiness of *The Electra* is unique. If we had only Shakespeare's *Titus Andronicus*, we would call him a disturbed semi-genius who wrote a few scenes horribly well. We'd draw the same conclusion if we had only Euripides' *Electra*. But we would not dismiss that play. Along with eccentric melodrama it has unique social realism.

Euripides starts with a prologue. A dirt farmer in front of his home in the hills near Argos talks frankly to us, recounting the evils of the House of Atreus from a commoner's viewpoint. His speech is as simple, sour and healthy as goats' milk. Homer can be down-to-earth; an old master's dog may lie on a dung heap in a royal courtyard and slaves and lords toil, talk and die together, but Homer passes no reformer's judgment on how his world works. In Euripides' *Electra* the barriers between wealthy rank and commoners' poverty buckle with class rancor. We are in a society uneasy with itself, high and low scrape against one another as disquietingly as in Athenian politics.

The farmer, Electra's husband, tells us that when a household servant saved Orestes from Aegisthus' fist and sent him to distant friends, Electra was still a child. She was not her brother's rescuer. Later, "when the burning season of young ripeness took her," he says, great princes came begging her bridal and Aegisthus was afraid. Aegisthus kept her unmarried and then, fearing an unwed pregnancy, planned to kill her. Her mother, Clytemnestra, saved her. Aegisthus settled for proclaiming a price on Orestes' head and degrading Electra by marriage to a commoner. The farmer tells us that his family was local,

> ...in breeding they shone bright enough, but in their fortune
> they ranked as paupers, which blots out decent blood.
> [Euripides, *Electra*, Vermeule translation]

Lines like that recur in Euripides with personal bitterness; he did not like to hear whispered that his mother had sold onions. Electra, says the farmer, is still virgin:

> I would feel ugly holding down the gentle daughter
> of a king by violence. I was not bred to such honor.
> [Euripides, *Electra*, Vermeule translation]

Electra comes out of their hut to go to the spring, water jar on head like any country wife. Their brief talk makes clear that this couple share a humane respect. She says,

> I am not forced, I chose this slavery myself
> to illuminate Aegisthus' arrogance for the gods.
> [Euripides, *Electra*, Vermeule translation]

She does not blame her man for their bitter life, nor he her. They go to their daily work.

Orestes and Pylades enter. Again Pylades seems a mute role. In this play and in Sophocles' version some lines could logically and effectively be his. Since scripts did not always indicate speakers, could it be that later transcribers assigned him no lines simply because of the three-speaker tradition?

Orestes has secretly sacrificed at his father's grave but will not risk going into the city; he is skulking here in the outback to get at his victims when they are away from their fortress. He also hopes to pick up news of his sister, who, he has heard, has been married to some farmer.

> Quick now! I see some sort of serving girl approach
> with a jar of fountain water on her shaven head —
> It looks heavy for her. Let us question the slave.
> [Euripides, *Electra*, Vermeule translation]

Electra's reentry is a startling gymnastic "turn," a folk dance with water jar on head. Weirdly, she dances to a passionate song of mourning. The eccentricity has to be intentional; it foreshadows how anomalous things are going to get. As the hidden men watch, a Chorus of country girls comes to tell how the city folk are making a festival pilgrimage through these parts on their way to Hera's shrine. Aegisthus is among them. They urge Electra to come; when she says her filthy hair* and torn rags don't fit a festival, they offer to lend her a dress. With that kind, folksy touch we could be in Yorkshire, the Yucatan, Appalachia or anywhere. Electra says no, she'd rather waste her life

---

* *"Filthy hair ..." "shaven head"? Which should it be? Probably "cropped hair" would translate Orestes' description better.*

> ...like wax in the sun,
> thrust and barred from my father's home
> to a scarred mountain exile
> while my mother rolls in her bloody bed
> and plays at love with a stranger.
> [Euripides, *Electra*, Vermeule translation]

Electra talks of her mother's sexuality and of her own barrenness till it becomes one of her themes.

The women see strangers, and there is genuine fear of unknown men in this countryside. When Electra cannot run past them to the hut, she actually kneels and begs not to be raped. The sight of this heroine kneeling terrified to a pair of men in her own dooryard undercuts any last preconceptions the audience has brought. This is not Agamemnon's undaunted daughter as portrayed before. Every detail seems planned to jolt, to demythologize the story and jostle its conventions.

An Athenian comedy had a traditional moment called the *parabasis*, a word that means both "stepping forward" and "an indiscrete rudeness." The Chorus leader, who might be the playwright himself, would stroll front, action stopped and he or the whole Chorus spoke their mind in a long riff, scolding, mocking, instructing the city with biting humor. He might tackle any problem or any person, since saying the outrageous was the comic muse's privilege and purpose. Euripides preempts the indiscretion of comedy now and brings it into tragedy. Orestes, talking to his sister, is suddenly haranguing the audience, an angry critic of them and their manners. I can only believe that the actor's stage move signaled to the spectators that this was, in fact, a *parabasis*.

> We look for good on earth and cannot recognize it
> when met with, since all our human heritage runs mongrel.
> At times I see descendants of the noblest family
> grow worthless though the cowards had courageous sons;
> inside the soul of wealthy men bleak famine lives
> while minds of stature struggle trapped in starving bodies.
>
> How then can a man distinguish man, what test can he use?
> The test of wealth? That measure means poverty of mind.
> Of poverty? The pauper owns one thing; the sickness
> of his condition, a compelling teacher of evil.
> By nerve in war? Yet who, when the spear is cast across
> his face will stand to witness his companion's courage?
> We can only toss our judgments random on the wind.

> This fellow here is no great man among the Argives,
> not dignified by family in the eyes of the world —
> he is a face in the crowd and yet we choose him champion.
>
> Can you not come to understand, you empty-minded,
> opinion-stuffed people, a man is judged by grace
> among his fellows; manners are nobility's touchstone?
> Such men of manners can control our cities best,
> and homes, but the well-born sportsman, long on muscle, short
> on brains, is only good for a statue in the park,
> not even sterner in the shock of war than weaker
> men, for courage is the gift of character....
> [Euripides, *Electra*, Vermeule translation]

"This fellow here is no great man...." Context has been broken out of. Recall every eye turning to Aristides when a just man was spoken of in Aeschylus' *Suppliants*? You and I, across the gulf of centuries, cannot know who is being flung at here and who is praised, but we can't miss the tone of voice. The fierce, partisan, judgmental function of comedy is conscripted into tragedy; someone the community has slighted is singled out for his undervalued worth. Also note the passing sneer at bodybuilders, a thing hardly met elsewhere among Greeks. Euripides' parents hoped he would be crowned as an athlete; he won some wrestling event as a youngster, but the training must have irked him. Abruptly, as though weary of deaf ears, Orestes turns to reenter the play.

It feels like obligatory melodramatics when Orestes keeps Electra in long suspense, saying he is a messenger from Orestes. Does he lie because of the country girls who overhear him? When he is finally recognized, he does not worry about them. Soon the play turns to gratuitous mockery of Aeschylus' version, a scoff at the idea that anyone could know Orestes had returned by his footprint being like that of his sister or his offering lock of hair being like hers. Those who did not approve of Euripides heard churlishness in that fling at the dead master poet—Aesop's ass kicks the dead lion. In realists' terms the objection is fair. Incorporated into a parallel play, this is literary reference, a newly discovered convolution of irony. Sophocles, too wellbred to mock the ghost of Aeschylus, won't have been displeased when Euripides was that nervy.

We hear more that is clearly about class. Orestes says,

> Uneducated men are pitiless but we who are educated
> pity much and we pay a high price for being intelligent.
> Wisdom hurts.

while a servant's line goes

> Often a noble face hides filthy ways.
> [Euripides, *Electra*, Vermeule translation]

We learn things about Clytemnestra that fit with her saving Electra from Aegisthus' murderous intentions. Electra herself, plotting to lure the Queen from the palace with news of a newborn child, says her mother still cares for her and will weep at the thought of a grandson's low breeding. Sharp ears will hear contradictions that hint at conflicted psyches. Orestes talks of killing his mother yet asks what he must do to "purify this mother from adultery." Apollo has advised him, but the young man still seems vague and needs prompting. In some tellings of the tale it was the community that tried and stoned Clytemnestra after Aegisthus was killed; Orestes' fault was in not intervening to save her. At this point in the play then, since Euripides has made it clear that he is unfolding the myth in his own way, anything still might happen.

Orestes takes advantage of Aegisthus' welcome of strangers to share in his rural banquet to the goddess nymphs at a roadside shrine. The killing (told, not shown) is unheroic, sacrilegious and nasty.

The trapping of the Queen, which we watch, is meaner and just as brutal. She comes, drawn by the lie about a grandchild. When mother and daughter meet, each has one hot speech of blame for what the other has done. Otherwise they talk like any unhappy kin, getting on with a painful relationship because family is what there is. Clytemnestra's side of the encounter seems the more sincere, since we know what Electra is planning. Euripides sketches a vain, depressive socialite, out of her depth, like sad Queen Gertrude in *Hamlet*, or something even more self-defeated. She brings a bevy of captive Trojan girls to attend on her and prefers their touch to her daughter's.

The brother and sister, once they slaughter her, are immediately overwhelmed with regrets. Electra cries out to her brother,

> ...I am guilty!
> A girl flaming in hurt I marched against
> the mother that bore me.

And to the corpse,

> Look, I wrap her close in the robe,
> the one I loved and could not love.
> [Euripides, *Electra*, Vermeule translation]

The siblings lash each other into a frenzy of self-reproach. They are their own Furies.

Then Castor and Polydeuces (uncles in that they are the star-dwelling brothers of Helen and Clytemnestra) appear. They could speak from the rooftop or descend in the crane to underscore their intrusion into a world where they do not belong. They resolve everything and nothing. They summarize what will happen to Orestes pretty much as Aeschylus tells it, and they say, among other things, that it is on Apollo that they place all guilt for this murder. Are they offering a flat condemnation of the god? Many think Euripides intended a grim "Let him who has ears hear." There is insight that knows it is not going to be heeded yet speaks because it cannot hold its tongue. Does any other author from the classical world have intentions interpretable so variously? Usually when we cannot be sure what a writer wants us to feel, it is bad writing. I'd settle for saying that of Euripides' *Electra* if it were not for its context. Its date can be guessed, and date illuminates intent and tone.

The last thing the divine brothers say before they vanish is that they are hurrying off to help a fleet sailing to Sicily. Castor and Polydeuces are the double Saint Elmo of the ancient world, patrons of storm-tossed sailors. Athens had sent out an insanely mis-motivated attack force against Syracuse in 415. Launched with grandiose hopes, it turned into the most disastrous of all the blunders of the Peloponnesian Wars. This play was almost certainly written between the sailing and the news of the fleet's miserable end. Almost certainly. Given Euripides' reckless disgust at war and his skepticism about divine goodwill, I could image him writing it even later, when so many young friends and kin were dead, maimed or hostage slaves. He could have been daring his audience to think out whether gods would aid a strike that had been ill-conceived, preemptive, promoted by lies and mismanaged. A sour irony: after the debacle, a few surviving prisoners of war in Syracuse won themselves better usage from their captors by reciting passages of Euripides!

The background, that campaign, lends rationale to why *The Electra* seems deliberately self-defacing, scribbled over, like one of Francis Bacon's great, horrible paintings. The play is brutish, nasty and brilliant with the reflected glow of the play before it and the plays around it. It was written just after *The Trojan Women*.

There may be other plays where beauty and savagely indignant human decency converge as completely as in *The Trojan Women*, but I don't know them. A Parisian (Anatole France, I think) at the funeral of Emile Zola, called him a "moment in the conscience of humanity." Euripides was that in writing *The Trojan Women*. It breaks (or annihilates) rules for how drama is made, taking up fatal moments of one woman after another, Polyxena (offstage), Cassandra, Andromache, Helen, all daughters or daughter's-in-law of Hecuba. Rules of construction are irrelevant. It indicts us human animals as war makers; it drags us back to old, tedious Troy in ruin and reanimates those women's names, the roster of sufferers. When Hecuba's wordless grandchild, Astyanax, is flung to his death from the walls of his home city, what writing can do, what writing can ask players to do, is done.

What writers and players can do, of course, is not enough. From here on up it is actions that must dig our road into the cliff face — if there is to be a road. Every time another nation makes another war, *The Trojan Women*'s relevance flairs, a livid flush to mark a fever. Korea, Vietnam, Chechnya, Guatemala, Tunisia, Tibet, Uganda, Iraq, Sudan have each, just in our short lifespans, prompted productions of *The Trojan Women* in France, Britain, the United States, Australia, South America, Russia and no doubt all across the globe. Nothing more than what that play says need be said. *Need* be said; things still *will* be said of course. We never shut up; we couldn't bear to.

One of the many extraordinary things about *The Trojan Women* is that it seems to be a rewrite, a "pentimento" (Lillian Hellman's phrase). Back in the mid 1920s Euripides had written a *Hecuba*. In it the Queen has the gruesome satisfaction of blinding at least one of the men who have destroyed her — and killing his children into the bargain. At play's end she is literally dehumanized into a demon dog. Today we lack a capacity for some aspects of tragic drama (I'll speak of that at the end of this book), but the willingness to look at brute violence in the *Hecuba* fits with what our own plays, films and novels can do. Yet Euripides, ten war years after writing the *Hecuba*, looked again at the Queen in the same circumstances, but took away from her even the hideous anesthetic of vengeance. In *The Trojan Women* Hecuba, like most war victims, is left with a nothing that encompasses all.

In *The Trojan Women* Euripides had expressed what he could

sanely express just before the Sicilian expedition; after that he explored madness in *The Electra*, *The Helen* and *The Orestes*. In a maniac world mad plays mean as much as sane ones. *The Helen* holds up absurdly the idea that Helen never went to Troy at all — she waited, chaste and sad, in Egypt for her husband, while the gods duped everyone into battling over a hallucination! That illusory Helen was not Euripides' invention. A Sicilian poet back in Arion's time, Stesichoros, went blind after singing rudely of Helen's elopement with Paris. Stesichoros composed a *palinode* (retraction song) denying that the real Helen had been carried to Troy — and he got his sight back. People must have thought Stesichoros' song a requisite lie to appease a vain heroine goddess. Homer's unvarnished version was the one common even in Helen's home, Sparta, where there was a shrine to her. Out of context Euripides' *Helen* seems romance adventure; in context it shrugs grimly at what men fight and die over.

In *The Orestes* a scramble of characters from the same story, including Helen (this time culpable again), her father, her daughter Hermione and Menelaus, all arrive at the House of Atreus just after Clytemnestra has been killed. All are debunked (that is, rolled out of bed). Everybody reproaches, everybody is filled with self-pity and self-loathing. A frightened servant gibbers absurd Greek. When possibilities of nightmare and opiate seem exhausted, Apollo appears. Orestes is married off by divine fiat to Helen's daughter, whose throat he was at the point of cutting. *The Orestes* is Euripides farewell play to Athens. There were no plays like these again until the twentieth century. Sam Shepard, Joe Orton and Antonin Artaud, collaborating over ouzo, might write *The Orestes*. It feels like yesterday and tomorrow.

To look honestly at the two *Electras* and their companion plays is to see war behind them and around them.

VI

Then and Now

A Twinge

Here in the Theater of Dionysos, 2005, Kim strolls at a bit of a distance, in her own thoughts. I recall reading of traces of a spring under the orchestra floor. Time and earthquake change water courses... In mid thought, a disturbance happens in my head. For a giddy moment trash, mud and the vitals of life well up and swirl together. Trivia about this place, shadows from plays and shadowy notions about the playwrights flood around me like water nixies, babbling fiction and factoid in a whelmed ear. The book *occurs*. The onset of a piece of writing for me often has brought a twinge of panic. To be obligated to so many words...

That minor twinge is followed by a major one. For an eyeblink this downslope of rubble looks like the concentric rings of Dante's Hell. To trace tragedy is to deal with the Peloponnesian Wars, the occasion for *The Trojan Women*. A jab of clarity shows how much *all* the Attic plays were products of war — and how seldom anyone says so. Tradition has us used to the spectacle. We lose sight of how odd, how unlikely a phenomenon tragedies are, how against the grain of hopeful human nature. Tragedy is a unique invention, a scary gift given to the Greeks because the ethical revolution and the freedoms of experimental democracy converged here, allowing the outrageous to be said. Aeschylus carved out a form during a postwar era, but Sophocles and

Euripides, living in wartimes no rational person could take pride in, made that form speak the unspeakable. Sophocles saw psychopathology because war makes psychopaths. Euripides saw the bizarre because war is bizarre. Their plays are owl-eyed in a wartime blackout.

A low voltage revulsion revs motor in my gut. I stare, to my dismayed surprise, through a meniscus of tears. *The Trojan Women* first played here, *here*, some March. This city's young soldiers, obeying orders, had slaughtered towns on the island of Melos and in many places. Some of those kids killed their own cousins. They obeyed. They were brave.

I've said I am here in Greece to remember. It's as true to say I am here to forget. This is no special sensitivity. Hundreds of thousands of my countrymen have been possessed, for months turning into years, with a mounting horror at our political drift. Our nation shares with the Near East a tightening fundamentalism; among us that works in concert with a rapid surrender of any principle. Islamic and Israeli fundamentalism seems to have at least the bleak, helpless excuse of sincerity. We have less of that as our fears preempt our freedoms, our compunctions, our wits.

Like Aristotles' three-mile animal, the whole is too big to take in. The part that for me says it all in one gagging mouthful has been our shrug at torture. Our functionaries discuss torture as "option," "to be left on the table," a proof of hard-willed leadership. They condone torture with a shrug and are not driven down the marble steps of our capitols. We are Athenians. Our governments truly are us, in effect, so we are complicit in all we do not protest. The one U.S. Senator who had himself endured torture as a prisoner made brief remonstrance, and the shamed good-willed felt a sick relief; then party loyalty silenced him. Old Solon put it as well as anyone since: Wrong doing is avoided in the state when people who are not wronged feel the same indignation as those who are. What we have accepted is unretractable; a nod and wink of cosmetic change by the executives only skins and films the ulcer. ("Skin and film" was not first coined about slow-witted kids stripping captives and filming abuses an administration encouraged, but it was coined about a state where something was rotten.)

Back home I'd worked on a satire on the theme of condoned torture — a few scores of like minds chuckled at it and there an end. I'd feared absurdly for my own sanity. To keep the extraordinarily rendered from hanging themselves, do WHINSEC graduates force-feed them valium against depression? I had prescribed myself a tourist trip, but in a journey to the past one finds the present.

Among Athenians, neck-deep, over their heads in their Peloponnesian Wars, their tragedians kept writing. Private life and *surface normalcy* went on in the city while Spartan expeditionary forces ravaged Attica and Athenian expeditionary forces ravaged the islands. That shows perhaps how healthy their body politic had once been. War alternately raged or smoldered from 431 to 404 — a foot soldier's lifetime. Yet every year Dionysia and Lenaea were kept, tragedies were composed and staged, collops from the Trojan War. What was Hecuba to them, that they should weep for her? She was them.

Why, among the innumerable, tedious wars of the world, should these Peloponnesian ones loom at us so? Because, like us, the Greeks almost *knew better*! Their plays, their philosophies, even their statues, pitchers and wine cups testify against them to that. Homer's *Iliad*, with its greathearted picture of the Trojan enemy, shows they knew better. Athenians weren't driven to their preemptive strikes by maniac Great Kings from above nor by brute ignorance from within. As things worsened, it truly was the popular party, the Athenian democrats, who furthered the war.

History does not repeat itself, but it plays recurrent variations on themes. In a theater ruin whose tradition war undid, the Peloponnesian Wars are to me what the Trojan War was to Athenians — far off enough to see the monstrous length of. That double exposure, Argos versus Troy overlaying Athens versus Sparta, accounts for the tragedies of Sophocles and Euripides, the peak and the closure. Those two playwrights sang at the end of a self-rule just before the onset of mammoth imperialisms, Seleucids, Ptolemies, Romans. The exposure looks triple now.

Realities in the theater of the world sit around us on more than 180 degrees of arc. We confront them fully by retreating way upstage. I stand in futile seizure as archaeology cuts open strata under strata of this seeing place. We've been here a long time, watching pride, violence and pride in violence pull down disaster upon our kind.

CITIZEN UNDER COMMODUS (a time of tortures)
    The slave boy sweeps slow, careful raising dust,
    Brushing a mean (in the skylight gold) between
    Effort and disturbance, taking tiles to task
    For being strewn with atoms. He might ask
    This whole evil world to be so clean.
    He simply does the simple chores he must.

> I know, with a small bemusement of contempt,
> His shaved head's crypto-Christian, some new kind
> Of displaced Jew (a fashion in the quarters)—
> Less dirt passed round among maids and porters;
> Honest help gets easier to find.
> One should be grateful good things can be dreamt.
>
> I read Lucretius, thank you, not the news;
> The latest crucifixions in the isles
> Are not new lately. Empire makes decree
> And atomists grow careful of debris.
> I gratefully dream reason, dodging the wiles
> Of guilt gods crouched for trouble. Thank the Muse
>
> For History, she sets me straight, recalling
> Times (say Athens or a golder era) when
> Men like me lived, plainly, fairly well
> Although a scream, say, smuggled from a cell,
> Boiled, a mote in their sunshafts, now and then.
> Now is shrill, a then is less appalling.
>
> As soft as broom straw brushes on baked clay,
> As soft as comfort sleeps its obligation,
> As stealthily as power roots its way
> Beneath this soil, the easements of the day
> Drowse a citizen, a slave, a nation.
> I watch. The dustbins fill. The servants pray.

Ordinariness sets in again. Kim waves from where Pericles' Odeon stood, a casual I'm-here signal. A woman has been walking up the tiers of old seats in my direction. Her tall hiking stick tamps the slope into submission underfoot European style, firm step by step. She looks elderly, with a back that pride wills upright though age would like to bend. At a downhill distance her bearing, Greekness and black dress make this fantasist think, Hecuba, before her ruin but after some nine years of siege might stride like that.

Her interest is in this site; she will not turn aside from her path because I am here, so she passes almost at my shoulder and our eyes meet. Hers are olive-leaf grey, sharp and pale. She nods to my existence and speaks the most ordinary thing one can hear in Greece, "Kalemera." If I understand that much language, her look says, I am worth the greeting; if not, no matter. Not Hecuba. Somebody. She passes upward out of my world into her own.

Greeks do not wish others a good day, as we do, nor peace as Jews and Arabs do, nor bid one another thrive as Slavs do. They wish one's day be beautiful: "*kale.*" They have been saying that to each other for at least three thousand years. Here that word, *beauty*, means good, it means fine, it means happy, sexy, fun, noble, exalted, pleasing to God and to human. Many have recognized it as a key to Greek survival. Linked with the word *day* it affirms the moment. Whatever is past, whatever is to come, be this day beautiful. Often in myth grey-eyed Athena passes unrecognized and leaves some useful gesture of wisdom. Life is no more peaceful for her passing through it, nor more thriving nor more good. But more beautiful? Yes.

"Kalemera, Athena," from a persistent fantasist.

Hubris in a Theater of War

Many Athenians continued to extol their city as savior of Greece, the beacon on the hill, the bastion of freedom. They looked back on their Good War in which they had truly played a leading and genuinely noble part. They could not understand why they were hated. We are in no position to reproach their imaginations for not getting beyond the borders of Attica to grasp what they were doing to their world. The wrongs were not at all one-sided; at Plataea Spartans slaughtered the male population, grandsons of their ally on that battlefield. They herded the women and children into slavery. Cynicism poisoned all mental springs. Small, ruthless bands of Athenian puppets were set up to rule island after island in the name of "democracies." One thinks of the depredations of alumni of the School of the Americas (the Pinochets, the Noriegas) in Central and South America; brutalities supported for what seemed good causes now come home to roost.

At its height Athenian theatrical tragedy arches weirdly over the social tragedy of Athens at low ebb. *Oedipus Rex, Medea, Iphigenia at Aulis*, along with *The Trojan Women*, and *Philoctetes* seem to me (and to better minds) best of the best and were all written in a city sometimes in straits nearly as desperate as Leningrad in 1942. The opening of *Oedipus Rex* demands respect for daring honesty. The play was staged within a year of that devastating pandemic of 430 and 429, brought upon Athens by the war. We should marvel at the granite-hard relevance in Oedipus' first lines:

> The town is heavy with the mingled burden
> Of sounds and smells, of groans and hymns and incense ...
> [*Oedipus Rex*, Grene translation]

Oedipus asks what is happening; the priest who answers points to a representative crowd of plague-stricken citizens either there onstage or, since those invalids are not the play's chorus, just possibly he points to the actual audience! Can Sophocles have been hinting that the best men of Athens provoked the plague the way Oedipus, best of Thebans, had brought plague to his city? Inspired writing sometimes says more than it intends. Theban citizen elders in the opening ode blame Ares, the hated war god, for this plague, and Zeus is begged to drive him away into the sea. War is not the cause of the plague in Oedipus' mythic Thebes, but war brought on the plague of Athens and was understood to have done so. Astonishing. The audience was offered no escapism.

After that plague, one more addition to the holy complex was built up on the Acropolis: the split-level Erechtheion. We know its "Porch of the Maidens," carrying the weight of their house on their heads. The Erechtheion is really three small temples huddled awkwardly into one, exquisite piecework with no overall plan except an eagerness to placate three different gods at once on a budget the war was pinching. Athens craved all the divine friends it could get. It had fewer and fewer human ones.

Aristotle was right to give *hybris* a ruling place in tragedy. It got there, however, by way of current events. Living with such men as Pericles and worse leaders, an awareness of the perils of hubris looms large. The three principle generals of the Persian Wars, Miltiades the Marathonian, Themistocles and the Spartan general/king Pausanias, all fell prey to success. They felt their victories as entitlements, and each was destroyed by his own pride more than by anything else. However well or ill the idea fits figures in tragic plays, it stood out as the flaw of flaws in the realities of public life.

One written tragedy that never played in the Theater of Dionysos is Thucydides' account of the Athenian expedition sent to slaughter the little island of Melos in 416. He writes it as a script. A commander parleys with a representative of the Melians, urging their unconditional surrender. *The Melian Dialogue* lasts longer than a real exchange would between invader and defender, exploring with chill patience the forces at work. No general or diplomat could ever be so honest. It is not in verse, but like a poet Thucydides wrote an x-ray of the diseased interior of the situation.

The Athenian says, mid argument, "You know just as well as we do that justice is only to be had between equal powers and that the strong take what they can while the weak yield what they must." When the Melian suggests a friendly neutrality, the Athenian says, "No, your hostility does not harm us as much as your friendship would, because in our subject cities' eyes that would prove our weakness, while your hatred proves our strength." Thucydides, an Athenian unfairly exiled, had clung to respect for his home city. If he could write *The Melian Dialogue*, what did those who really hated Athens think of her!

In the late throes of the Peloponnesian War Alcibiades came to the fore in Athens, a relative brought up in Pericles' household. There, as a scolded teenager, he'd had the cheek to tell his guardian, "Better not raise a lion in your house, but if you do, treat him like a lion!"* Alcibiades was popular, charming, manipulative, clever and treacherous, an incarnation of entitled hubris. Athens admired him, quoted him, appointed him and followed him to its ruin. He initiated the Sicilian campaign. He betrayed Athens for Sparta, Sparta for Persia and the Persia again for Athens. His feckless adventures could make stuff for tragedies or at least satires on our drunkard thirst for national heroes and missions accomplished. Athens' ruin truly was collective, but Alcibiades embodied in himself its flashy vice.

One play of Sophocles had a title that is not the name of a person nor the choral group; his lost *Hybris*. We don't know who it was about; *what* it was about is obvious. Aristotle, who knew his favorite playwright's works, may have focused on the word especially because it had struck Sophocles as apt.

Though Euripides most noticeably exposes Homer's aggrandized warriors as scoundrels, Sophocles' portrait of Odysseus in his next-to-last play, *The Philoctetes*, carried that impulse to extreme. Homer's age-mates liked tricksters (as long as they were on the home team); later generations noticed that though trickery is comedy to those who think, it is bitter to those who feel. *The Odyssey* is animated by the man's enormous yearning to get home. Nostalgia can be a love; in Odysseus

---

This quote is reconstructed from Plutarch quoting Aristophanes quoting some detractor of Alcibiades — or perhaps Aristophanes quoting Alcibiades bragging about his own insolence. If not literally a thing Alcibiades said to Pericles, it serves as splendidly false, revealing the man.

it is a passion so deep that he himself grows lovable. But in too many stories Odysseus is just a scheming liar. Athens in Sophocles' old age had its fill of such men.

In *The Ajax* Odysseus does the right thing — too late, but he does it. In *The Philoctetes*, the last of his own plays Sophocles lived to stage, Odysseus is nastier. Sophocles did not easily give up the gladder sense of the folk hero as deviser of ways out of tight corners. But by 405 it will have been very hard, even for a poet in his nineties, to have faith in ways out. The city had been desperate after the Sicilian campaign failed, and eighty-some-year-old Sophocles in 411 had been one of a group appointed to select a committee of Four Hundred to govern in that emergency. It was an ill-advised retreat from unthinking democracy into uncaring oligarchy. The Four Hundred, once in command, started spying on fellow citizens and launched government-sponsored murders. Their rule did not last out the year, but it must have haunted Sophocles to have helped them to the power they abused.

The Philoctetes is little known. *The Oedipus Rex* is a superb construct, but I admit I have found it hard to love. *The Philoctetes* is easy. I have never directed it, mostly because it has not a single woman's role, although the right, strong young actress might be fine as Achilles' son, Neoptolemos.

I suspect this plot gave Robert Louis Stevenson his idea for *Treasure Island*: shrewd scoundrel tries to use youngster to steal treasure from a half-mad sailor he had marooned long ago. Philoctetes had been a follower of Heracles, who, dying, bequeathed him a bow and arrows. Troy would never fall until that bow was drawn against it. Voyaging with the Argives toward Troy, Philoctetes trod on a snake in an island shrine. The unhealing bite festered maddeningly, and Philoctetes would scream when the fits of pain shook him. The wound stank. Odysseus had him put ashore on desolate Lemnos Isle and sailed away.

Ten years have passed. Neoptolemos, dead Achilles' son, has joined the Argives, but the siege is at stalemate: the bow left with Philoctetes, it is now learned, is the needed talisman. Odysseus brings Neoptolemos to the island, instructing the boy to befriend the castaway, beg or steal the bow and carry it off. As a good playwright, Sophocles makes the constraints of dramatic compression serve him; Odysseus first tells Neoptolemos the whole truth only as they land. Instead of feeling like bare exposition, the moment shows us the youngster being treated as cat's paw, not as sharer in the scheme. We watch in Neoptolemos the awakening of compassion and moral strength and in Philoctetes the flinty depth of his anger at his wrongers and at the mystery of undeserved suffering.

There is magic in Sophocles' representation of what loneliness has done to the soul of this man. Along with the rancor and anguish he has found a strange love for the beauty of the desolation where he has lived. Nature, the birds, the rocks and the wild nymphs unseen become presences because Philoctetes has made friends of them; the only friends to be had. Sophocles understood the beauty of wilderness and how it can sustain a spirit otherwise starved.

The large decisions in the play are three. Though fame-hungry, the boy gives up the respect of the Argive captains by at last refusing to rob Philoctetes. Philoctetes refuses to exchange his bow even for promise of a restored place in the ranks of the Greeks—better this unutterable loneliness than gratifying Odysseus and others who had treated him so.

The last choice is brought by a divine intervention, but is too powerfully written to feel arbitrary. Heracles himself appears and tells Philoctetes to go rejoin his fellows and be healed. That and young Neoptolemos' decency redeem humanity for this hardy old victim, at least enough to make a return to the common world bearable. Shakespeare's equally late *Winter's Tale* closes with this kind of redemption; the implausibility is swept away in performance by an irresistible swell of verbal music. Did Heracles use the machine hoist? Perhaps, but speaking from the roof would do.

By his Athenian wife, Sophocles had a son, Iophon, a boy with some talent as a poet. Later, by a wife from one of the islands, he had another son, Ariston. In the last of the war years the serene façade of Sophocles' life seems to have cracked. Iophon, they say, was hurt and angered by Sophocles' preference for Ariston's boy, a name-sake Sophocles. If the story is true, Iophon took his father to court on the grounds that the old man had grown vague-minded and could no longer manage family affairs.

Sophocles brought the play he was currently at work on, *Oedipus at Colonos*. In it old, battered Oedipus, driven from home, rages against his rebellious sons—who have learned that his bones will bless any land where they are ultimately buried. Juxtaposed to the bitter fury in the play, the choral lyrics praise the groves and pastures of Colonos. (By now Spartan invaders had hacked those groves down and burnt the fields.) I quoted one verse earlier. Sophocles stood up and read.

> Come praise Colonos' horses, and come praise
> The wine-dark of the wood's intricacies,
> The nightingale that deafens daylight there,
> If daylight ever visits where,
> Unvisited by tempest or the sun,
> Immortal ladies tread the ground
> Dizzy with harmonious sound,
> And have great Bacchos reveler
> For gay companion.
> [Sophocles, *Oedipus at Colonos*,
> Yeats translation, Macmillan, 1934]

The case was dismissed.

I have a conjecture about that story, a piece of fiction; any are welcome to make what they will of it. The trial, remember, took place (if it took place) during the last of the losing war, when divisive recriminations were seething in Athens. The superstitious, patriotic rage that was eventually to kill Socrates was already on boil. Euripides left town. I picture Iophon seeking to have his father declared *non compos mentis* to shield the old man (and the family) from blame for a share in having brought the Four Hundred into power. Sophocles did not appreciate or grasp the motive, and his anger went very deep. Even the wisest of the old live partly in the climates of past years. Sophocles could not have believed himself in any danger from his public; it was easier though bitterer to see in the lawsuit the machinations of a jealous son! The blind rage of Oedipus against his sons at *Oedipus in Colonos* suggested this version to me. Of course there is no drawing real insights into a writer's life from imaginative works.

THE ART OF OLD AGE

We all know (with contempt or empathy) the legitimate conservatism of age. That clutch at what is known and owned comes with the arrival of a real sense that all will soon be lost. There is, I think, in some rare minds, a state beyond that conservatism.

We meet the comic, common version of it in the very old people who will abruptly speak their mind, civil or not, kind or not, relevant or not. We blame their careless frankness on failing wits or deafness and its maddening solitude. But a daring is at work in them, or rather at play, a daring neither cowardly nor brave but free floating. They have one foot not in the grave but definitely off-planet. Great artists who enter that state can leave an extraordinary legacy.

A deep book waits to be written (by someone more knowledgeable than I) called *The Arts of Old Age*. There are Goya's eerie paintings on the walls of his "House of the Deaf Man"; there are Michelangelo's Slaves writhing themselves out of their stone, Ibsen's *When We Dead Awaken* with its onstage avalanche and impossible sculptures, Beethoven's ultimate Quartets. The makers of such things are not recapitulating or clinging; they fling free into strange voids and innovate as daringly as they ever innovated in youth. In *Oedipus at Colonos* a mad nonagenarian takes the plunge into an incomprehensible personal salvation as the rest of his world goes to Hell around him. If you had a happy childhood in some one place, substitute its name for Colonos. "Furious Old Man at the Most Beautiful Spot" would be a Japanese-sounding but fair translation for Sophocles' title. The craftsmanly pride in play construction, demonstrated in *Oedipus Rex* and *The Philoctetes*, is shrugged off. Try reading the plot summaries in circulation of *Oedipus at Colonos*; the play's power is not in its story! Sophocles is off on some expedition with Goya, Michelangelo and Beethoven. I'd love to be able to guess what they seek, what they find. It is definitely not serene resignation. Francis of Assisi spoke familiarly of "brother fire" while he underwent, without anesthetic, a cauterization for cataract. Now that really is an unblinking look at the terrible!

As Sophocles conceives him, the best of Oedipus' times had been rash, we'd say paranoid. The Sphinx could have conceded her riddle and leapt off her cliff just because he was that scary! I've admired *The Oedipus Rex* more than liked it because Oedipus is so brazenly self-righteous. Sophocles does not bother to dovetail facts between that play and this one but his sense of the central character has not at all changed. I suggested an inner Sophocles at odds with an outer one because of these plays. The fictional Oedipus rages in works written far apart from each other but feels completely of-a-piece; he must have been not just thought out but *felt and owned*. Oedipus was some aspect of Sophocles, yet certainly not the persona the playwright turned to the world.

Did Euripides ever touch that kind of creative age I am groping to describe? Euripides' home life we know even less well than Sophocles. He lived very privately. Every birthright Athenian male was subject to public office by lottery but only if he put his name on the list. An *idiotes* like Euripides simply did not bother. He assembled a private library, remarkable in his day. He married twice, both times unhappily. He divorced his first wife for an affair with his own trusted copyist; his second wife left him. He was luckier in his sons and daughters, especially his youngest, Choerile. She, I read in some piece of speculation, was rumored to have helped her father write the plays. That would be fascinating if true; I wish I'd kept better track of odds and ends run across. Choerile's existence has been doubted, by some on the grounds that the name meant "piggy" and had obscene connotations. The same objection can be raised against the name Portia among Romans yet they used that name with cherished daughters. Besides, Euripides will have named her for Choerilus, one of the lost playwrights who rivaled young Aeschylus back in the 480s. Nobody doubts that Choerilus existed. As for names, Aeschylus, which seems to mean "shameful," is just as improbable!

A charge of impiety brought against Euripides in 410 culminated in a trial. He was acquitted, but after the 409 Dionysia he accepted an invitation from the city of Magnesia up in Thessaly. It was time for an *idiotes* to get out of town and by now such northern cities had good theaters of their own. They appreciated drama from Athens and had less desperate finances. (The theater one can find in Magnesia now is built over the one Euripides knew.) Agathon, the inventive tragedian whom Socrates tries to talk with at the end of Plato's *Symposium*, also went north at about the same time.

Euripides moved on from Magnesia the next season, not home but to the court of the great-grandfather of Alexander of Macedon. There he finished his last Athenian tragedies, *Iphigenia in Aulis* and *The Bacchai*. He must have been conscious of the ouroboric snake biting its own tail: *The Bacchai's* subject was the first theme of Arion, the triumph of Dionysos! He could not have known this would be the last tragedy to survive the teeth of time, but he may have felt it was his own last. This *Iphigenia,* unlike his earlier play about her, is a bleak shudder at war-driven human sacrifice, but *The Bacchai* does not feel cynical — it has passed beyond that into a... what? A radiant murk? It feels to me like Art of Old Age. Euripides was only in late middle life by healthy Greek standards when he retired from his city, but *The Bacchai* comes from a different mental realm than the other plays. It makes me suspect that like Shakespeare in retirement he foresaw an end.

Written at a distance from the Theater of Dionysos, *The Bacchai's* staging demands are extravagant: an earthquake shakes down a prison house and frees the young god. The wonderful-sounding mechanical gimmickries of the next two centuries, thunder devices, lightning devices and more, would serve it well. Perhaps the theater structure of the Macedonian king had already surpassed this Theater of Dionysos in technics. There is, after all, something barbarous in the seductive temptations of costly stage apparatus.

The play seems to speak a reversal of all Euripides must have thought and felt in the last twenty years; it is impossible not to take the divine Dionysos in this play profoundly seriously. He, *It,* is a supernatural force, overwhelming and divinely cruel to opposition, as terrible and authoritative as Jehovah, as lightly laughing as a conscienceless child. Dionysos returns to a home city that rejects him, hypnotizes his cousin, King Pentheus, into dressing as a woman and venturing out to spy on the revels of the bacchai, the new cult's frenzied followers. Pentheus' own mother, maddened, is among them as they tear the luckless king limb from limb. She comes on stage with his head as a trophy, and we watch her slowly realize what she carries. Dionysos' last words are a banishment pronounced on all survivors of his own offending family, an uncomfortably resonant closure for an expatriate whose doomed home city had so little welcomed him.

It was told in Athens that Euripides had gone walking alone in the Macedonian king's hunting preserves and been torn to pieces by the royal hunting hounds.

Sophocles in 406 dressed his last chorus in black to salute news from the north of Euripides' death and remind his fellow citizens what they had lost in that writer. Only a very old man could get away with such a gesture at such a time. All around him his city was losing far more than a playwright. Sophocles too died within a few months. The dazzling century's playwrighting and Athens as a power ended almost together.

Charon's Steps

Athens fell in 404 into the brutal hands of a Sparta too exhausted to strangle its victim. The Athenians must have seen their fate as even bleaker than it in fact was. The able-bodied were set to tearing down, stone from stone, the city's defensive walls. Athens was ruined as a political force, powerless beyond its own doorless gates. Would it become a Troy, a deserted mound where solitary herd boys one day might guard a few cows or snare wild thrushes for a pie? As we stare at seemingly inevitable destructions even of the human animal, it is bracing to look at the difference between what was foreseeable in 404 and what actually happened. Athens and life dragged on, often third rate but alive.

In a few years they had enough autonomy once more to put one of their own citizens to death if they chose, and they chose old Socrates. Alcibiades had, as a youngster, been a follower of Socrates. So had Critias, one of the hated oligarch puppets Sparta left briefly in charge of Athens. That tipped the scales. Socrates (like his acquaintance Euripides) was blamed for corrupting a whole generation's morals. A certain Meletos formally laid the charge. Meletos was an unsuccessful writer of tragedies; he succeeded at jurisprudential farce. No wonder Plato, Socrates' loving pupil, grew to distrust poets and democracies as well. The dank little cave, Socrates' prison, over beyond the other side of the Acropolis from here, can still be seen and smelled.

Perhaps Socrates, more fully than any playwright, embodied the way of thinking that made Attic drama and Attic democracy the comates they were. Back some years, while Socrates as a stonecutter could have been among the crews at work on the Parthenon, a young man interested in new philosophy had had the temerity to ask at Delphi who was the wisest man in Greece. With the offhandedness of a power weary of silly questions, the oracle had given for once an unambiguous answer. The wisest man, word from the temple said, was Socrates the Athenian. At the time Socrates was relatively obscure, a talkative eccentric in a city where many exponents of "schools" felt themselves worth the title of wisest. Flabbergasted, Socrates concluded that the oracle was being ironic, that he was wisest in being one who knew that he did not know. Only a profound humility knows that about its knowledge. Such humility produces that brilliantly attractive thing, a true listener. It allows sincere respect for other minds. Socrates clung all his life to that proposition of not knowing, though he believed in the worth of the quest for knowing so passionately that he finally chose to die rather than give it up.

What has that paradox to do with democracy — and with drama? Everything.

Democracy is only worth the struggle and tedium if one believes ("knows," we say incautiously) that individuals have worth just for being individuals. We hold that truth self-evident. Yet we must live with and even respect the voices of people who know things opposed to what we happen to know — things that are therefore (we know) absurd, outrageous or blasphemous, since we disagree with them. Put bluntly, we must put up with one another. We must suffer fools, gladly or not, and demand only that they suffer us in turn. To live in democracy sets an odd limit to what knowing can mean: we need to admit with Socrates, "I know that I don't know," and yet like Socrates to feel impassioned and emboldening beliefs. Admittedly, that is paradoxical. Preserve us from unparadoxical totalitarianisms!

Socrates did not come up arbitrarily with his idea; he was putting into blunt words his unspoken inheritance. Greek religion, less than most, claimed to know: it respected, feared, enjoyed or cringed from powers that come and go in life and revered the power one might infer behind those powers. But it hardly ever claimed to know the rules it groped to follow. It had the flaws and advantages of the uncodified mind. Its dogma, if it had any, was kept under wraps at places like Eleusis; one could take that or let it alone.

That open-endedness, as I've already said, I take to be an essential of the Greek mindset and of Attic drama. It is what I value most in my own country, and rankle most at seeing diminish. Truth is not to be had as money is had in a wallet (the phrase is from Lessing's *Nathan the Wise*). Old Solon called Thespis' poetry lies, but most Greeks respected poetry religiously. Poetry was understood to play on a commons, a park where fiction and truth share possession. In the special poetry of drama, two voices, at minimum, have their say. We in the audience are at liberty to decide that truth is wholly on one side or the other in the conflict, and the playwright, who is human, is apt to tilt some moral scale in favor of the protagonist, but the room for argument produces a model of that elusive thing, political freedom. At least by implication it restates the humbling confession, "We know that we do not know." When Athens executed Socrates, it was casting off more than one seventy-year-old. It was unwittingly giving up on what had been its own essence. Tragic drama atrophied.

Theater, of course, can emerge without democracy. There was no political valuing of dialogue in the Imperial Pear Garden of ancient China, where palace entertainers first played, nor in the minds of performers in the stony brook bed where Noh emerged in Japan. Certainly it had no part in the lives of the monks or nuns in clammy Romanesque chapels as drama refound itself in the Medieval West. But Attic tragedy (and comedy too) is a unique kind of drama. Part of the uniqueness is the terribleness I've tried to speak of, but part is that drama and a democratic experiment shared time, space and spirit. At the best moments tickets were available here in this Theater of Dionysos to rich and poor of any party or faction. To be here was dialogue.

One irony about Plato's late-in-life conclusion that poets did not belong in an ideal state is that he himself had been, as a youth in Athens' dark hours, a poet, just young enough not to be shipped off on the Sicilian Expedition. We have a touching love poem probably from him, and his dialogues are, in a real sense, plays. They are more poetic (by our definitions) than a lot of philosophy that Greeks wrote in verse. It would have been natural for him to have tried his hand at tragedy as a youngster. Whether or not he did, he learned from the art. He is ungrateful heir to Sophocles and Euripides, more so, we must guess than many of his contemporaneous dramatic poets now lost and forgotten.

Choerile was able to produce her father's plays. When she did his *Bacchai* and *Iphigenia in Aulis* plus another tragedy, they won first prize. But theater conditions were changing radically. It was now hard to find producing *choregoi* in Athens who could put up money to hold the feast of Dionysos in style. Inventiveness gave way to repetition, partly to reuse old costumes, more significantly from change of spirit. The big productions happened in other cities.

Sparta really did collapse into a heap of turf but only after centuries.

Mental life carried on cautiously. Philosophers left the agora and the theater, retreating to the elite shelter of sacred groves, the Academeia and the Lyceon. Reverence for hallowed places protected the irreverences of those schools. Plato and Aristotle are the most famous Athenians of the Three Hundreds, but their patrons were from abroad. The greatest of Greek math and geometry were yet to come and in far-flung cities. Despots and emperors could safely support the studies of Euclid and his like, or, without support, mathematicians could carry on with counting stones and a sand table. Religious syncretism gradually replaced metaphysical adventurists; the devout, self-satisfying "I know the secret" replacing the creative "I wonder." Democracy had disgraced itself in the world's eyes although it lingered, off and on, in the reduced Athens of the next fifty or so years. After that, no one would trust democracy again for twelve centuries, till the Icelanders tried it.

This atrophy relates, by the way, very tangentially to why the Charon's steps were little used in the theaters that followed. I promised some answer to that insignificant question, and I offer three.

First, there are the remnants of that prehistoric spring under the orchestra. Earthquake is always changing water courses, and there is a drain trench around this orchestra floor now, deeper than rain runoff needs. Perhaps the underground passage simply flooded. The era was cautiously sensitive about offending Dionysos' mother Semele, that is to say, Earth. The earth's signal of disapproval could close the passage. The mystique of Athens did not cease along with its creative power and in mere respect of mystique; other theater builders would have been less likely to construct something the Athenians no longer used.

A more satisfying guess would be that in the 300s B.C. and later there was typically, between *skene* façade and orchestra, a stage with wooden flooring. The wood is gone, but here in the Theater of Dionysos I lay my palm on the basso-relievo vertical face that was that stage's front. When the action gravitated up there and the orchestra became exclusively for choral dancers, the trap would be built into the stage floor planks.

I am most at ease with a third explanation. After the dazzling century certain mental springs dried up. The shocks of military collapse promoted not religion but religiosity. So what happened to the daring of the Unnamed Revolution, the zeitgeist animating Greece and the world, which I pointed to in Chapter II? Well, in Athens commercial imperialism and the aftermaths of war happened to it. Neither a war nor thoughtless greed could raise levees against the great flood of that revolution, but they eventually turned its currents awry. Formalism and tradition overwhelmed exploration; theater performance drifted more and more back toward ritual. And ritual more and more forward toward desiccation. Neither free lifestyle nor open inventiveness is the human norm; in most eras the impulse to be near the center of the herd is stronger than the impulse to be at its edge. The Greekness that spread far and wide was mannerist, an imitation of things Greeks had once felt and been. Theater fashion reflected this.

Costumes, always stylized, now grew standardized. As in Beijing

Opera and Noh and Kabuki, costume colors came to signal character type. Masks were made larger with wider, gaping mouths to serve the huger theaters of empire. They became megaphones. The Roman word for mask means "sounder-through," *per-sona*. In order not to look absurdly big-headed, actors wore higher and higher stilted shoes, padded bulky costumes and finally a kind of high-piled top-knot, the *onkos* ("the heap"), above the mask.

Free motion became difficult in the stage costumes that evolved. The high headgear and platform boots were no longer special effects for, let's say, a chorus of Aeschylean Titans; they were now the standard gear all figures in tragedy wore. Such outfits were not for crouching or crawling in a tunnel. Directors have always liked traps better than performers do, who actually have to squeeze in and out of them. If one must inconvenience oneself for an effect, better to do it on the trapezelike *mechina* that lowers you to the stage in everyone's full view — the oohs and ahs last longer.

Alexander of Macedon's armies spread the outward signs of their way of life. Later Romans mimicked that lifestyle though their own armies had smashed the life out of it, leaving only style. Thousands more tragedies were written. Each generation felt its parents' plays less interesting than those of its own present day — and less respectable than what had been written once in Athens. Plays filled the libraries; in Egypt copies began being used to stuff mummies. All that papyrus and parchment was to help fuel the great burnings in Alexandria, Baghdad, Ephesus and Rome. It tended to be old, tampered texts of Athenian Aeschylus, Sophocles and Euripides that got recopied and valued. Not every century can dazzle.

Then Afterthought Said...

At outset I promised I would only describe a bit of tragedy's evolution, not define tragedy. Looking back, however, I discover that I did give away in one sentence my own meager definition of that mystery.

Definitions matter profoundly to sharpen language as a tool, but in the arts there is something pathetic about them. Arts grow beyond whatever definitions there have been up to the moment. Nonetheless we all persist, like Thales, in feeling that some essence underlies what we see and touch, something unitary unifies, something definite defines.

When I was first interested in theater, people were still asking, "Is it possible, in our times, to write real tragedy?" *Death of a Salesman*, for example, was hailed as an American tragedy. That was very high praise — which the play deserves. However, the question about writing tragedy came to seem less and less meaningful. A play resonated, moved, intrigued, or else it didn't. Whether or not it should be called a tragedy felt irrelevant. Minds had more pressing things to ask than what Aristotle meant in saying a tragedy "by pity and by terror accomplishes a cleansing."

But certain plays do something mysterious to us that other plays just don't. It is impossible not to wonder what that something is, how it works. My own suspicion is that it has much to do with language.

If English (or German or Russian) is your native tongue, chances are that only the plays of Aeschylus, Sophocles, Euripides and Shakespeare do that mysterious thing to you. If you are French (I accept on faith) you may also be susceptible to it via plays of Corneille and Racine. French poetic assumptions are unique enough to justify the critic's half joke: poetry *is* what is lost in translation. If a style of poetry can make or break our appreciation of the tragic effect, that effect must be closely bound up with poetry.

My five year old step-daughter, Gabrielle, once came to see a dress rehearsal of *Electra* I had done. She was in bed by the time I got home, but I still have the review she wrote and left me on the kitchen table:

> The play is Electra. Too much killing.

She laid a small finger exactly on the knotted problem. Why on earth *enjoy* representations of rage, misery and death?

Murder mysteries and thrillers are probably enjoyed because they inject adrenalin painlessly — they show us evils resolved. In a typical contemporary murder mystery the crime is "solved" and our naïve psyches equate solving the external puzzle of who did the crime with righting its essential wrong. But the plays we call tragedies act slowly and subtly. I have fretted off and on about the ramifications of Gabrielle's objection. Our decency objects to our behavior in art just as in life: too much killing. Aristotle's quasi-answer was that tragedies offer a cleaning out or "scouring down," a *catharsis*. He drew the term from familiar liturgy: "Dionysos Catharsios" was one of the god's ritual titles.

Aristotle might have been astonished that twenty-five hundred years were to echo his wording as the ultimate definition of an art form that offers such puzzling satisfactions.

The closest I have to my own answer to the puzzle slipped out a few pages back when I wrote of "a juxtaposition of the terrible and the lovely which makes great tragedy disconcerting and mystifying." Tragedy in its worthwhile sense is not a genre; it is an effect, an eerie appeasement that we get, very rarely, when a play confronts us with the worst life can do and restores and reconciles us at the same time.

We are not often brave enough or stupid enough to look squarely at just how horrible things can get; usually that serves no purpose. Life's own evils are sufficient to a given day. Lately some playwrights, most brilliantly Christopher Durang, have made comedy of glimpses into that banal bleakness. Bad stand-up comics now imitate him, delivering a brand of depression-porn or complaint litany — and we laugh uneasily. The undervalued and unique playwright Christopher Fry pleads the opposite case from Durang's. In *The Lady's Not for Burning* his condemned heroine, in love, asks,

> What is to be done? Something compels us into
> The terrible fallacy that man is desirable
> And there is no escaping into truth.

And later in the same comedy her disillusioned man marvels,

> The night's a pale pastureland of peace
> And something condones the world incorrigibly.
> What (he goes on to ask) is this vaporous charm?
> [Christopher Fry, *The Lady's Not for Burning*,
> Oxford Univ. Press, 1950]

To suggest that the tragic effect occurs when beauty and terror juxtapose, rather than when pity and terror juxtapose, may seem simply to swap a bad vagueness for a worse one. Beauty feels especially indefinable. Very privately and *very* tentatively I do define it.

Religions, by their exclusionary self-satisfactions and their fits of murderousness, have made it embarrassing, almost immoral, to speak of metaphysical or spiritual dimensions in things. Decent people have a visceral impulse to leave that talk to vote seekers and well-heeled preachers on television. Being born again looks from the outside like being infantile again, and Greek religion, such as it was, feels respectable in comparison because it leaves itself room to acknowledge it might be wrong. It senses what absurdly tiny fragments of insight we have capacity to hold when we look in the direction of the truly enormous.

Nonetheless we all do end up believing this or that. (I hear readers sigh: "Now this book will go soft and runny like an ill-cooked egg!") Obviously what we call beauty is not a quality, or a *thing*, but an experience. It comes over us, I believe, when looking or listening pierces *through* the thing perceived, sees through it as we see through stained glass into something very like light behind it. Aldous Huxley suggested we feel acquisitive about gemstones because their translucences and refractions are vaguely like that experience of *seeing through*. Those glassy pebbles are uniquely beautiful to us for being tangible metaphors for how beauty happens. Even the banal, overpriced diamond may not be as trivial a trinket as it has seemed. The glad joy one calls "beauty" in a physique is easily explained by biology: those two magpies down there in the pine beyond the fallen *skene* are aflutter with seeing that in one another just now; it is Dionysiac springtime. But the joy taken in the unique red of a Greek poppy, in a sunset through the bruised magenta haze of a commercial city like modern Athens, or a pale night's pastureland of peace — those are less easy to shrug off. I suspect that poetry's tangible network of sound and sense trains us, if we give it the chance and time, till through it we see that transcendent translucence. Greeks gave poetry that chance and time, as Elizabethans did. They trained themselves to hear sweet sounds articulate together. Both eras achieved plays that have an effect unlike any others: plays that look at the worst life can inflict and yet *condone the world incorrigibly*. Kalemera. The name that Greeks eventually gave to the impulse to write tragedies was Melpomene, "She Who Sings Sweet."

Four writers seem to produce that effect almost unerringly, Aeschylus, Sophocles, Euripides and Shakespeare. What had flailing Athenian democracy and rigid Elizabethan monarchy in common to account for their access to this experience? Perhaps among both peoples some lived on a finely balanced edge between religion and skepticism, the vantage that neither codifies nor rejects things visionary. I suspect they saw the tragic beauty not when giving answers but when asking questions — and asking through poetry. Also, Athenians and Elizabethans both had strong stomachs. They shared the virtue — and vice — of accepting the universe as is.

The tragic effect is tragic beauty. It is, I'm afraid, repugnant to reason; beauty found consorting with misery must be suspect. We should go there only briefly, once or twice a year, in festal mood, and not linger to draw conclusions. Like much that is dappled, baffling and messy, tragic beauty seems to exist. Like life we value it unreasonably, preferring it to our ultimate, friendly death (Christopher Fry's phrase). Is tragic beauty mere medication for pain in a cancer ward or an insight into the Mind steering all things through all things, willing and unwilling to be called by the name of Zeus? According to temperament and experience you will believe it is one or the other — or something else altogether.

I claim no finality for this tentative proposal as to what tragedy might be. If there is significance in this book, it must not be in one more defining of tragedy but in a flickering image of three playwrights and their work on a screen of woven digressions. Necessity mothers make-do; invention's real mother is digressive cross-pollination. A digression interlocks the disconnected; poetry in the light of physics, of the archaeology of Crete, of scarcity of cabbages and scariness of kings. Praising digression, one praises poetry and collaterally the universe.

Lately relevance has been a great cry. For good reasons our best minds have been at work to uproot much that was vile in our attitudes toward gender, race and class. That work has entailed looking sharply at the passing moment to the exclusion of much else. Despite failures, that effort is the best part of our era. But handsome things have gone to the compost pile too, just for supposedly lacking relevance. That is poor grounds for excluding anything.

The cosmos (digression suggests) is entirely interrelated, in a way consistent. We can be curious to see galaxies of irrelevant stars, trillions of miles across, following the pattern that water follows when we flush a toilet or that a chambered nautilus builds into its shell. Which is image of which? We know we don't know. We hear words diversify to talk of things in a shifting society just the way the immigrant finches Darwin watched in the Galapagos diversified to feed on the fruits or bugs of their new little environment. *Climax* evolved from meaning "ladder" to meaning "drama's high point" once there were dramas; *hypocrite* evolved from *answerer* to *actor* when a profession emerged in need of a name, and then evolved on from *actor* to *pretender* because of theater's boggy margin between show and substance. One evolution mirrors another. To recognize evolutions is simply, complexly, to believe in cause and effect. To recognize how effects radiate is to respect digression.

VI. Then and Now

Our cosmos keeps making metaphors like a poet; A is like B in this way; B is like C in that. Like a poet the cosmos uses rhythm, vibrations of light and sound, beats of hearts, fluxes of tides, cycles of years. Like a poet it makes imagery, reflecting one thing upon another, including the deeply strange reflection of exterior things into us, what we call conscious mind. Then mind produces the even stranger reflection of itself back out into the world, mind over matter, moving and rearranging things through acts of will and works of art.

Aeschylus, Sophocles and Euripides, poets of bleak times, were each a small cosmos. Each of us equally is, but in bleak times they were more equal than most.

Hear one last fragment of Aeschylus, a stanza from the opening chorus of *The Oresteia*. Two great translations are paired, the one on the left by Richmond Lattimore and the one on the right by Robert Fagles, not to hear one as better than the other but because in the stereophonic sound of the two we might pick up Aeschylus' authentic voice speaking of tragedy.

Zeus, who guided men to think,	Zeus has led us on to know,
Who has laid it down that wisdom	the Helmsman lays it down as law
Comes alone through suffering,	that we must suffer, suffer into truth.
Still there drips in sleep against the heart	We cannot sleep & drop by drop at the heart
Grief of memory; against	the pain of pain remembered comes again
Our pleasure we are temperate.	and we resist, but ripeness comes as well.
From the gods who sit in grandeur	from the gods enthroned on the awesome rowing-bench
Grace comes somehow violent.	there comes a violent love.

Bibliography

I owe much to forewords, afterwords and footnotes in translations that I've read or skimmed. I naively trust those who have lived on intimate terms with the Greek texts. I've never understood why more recent authorities should automatically be better than older ones; having lived even the tiniest bit closer to the world the plays were written in should be of some advantage.

This bibliography is not complete. I tend to buy paperbacks, and they have tended to scatter — theater is an occupation of migrant workers. In this list I try to respect and remember some books I have relied on over the years as well as those which, read or relooked into lately, brought this piece of writing into some focus.

Aeschylus. *The Oresteia*. Translated by Robert Fagles. New York: Viking, 1975. (Even if Fagles' translation were not as wonderful as it is, his notes to various lines would be a huge enrichment of the plays.)
    ———. *The Persians*. Translated by Seth Bernardete. In Grene, David, and Richmond Lattimore, eds., *The Complete Greek Tragedies*. Chicago: University of Chicago Press, 1992.
    ———. *Prometheus Bound*. Translated by Paul Roche. New York: New American Library, 1964.
Banham, Martin, ed. *The Cambridge Guide to Theatre*. New York: Cambridge University Press, 1995.
Barr, Stringfellow. *The Will of Zeus: A History of Greece from the Origins of Hellenic Culture to the Death of Alexander*. Philadelphia: Lippincott, 1961.
Brown, John Russell, ed. *The Oxford Illustrated History of the Theatre*. New York: Oxford University Press, 1995. (The Greek Theater section in this by Oliver Taplin seems especially good.)

Durant, Will. *The Story of Civilization*. Vol. 2, *The Life of Greece; Being a History of Greek Civilization from the Beginnings, and of Civilization in the Near East from the Death of Alexander, to the Roman Conquest.* New York: Simon & Schuster, 1936.

Euripides. *The Bacchae.* Translated with an introduction by Michael Cacoyannis. New York: New American Library, 1982.

_____. *Electra.* Translated by Emily T. Vermeule. In Grene, David, and Richmond Lattimore, eds., *The Complete Greek Tragedies.* Chicago: University of Chicago Press, 1992.

The Greek Historians. The Complete and Unabridged Historical Works. Edited with an introduction, revisions and additional notes by Francis R. B. Godolphin. New York: Random House, 1942.

Grene, David, and Richmond Lattimore, eds. *The Complete Greek Tragedies.* Chicago: University of Chicago Press, 1992.

Hamilton, Edith. *The Ever-Present Past.* Prologue by Doris Fielding Reid. New York: Norton, 1964.

_____. *The Greek Way.* New York: Norton, 1930.

Hartnoll, Phyllis, ed. *The Concise Oxford Companion to the Theatre.* New York: Oxford University Press, 1972.

Herodotus. *Herodotus: The Persian Wars.* Translated by George Rawlinson. In *The Greek Historians. The Complete and Unabridged Historical Works.* Edited with an introduction, revisions and additional notes by Francis R. B. Godolphin. New York: Random House, 1942.

Kagan, Donald. *The Peloponnesian War.* New York: Viking, 2003.

Kitto, H. D. F. *Greek Tragedy: A Literary Study.* London: Methuen, 1939.

Nahm, Milton C., ed. *Selections from Early Greek Philosophy.* New York: F. S. Crofts, 1947.

Nicoll, Allardyce. *The Development of the Theatre.* New York: Harcourt, Brace Jovanovich, 1966.

Pickard-Cambridge, A. W. *The Theater of Dionysus at Athens.* Oxford: Oxford University Press, 1946.

Podlecki, Anthony J. *The Political Background of Aeschylean Tragedy.* Ann Arbor: University of Michigan, 1966.

Rosenmeyer, Thomas G. *The Art of Aeschylus.* Berkeley: University of California Press, 1983.

Sophocles. *Antigone; Oedipus the King; Electra.* Translated by H. D. F. Kitto. Edited with an introduction and notes by Edith Hall. New York: Oxford University Press, 1994.

Taplin, Oliver. *The Stagecraft of Aeschylus: The Dramatic Use of Exits and Entrances in Greek Tragedy.* Oxford: Clarendon, 1977.

Yeats, William Butler. *King Oedipus* and *Oedipus at Colonus.* In *The Collected Plays of W. B. Yeats.* 2d ed. London: Macmillan, 1952.

Also, two quirky salutes:

1. A while ago in a bookstore (without credit card or even pencil), I opened a recent book about Euripides by a voice that struck me deeply, an angry voice. It felt like work of a veteran of Korea, Vietnam, Iraq or perhaps one of our unhappy, covert adventures in South America. I deter-

mined to remember the author and title — the book matters. Weeks of private life intervened; the names were gone. I salute that book's recognition that Attic tragedy is a child of Dionysos by adoption; Ares is its real father.

2. Harold Bloom's *Shakespeare: The Invention of the Human* (New York: Riverhead Books, 1998) helped me dare (for good or ill) to mingle private experiences with a huge theme. Not that Mr. Bloom does that — his daring is of a wider kind — but reading him has buoyed me.

Index

Abu Ghraib 123
Academeia 186
Achilles 23, 46, 128
acoustics 44 (footnote)
Acrocorinth 17
Acropolis 5, 27, 40, 41, 43, 88, 176, 184
acting 23, 28, 38, 50 passim, 58, 87
Aegean Sea 17, 35, 64, 96
Aegeus 153
Aegisthus (in Aeschylus) 94, 101, 104
Aegisthus (in Sophocles) 155, 156
Aegisthus (off-stage in Euripides) 163, 167
Aeschylus' birth date, question of 32
Aesop 166
Agamemnon 12, 69, 94, 96 passim, 128, 154
The Agamemnon 49, 95 passim, 131
Agatharchus 134, 158
Agathon 125, 182
Ahasuerus (Xerxes) 67
The Ajax 127 passim, 178
The Alcestis 147
Alcibiades 177, 184
Aletes 158
Alexander the Great 8, 13, 182, 188
Alexandria 188
Amazons 14
Anaxagoras 9, 63 passim, 84, 92, 142, 159
Andromache 169
Angels in America 114
Anouilh, Jean 135
Antigone 162
The Antigone 73, 127, 134, 140, 150, 161

antistrophe, "counter turn" in choric dance and verse 19
Anthony and Cleopatra 82
Aphrodite 61, 62, 65
Apollo 40, 51, 61, 84, 105, 108 passim, 116, 147, 167, 170
ara, "curse" 93 passim, 99, 105, 114
Arcadia 16, 36
Archilochus 42
Areopagus, "Ares' Rock" 21, 94 passim, 112, 113
Ares 9, 61, 176
Argos 12, 20, 60, 62, 69, 70, 94, 120, 157, 163, 173
Ariadne 11
Arion 15, 17 passim, 23, 24, 182
Aristides 35 passim, 40, 41, 59, 69, 80, 166
Ariston 179
Aristophanes 9, 68 (footnote), 80, 125, 177 (footnote)
Aristotle 30, 47, 97, 119, 148, 160, 172, 176, 177, 186, 189
The Art of Aeschylus 73
Artaud, Antonine 170
Artemis 14, 160
Aspasia 127, 161, 162
the Assembly (Athenian) 22
Astyanax 169
Athamas 46
Athena 22, 25, 108 passim, 128, 132, 175
Athos, Mt. 35
Atlas 6, 85

Atossa 37, 75
Atreus 93 passim, 114, 155
Attica 27

Babylon 37
The Bacchai 3, 27, 182, 183, 186
Bacchos (cult name for Dionysos) 15, 74, 180
Bach, J.S. 120
Bacon, Francis (painter) 168
Baez, Joan 24
Bagdad 188
barbaroi, "non-Greeks" 122
Barr, Stringfellow, *The Will of Zeus* 26, 27
beat 13
Beethoven 181
Beijing Opera 187
Bloom, Harold 116
Bosch, Hieronymus 74
Bosphorus 96
Bread and Puppet Theatre 25
Brecht, Bertholt 135
Britain 75
Brook, Peter 61
Buddha 66
burial rites 129 passim
Byron 7
Byzantium 13, 162

Caldwell, Zoe 153
Carthage 43, 55, 120
cartharsis, "scouring down" 189
Cassandra 98 passim, 169
Castor 168
Ceos Island 35
Cephisus 126
Chaos 84
Charon's Steps 77, 80, 108, 131, 187
Chile 150
China 37, 56, 185
Choerile 182, 186
Choerilus 182
Chomsky, Noam 24
choregos 52, 59, 137, 186
chorodidaskalos, "chorus teacher" 126
chorus: as "backup" 23; central in early plays 60; choric moves 50; diminished involvement 149; divided exit in *Seven Against Thebes* 72; of fifty 18; flown 88; human conversing with divine 39; less central in Sophocles 133; less defined as characters 140; number in Euripides' *Suppliants* 160; size of 47, 48; size reduced 78; special dialect 49; varied roles in trilogy 82–83; of women 48, 49
Chrysothemis 155
Cilissa 103, 104
Cimon 81, 90, 95, 119, 137, 147, 151
Cirque du Soleil 89
Clazomenae 64
Cleisthenes 34, 59
Cleo 50
climax, "ladder, staircase" 192
Clytemnestra: in Aeschylus 78, 94 passim, 161; in Euripides 153, 161, 163 passim; in Sophocles 154 passim, 161
Cocteau, Jean 97
Codros, King 21
College of the Americas 175
Colonus 126, 157, 179
comedy 29, 59, 63, 124, 125, 149
Commodus (Roman Emperor) 8, 173
comoidia 124
Confucius 66, 67
Constantine, 1st Christianized Emperor 7
Corinth 17, 21, 41, 59, 119, 151
Corinth, Isthmus of 21
Corinthian Aphrodite, brothel temple of 20
Coriolanus 89
Corneille 189
coryphaeus, "crew head" 52
costume 18, 51, 54, 83, 187, 188
cothurnoi 83
Crane, Hart 99
Creon 135, 143, 144
Crete 11, 125
Critias 184
Crusades 7
Cyclopes 55, 85
Cyclops 47
Cyneigiros (Aeschylus' brother) 35, 36

Daedalus 11 ("dancing place" designer)
Damon 126
Danae 130
Danaids 71
Danaus 54, 60 passim
Dante 171
Darfur 71
Darius 32, 37, 75, 76, 78
Darwin, Charles 192
Datis 32, 35 passim
Daughters of Ocean (aka Oceanides) 86, 149
Death of a Salesman 189
De Boer, Jelle 14 (footnote)

Declerq, Nico 43 (footnote)
deforestation 152
Deianeira 133
Dekeyser, Cindy 43 (footnote)
Delos 14
Delphi 14, 37, 39, 61, 84, 105, 107, 110, 130, 147, 184
demes, "parishes" 34
Demeter 15, 33, 62
Democritos 9, 124
Diana 14
Dickenson, Emily 1
Dionysia, City (aka "the Dionysia," "The Great Dionysia," and "The Festival of Dionysos") 6, 26, 27, 28, 38, 52, 59
Dionysos, 23, 34, 50, 117, 147, 182, 183, 187, 189
The Discus Thrower 59
dithyrambs 23, 26, 28
Dörpfeld, Wilhelm 77
Draco 11, 21
drama, "doings" 29
dramatic contests conduct of 44 passim
dummy (as actors' stand-in) 87, 99, 131
Duncan, Isadora 50, 160
Durang, Christopher 190
du St. Read, Leslie 54
Dylan, Bob 50

eccyclema, "out-roller" 101, 107, 108, 110, 130, 149, 158
Egypt 21, 37, 39, 42, 117, 122, 170
Egyptian liturgies 21
Eilythyia 14
Electra: in Aeschylus 102, 162; in Euripides 162 passim; in Sophocles 16, 127, 154 passim, 162
The Electra (Euripides) 154, 162 passim
The Electra (Sophocles) 154, 189
Elektra (opera) 154, 157
Eleusis 15, 28, 33, 92, 117, 137, 185
Eliot, T.S. 98 (footnote)
emmeleia, "in-tune dance (?)" 50
Empedocles 65
Ephesos 14, 188
Ephesus 17
Ephialtes 59, 95, 119
Epicurus 9
epigones, "the late-born ones" 10
Epiphany (Christian holiday) 19
Erechtheion 176
Eretria 36, 75, 80, 130
Erigone 158

Eros 162
Esther 67
Eteocles 72
"Ethical Revolution" 67, 132, 171, 187
Etna 55, 120
Euboa Island 36, 43, 76
Euclid 186
The Eumenides 48, 62, 103, 107, 150
Eumenides (Furies) 31, 106
Euphorion (Aeschylus' son) 119
Euripides' birth date 43
Euripus 43
Evadne 160
Eve 111
existentialism 31
exodos (aka *exodios*), "roadway out, exit" 54
The Exodus 55

Fagles, Robert 193
The Fall of Miletos 40, 52
Fo, Dario 153
The Four Hundred 178, 180
Francis of Assisi 181
The Frogs 68, 80
Fry, Christopher 190, 192
Furies (Eumenides) 31, 106, 157, 168

Galapagos 192
Galatians 9
Ganges 66
Gauls 9
Gela 120
Genesis 111
Gertrude, Queen 167
Gibson, Mel 132
Gielgud, John 136
Giradoux, Jean 154
The Glass Menagerie 97
Goethe, J. W. 153
Gordion Knot 13
Gorgias 142, 143
Gorgon, 25
Goya 84, 181
Gray, Thomas 140
The Great King, title of Persian rulers 12, 122, 173
Greek National Theater 31
Greek poetry: challenge of translation 145; dithyrambs 23; iambics in drama 41; poetic rhythms 16; public art vs. private 79; separated from music 23; stichomythia 142; word order and lost melody 17
Greek Revival architecture 10

Index

Grene, David 73
Grimm brothers 62

Hades 15, 93
Haemon 143, 162
The Haggada 20
Hale, John 14 (footnote)
Hamilton, Edith 47, 78
Hamlet 63, 167
Handel's *Messiah* 20
Hecate 14
Hecht, Anthony 71
Hecuba 160, 161, 169, 173, 174
The Hecuba 169
Hegel, G.W.F. 73
Heiro of Syracuse 90
Helen 94, 130, 168, 169
The Helen 170
Hellman, Lillian 169
Hepburn, Katharine 153
Hephaestus 87
Hera 86
Heracles 35, 133, 178
Heraclitos of Melitos 10, 15, 65
Hermes 86, 91, 108
Herodotus 9, 20, 43, 137
Hesiod 84
Hippias 32, 34, 36, 37
The Hippolytus 162
Hofmannsthal, Hugovon 154
The Holy Ghost 93
Homer 12, 17, 23, 67, 75, 85, 96, 98,
  126, 163, 170, 173
homosexuality 162
Horace 62
House of the Deaf Man 181
House of the Maiden (Parthenon) 110
Huang Ho 66
hubris (aka hybris) 160, 161, 176
human sacrifice 16, 41, 93, 182
Huxley, Aldous 191
The Hybris 177
Hymettos Mt. 5, 65
Hypatia of Aexandria 124
Hypermnestra 62, 144, 162
hypocrities, "expounder, actor" 137, 192

Ibsen, H. 1, 181
Iceland 187
Ictinus 126
Idi Amin 18
idiotes, "apolitical person" 34, 182
Ikarion 23, 29, 35
The Iliad 12, 17, 23, 43, 46, 160, 173
Ilium 46

Imperial Pear Garden 185
India 28, 56
Indus 13
The Infernal Machine 97
Io 57, 86
The Ion (Euripides) 147
The Ion (Plato's dialogue) 51
Ionians 17, 32, 39, 42
Iophon 179, 180
Iphigenia 154
The Iphigenia 153, 161
The Iphigenia at Aulis 175, 182, 186
The Iphigenia in Tauris 160
Iran 66
Iraq 150
irony 157
Isis 86
Israel 67
Isthmian Games 59
Isthmus (of Corinth) 41
Italy 125

Jacob 66
Japanese 75
Jehovah 183
Jerusalem 66
Jesus 27
Job, Book of 92, 93
Joppa 93
Julius Caesar 82

Kabuki 131, 188
Kagan, Donald 151
Keller, Helen 132
kithara (or *cithara*) 16, 43
Kitto, H.D.F. 132 passim
Knossos 11
Kronos 84, 86
Krotos 43
kudos 18, 52
Kushner, Tony 114

labrys 11
Labyrinth (on Crete) 11
The Lady's Not for Burning 190
Las Vegas 20
Lattimore, Richmond 32, 38, 42, 55, 193
Laurion 40
League of Delos 59, 69, 81, 122, 150, 151
Lemnos 178
Lenaea 46, 52, 173
Leningrad 175
Lesbos 17
Lessing, G. 185
Li Bo 1

The Libation Bearers 49, 101
The Lion King 89
The Lovers of Achilles 162
Lucretius 124
Lyceon 186
Lycurgos (finance minister) 8
Lydia 20, 64
lyric tragedy 48
The Lysistrata 5

Macbeth 92, 111
Macedon 182, 183
MacLeish, Archibald 58
Magnesia 182
Marathon 6, 12, 23, 35, 38, 39, 43, 70, 75, 76
Marcos, Imelda 92
Marlow 42
masks 24 passim, 54, 87, 188
The Masterbuilder 118
mechene, "hoist, crane" 88, 149, 168, 179, 188
The Medea 153, 161, 162, 175
Medusa 25
Mei Lai 41
Meletos 184
The Melian Dialogue 176, 177
Melos 172, 176
Melpomene 23, 191
Menelaus 12, 94, 117
messenger 141
Michaelangelo 181
A Midsummer Night's Dream 56, 115
Miletos 17, 32, 35, 39, 43
Miltiades 36 passim, 38, 70, 176
Milton, John 125
Minos 11
Minotaur 11
Mnemosyne 23
Mohammed 27
monotheism 7, 125
Moore, John 131
Moses 27
Mourning Becomes Electra 154
Mozart 1
Murasaki 1
Murray, Gilbert 145
Muse(s) 23
Museon 96
music: actors also singers 138; aharmonic 79; Euripides not his own composer 159; modes/scales 49; notation lacking 23
Myrrhine 5
Mystery cult at Elusis 33, 92

mythos, "story, plot, talk" 57
Mytilene 17

Nahum, M.C. 66
Nathan the Wise 185
The Nausicaa 131
Naxos 137
Neoptolemos 178 passim
New York 75
Noh 186, 188
Noriega, Manuel 175
nudity on stage 108

Odeon: Greek 136; Roman 8, 137
Odysseus 23, 129, 132, 177, 178
The Odyssey 12, 17, 23, 43, 177
Oedipus 10, 71, 73, 93
Oedipus at Colonos 57, 126, 127, 134, 179, 180, 181
Oedipus Rex 73, 127, 157, 158, 175, 178, 181
Okeanos (aka Ocean) 84, 90
Old Testament 92
Olivier, Laurence 89
Olympia (in Peloponnese) 12
Olympiads 4, 12
Olympic Games 12
Olympus, Mt. 84
O'Neill, Eugene 154
onkos, "heap" 188
orchestra, "dancing place" 6, 27, 53, 187
The Oresteia 31, 41, 48, 54, 76, 94, 154, 193
Orestes: in Aeschylus 31, 82 passim, 102 passim; in Euripides 160, 163 passim; in Sophocles 154 passim
The Orestes 150, 170
Orff, Carl 19
Orgasmo Adulto Escapes from the Zoo 153
Oropus 130
Orton, Joe 170
ostracism 34

palinode, "retraction-song" 170
Pan 36, 46
Pan, Cave of 5, 37
Papas, Irene 153
parabisis, "step forward, indiscretion" 165
parodos, "side road" 53, 105, 115
Paros 38
Parthenon 6, 7, 150, 184
passion plays 132
Passover 20
pastoral style 9
Pausanias (General) 70, 176

The Pearl Theater 75
Peloponnese 41, 70, 94
Peloponnesian League 69
The Peloponnesian War 152 (footnote)
Peloponnesian Wars 151, 152, 168, 173, 177
Pelops 93 passim
Penn, William 34
Pentelikon, Mt. 88
Pentheus 183
periactoi, "turn-arounds" 103, 130
Periander 18
Pericles 35, 37, 59, 126, 127, 136, 137, 150, 152, 161, 162, 177
Pericles, Prince of Tyre 82
Peron, Eva 136
Persepolis 13, 42
Persian Wars 37, 63 passim
Persians 31, 36, 64, 67, 75
The Persians (Aeschylus) 42, 48, 53, 54, 59, 68 passim, 83, 89, 98, 118
The Persians (Phrynichus) 53
persona, "sounder-through" 188
Pheidippides 36, 37
Phidias 126, 150
Philocles 119
Philoctetes 178, 179
The Philoctetes 127, 128, 134, 175, 177, 178, 181
The Phineas 46
The Phoenician Women 53
Phrynichus 40, 47, 49, 53, 55
Pickard-Cambridge, A. 77
Pinochet 18, 175
Pireus 35, 40, 88, 93
Pisistratidae (aka sons of Pisistratos) 28, 32, 52
Pisistratos 22 passim, 53, 59
plague 162, 176
Platea 36, 37, 43, 70, 136, 175
Plato 125, 161, 184, 186
The Pliades 93
plot structure 55 passim
Plutarch 177 (footnote)
Podlecki, Anthony 68 passim
The Poetics 97, 119
Political Background of Aeschylean Tragedy 68
political theater 27
Pollux 78
Polonius 90
Polydeuces 168
Polyxena 169
Porch of the Maidens 176
prologue 163
Prometheus 82 passim

Prometheus Bound 48, 57, 58, 82, 99, 107, 120
Prometheus Firebringer 85
Prometheus Firekindler 47, 85
Prometheus Unbound 83
The Proteus 117
Purim 67
Pylades 102, 154, 157, 164
Pythia 14, 107
Pythian Games 14, 59
Pytho 14, 84

Racine 189
Rama, Franca 153
Rand, Ayn 134
Ransome, John Crowe 135
Redgrave, Vanessa 153
Renault, Mary 11, 55
The Republic 161
rhapsodes, "song-weavers" 23, 46
Rhea 84
Roche, Paul 92
Rome 33, 165, 188
Roosevelt, F.D. 35
Rosenmeyer, Thomas G. 73

Sacred Way (Athens to Elusis) 28
St. Anthony 33
Salamis (island and battle site) 40, 43, 58, 59, 75, 93, 125, 147
Salamis, Gulf of (aka "the Bay of S." and "Bay of Elusis") 6, 13, 41
Samos 134, 150, 151, 158
Sappho 161
Sartre, Jean Paul 154
satyr 18, 23, 47
satyr play 28 passim, 46, 85, 148
Schrödinger 51
second character in drama 38
Second Sacred War 147
Semele 187
Semnai 114
The Seven against Thebes 48, 54, 68 passim, 118, 135, 139
Shakespeare 8, 17, 42, 56, 82, 111, 116, 145, 163, 179, 182, 189, 191
Shaw, Fiona 158
Shepard, Sam 170
Shylock 49
Sicily 17, 43, 55, 58, 65, 119, 120, 125, 168, 177, 178, 186
Siddhartha (aka Buddha) 66, 67
Sidon 42, 49
skene, "tent, hut, booth" 6, 53, 88, 95, 96, 102–104, 124, 130, 149, 187

skeuopoios, "supplier" 54
skole, "leisure" 65, 184
Smyth, H.W. 33
Socrates 9, 51, 136, 143, 182, 184, 185
Solomon 67
Solon 22 passim, 72, 161, 172, 185
sophists 142
Sophocles (grandson of poet) 179
Sounion, Cape 36
Sparta 12, 33, 36, 40, 41, 43, 68, 69, 75, 94, 137, 147, 148, 150, 170, 179, 183, 184, 186
sparte, "the scattered ones" 12
Sphinx 181
spine 13
Stalin 92
stasimon, "a standing still" 50
Steiner, Rudolph 50
Stesichoros 170
Stevenson, Juliet 136
Stevenson, Robert Louis 178
stichomythia, "line-of-verse-talk" 142, 143
Strauss, Richard 157, 158
strophe, "a turn" 19
Stuyversant, Peter 34
The Suppliant Women (Euripides) 78, 131, 160
The Suppliants aka *The Suppliant Maidens* (Aeschylus) 48, 54, 60 passim, 68 passim, 94, 120, 166
Susarion 29, 124
Sybaris 19
The Symposium 125, 182
Syracuse 43, 53, 58, 168

Taenaron, Cape 20
Taliban 75
Tantalus 93
tapes, "woven thing, rug" 99
Taymor, Julie 89
The Tempest 119
Terkel, Studs 24
Teucer 129
Thales 64, 188
Thamyris 125
Tharp, Twyla 131
Thebes 71, 151, 160
Themistocles 35 passim, 40 passim, 53, 69, 80, 176
Theocritos 9
Thermopylae 41
Theseus 11, 115, 153, 160
Thespis 15, 21, 24 passim, 39, 47, 51, 58, 148, 185

Thessaly 182
Thimotheus 159
The Thirty Years Peace 150, 151
Thomas, Dylan 99
Thucydides 151, 176, 177
Thurii 150
Thyestes 94 passim, 100
Titans 83
Titus Andronicus 163
Tlepolemos 137
The Torah 53, 67
Tower of Demosthenes 52, 123
Toynbee, Arnold 9
The Trackers 47
tragoidia, "goat-song" 29, 30, 118, 124
Treasure Island 178
trilogy (as three act play) 118
Tripod Street 52
The Trojan Women 145, 153, 160, 169, 171, 172, 175
Troy 12, 69, 95, 124, 170, 173, 178
Typhon 84
Tyre 42, 43
tyrsis, "fort-tower" 18
Twelfth Night 19

the unities 56, 97

Virgin Mary 130

Walpole, Hugh 128
The Wasps 49
Wesleyan University 14 (footnote)
When We Dead Awaken 181
WHINSEC (formerly "School of the Americas") 172, 175
Whitman, Walt 39, 129
Wilde, Oscar 119
Wilson, Woodrow 34
The Winter's Tale 179
women in audience 45
The Women of Etna 55 passim
The Women of Trachis 127, 133, 162
women's roles 48, 49, 159, 161
World Trade Towers 75

Xerxes 39 passim, 61, 75, 81, 98

Yeats, W.B. 2, 16

Zeus 15, 57, 61, 65, 84 passim, 91, 113, 176, 192, 193
Zola, Emile 169
Zoroastrianism 37, 65, 91

www.ingramcontent.com/pod-product-compliance
Ingram Content Group UK Ltd.
Pitfield, Milton Keynes, MK11 3LW, UK
UKHW042002140426
5217IPUK00015B/938